Short Takes

Short Takes

MODEL ESSAYS FOR COMPOSITION

Seventh Edition

Elizabeth Penfield

University of New Orleans

New York   San Francisco   Boston
London   Toronto   Sydney   Tokyo   Singapore   Madrid
Mexico City   Munich   Paris   Cape Town   Hong Kong   Montreal

Editor-in-Chief: Joseph Opiela
Senior Acquisitions Editor: Steven Rigolosi
Marketing Manager: Carlise Paulson
Supplements Editor: Donna Campion
Production Manager: Mark Naccarelli
Project Coordination, Text Design, and Electronic Page Makeup: Nesbitt Graphics Inc.
Cover Design Manager: Wendy Ann Fredericks
Cover Designer: Kay Petronio
Manufacturing Buyer: Al Dorsey
Printer and Binder: R.R. Donnelley & Sons/Harrisonburg
Cover Printer: Phoenix Color Corps.

For permission to use copyrighted material, grateful acknowledgment is made to the copyright holders on pp. 335–338, which are hereby made part of this copyright page.

Library of Congress Cataloging-in-Publication Data
Penfield, Elizabeth, 1939–
    Short takes : model essays for composition / Elizabeth Penfield.—7th ed.
        p. cm.
    Includes bibliographical references and index.
    ISBN 0-321-07223-5 (pbk.)
    1. College readers. 2. English language—Rhetoric—Problems, exercises, etc. 3. Report writing—Problems, exercises, etc. I. Title

PE1417.P43 2002
808'.0427—dc21   2001020386

Please visit our website at http://www.ablongman.com

ISBN 0-321-07223-5

5 6 7 8 9 10—DOH—04 03

CONTENTS

Freeze Frame: Reading and Writing   1

1   On Using Description   12

The Mute Sense   Diane Ackerman   22

"Smells detonate softly in our memory like poignant land mines, hidden under the weedy mass of many years and experiences."

The Bridge   Jason Holland   26

"The bridge was county property, but my friends and I felt like we were the owners. It was a mutual relationship. We owned the bridge, and the bridge owned us."

El Hoyo   Mario Suarez   30

"From the center of downtown Tucson the ground slopes gently away to Main Street, drops a few feet, and then rolls to the banks of the Santa Cruz River. Here lies the section of the city known as El Hoyo."

Frightened by Loss   J. Merrill-Foster   34

"Widowed, alone, children and grandchildren flung wide from California to New England, she fills her days with little things."

Left Sink   Ellery Akers   38

"In the world of the bathroom the light shelf was a delicatessen of the highest order. Light Buddha sat there night after glorious night, lazily snapping up moths as they fluttered past. The other two frogs seemed content to stake out the sinks, which weren't quite as dependable a food source, though they weren't bad."

4   On Using Example   **108**

8 On Using Cause and Effect   230

9 On Using Argument 262

10 For Further Reading: Pro and Con   304

On Legalized Gambling

On Hunting

On Film

11 Additional Writing Prompts 325

THEMATIC GUIDE

PREFACE

This book combines the old and the new. Back when the first edition was only an idea, I was teaching freshman English in a highly structured program that emphasized both the rhetorical modes and the final product. My dilemma then was one that many teachers still face: how to incorporate the modes with invention and the whole tangle of the writing process. But once I focused on the aims of discourse, the modes fell into place as means, not ends, and as patterns of organization used in combination, not just singly. There remained the problem of the textbooks, many of which contained essays of imposing length and complexity, essays that intimidated and overwhelmed many a student. Often, any essay that was short was so because it was an excerpt. *Short Takes* was the result of my frustrations. The seventh edition still reflects the rhetorical framework of the first one, but it is a flexible framework. You can even ignore it and use the thematic table of contents. But if you find the modes useful, you'll see them here.

This edition remains a collection of short, readable, interesting essays written by professionals and students, and the commentary continues to focus on reading and writing as interrelated activities. Much, however, is new. "Freeze Frame," the initial essay that sets the tone for the book by emphasizing reading and writing as active and interrelated processes, is aimed directly at the student. In addition, I have added

- Writing prompts by mode and by theme, including personal essays, responses to readings, and research projects
- A selection of more challenging essays, one at the end of each chapter
- "For Further Reading: Pro and Con," which contains differing views on contemporary topics—home schooling, legalized gambling, *The Blair Witch Project,* hunting—with minimal apparatus
- New essays, 25 of them

At the same time, those features that teachers particularly liked are still here.

- Introductions to each chapter directed to students and emphasizing the writing process (as well as the kinds of choices and decisions all writers face)
- Suggestions for writing journal entries and essays
- Descriptions of the author, the context for the essay, and its notable stylistic features
- Diversity of authors, styles, and subject matter
- Complete essays, not excerpts

As always, I welcome responses from students and teachers to this new edition, along with suggestions for the future. You can email me direct (ttsafari@rof.net) or write to me in care of Longman's Developmental English Editor at Longman, 1185 Sixth Avenue, 25th Floor, New York, NY 10036.

If you are familiar with previous editions, you'll also notice that the sequencing of the chapters has changed. Description and narration are now followed by definition because it plays such an important role in expository and argumentative writing. Each chapter builds on the previous one and leads to the one that follows, culminating in argument, but argument with a difference. The chapter on argument is a basic introduction, an extension of the kind of emphasis on thesis and evidence that exists throughout the text. Within each chapter, the essays are presented in order of difficulty. All the supplementary information—the chapter introductions, background information, notes on style, questions on the essays, and suggestions for writing—balance process and product, working on the premise that the two, like reading and writing, are so closely interrelated that one cannot be considered without the other.

THE ESSAYS

This edition contains 57 essays, 25 of which are new. Most are indeed short—about one thousand words at most—and as such should easily lend themselves to scrutiny and emulation, because most of the papers assigned in composition courses fall in the four hundred to one thousand word range. A few of the essays are longer and rely on the kind of research that students may be asked to carry out. And a few illustrate forms that differ from the classic short essay: the problem/solution organization often found in argumentative pieces; an opinion piece followed by two letters to the editor; and pro/con essays. One essay also serves as a basic introduction to the Modern Language Association's system of documentation. All of the essays are complete pieces, not excerpts, illustrating the basic arms of discourse and standard rhetorical modes.

To write is to choose among alternatives, to select the most appropriate organization, persona, diction, and techniques for a given audience and purpose. Each of the essays included in this edition was chosen because it exemplifies the author's choices, and the apparatus emphasizes those choices and alternatives. The essays, therefore, serve as illustrative models of organization and stylistic techniques available to the writer. The essays were also chosen because their authors represent different genders, ages, and cultures; as a result, the subjects of the essays are accessible and their perspectives are lively, qualities that also allow them to serve as sources of invention, as jumping-off places for students to develop their own ideas in their own styles.

RHETORICAL MODES AND THE AIMS OF DISCOURSE

Anyone who has used a reader with essays arranged by mode has probably run into two problems: first, few essays are pure examples of a single mode; second, most collections of essays treat argument—an aim of writing—as though it were the equivalent of description, comparison/contrast, and so on. *Short Takes* addresses these inconsistencies by emphasizing the difference between mode—how an essay is organized—and purpose—how an essay is intended to affect the reader—and by pointing out how writing frequently blends two or more modes.

Because essays usually employ more than one mode, the essays here are grouped according to the *primary* rhetorical pattern that guides their organization; the questions that follow each essay point out the subordinate modes. As for the aims of discourse, the essays represent the various purposes for writing. The writers' self-expressive, informative, and persuasive purposes are underscored in the discussion questions. In addition, the apparatus connects academic writing and the kind of writing found outside the classroom.

Example, description, or other standard modes are used in developing all kinds of nonfiction prose—self-expression, exposition, and argument. Of these three types of writing, self-expression is the easiest and argument the most difficult. For that reason, argument has its own special chapter exemplifying the classical appeals: to reason, to emotion, and to the writer's credibility. Because lively discussion often leads to good writing, in the final chapter you'll find a number of pro and con essays on subjects that lend themselves to debate.

APPARATUS FOR READING AND WRITING

The apparatus makes full use of the essays. Chapters 1 to 9 begin with a brief introduction to the student that depicts the mode or purpose under discussion, showing how it can be used in formal essays and in practical, everyday writing tasks. The introductions point out specifically how the modes can be shaped by considerations of audience, purpose, particular strategies, thesis, and organization, ending with advice on finding a subject, exploring a topic, and drafting a paper. This division of the writing process approximates the classic one of invention, arrangement, and style but is not intended to imply that these are separate stages.

To emphasize both what a text says and how it says it, each essay in Chapters 1 to 9 is preceded by background information on the author and the text and a brief discussion of a stylistic strategy. Two sets of questions—Thesis and Organization and Technique and Style—follow the essay. Then ideas for journal and essay writing are presented. Throughout, process and product, as well as reading and writing, are interrelated, emphasizing the recursive nature of the act of writing. Writers constantly invent, organize, and revise; the lines that distinguish those activities are narrow, if not downright blurred.

The suggestions for writing following each essay contain a number of options for both journal entries and essays, all related by theme, organization, or ideas to the work that has just been read. The assignments allow a good deal of flexibility: some lend themselves to general information or personal experience, some to research papers, and some to the classic technique of imitation. Once students select a subject, they will find flipping back to the introduction helpful. There the section "Exploring the Topic" shapes questions so that no matter what type of paper they are writing, students can generate information about it. "Drafting the Paper" then helps students organize the material and points out some of the pitfalls and advantages inherent in a particular mode or aim.

THE TEACHING AND LEARNING PACKAGE

A full array of supplements is available to support *Short Takes: Model Essays for Composition.*

An Instructor's Manual (0-321-07225-1) offers teaching suggestions and comprehension quizzes for each reading.

In addition, Longman offers a variety of other free or inexpensive supplements with this text. Ask your Longman sales representative for more information about the following:

- *100 Things to Write About*—100 writing prompts
- Discounted Penguin novels and works of nonfiction
- Discounted dictionaries, both hardcover and softcover
- The Longman Englishpages website: **http://www.ablongman.com/ englishpages**
- The Writer's ToolKit Plus CD-ROM for developing writers
- Daedalus Online
- *Researching Online*—an introduction to online research for students
- *Teaching Online*—a guide to integrating the Internet into the classroom
- Electronic Test Bank for Writing
- Competency Profile Test Bank
- Diagnostic and Editing Tests
- 80 Practices
- ESL Worksheets
- A Guide for Peer Response

ACKNOWLEDGMENTS

I have many people to thank for their help in bringing this book to publication: Liza Rudneva for her good advice and flexibility; Hope Rajala and Leslie Taggart, and Karen Helfrich for their able assistance with past editions; James Postema, Nancy Braun, and Kim McDonald for their help and their students; and Theodora Hill for her sound recommendations, patience, and help with the more mundane aspects of preparing a manuscript. Louis Bruno's careful copyediting of this edition is much appreciated. The following reviewers all provided guidance and advice that improved the manuscript: Alice Adams, Glendale Community College; Jonathan Alexander, University of Cincinnati; Kristine Bair, Fort Hays State University; Janel Davis, Saddleback College; Michel DeBenedictis, Miami-Dade Community College; Karl Edwards, Ricks College; Carol Goclan, Belmont Technical College; Peter Lindblom, Miami-Dade Community College; Frank Kelly, SUNY Farmingdale; James Murphy, Southern Illinois University; Joel Perez, San Diego Mesa College; Nancy Schneider, University of Maine at Augusta; and Lynne Weller, John Wood Community College.

ELIZABETH PENFIELD

Freeze Frame
Reading and Writing

This Book

1   In filmmaking, a "short take" is a brief scene filmed without interruption. Similarly, short essays move quickly toward their conclusions, with only the small breaks caused by paragraph indentations. Those are the kinds of essays you will find in this book, short essays that explain, argue, express the writer's feelings, or simply entertain. The essays carry out their purposes by drawing on various patterns of organization, patterns that can describe, tell a story, define a subject, provide examples, set up comparisons, or analyze a process or a cause and effect. These are the same patterns you will draw on when you write your own papers. The essays, then, can serve as models.

2   And just as the essays collected here are "short takes," this essay is a "freeze frame," as though you had stopped the film on one particular shot to get a better look at the details. That's just what this essay will do, stop and take a close-up look at what goes on when you read and when you write.

You, the Reader

3   A skilled reader interacts with the words on the page: reshaping, evaluating, selecting, analyzing. After all, you have your own world, one made up of everything you have experienced, from your first memory to your last thought—all of which you bring to what you read. An essay about why people love to walk on beaches, for example, will remind you of any beaches you know, and your associations will probably be pleasurable. As you begin the essay, you discover that the writer's associations are also pleasant ones, reinforcing yours. You read on, constantly reassessing your ideas about

the essay as you add more and more information to your first impression. Now and then, you may hit a sentence that at first doesn't make much sense, so you stop, perhaps to look up an unfamiliar word, perhaps to go back and review an earlier statement, then read on, again reevaluating your ideas about what the author is saying and what you think of it. The result is analytical, critical reading—not critical in the sense of judging harshly but critical in the sense of questioning, weighing evidence, evaluating, comparing your world to the one the writer has created on the page.

4   The idea of revising and tinkering is usually associated with writing, less so with reading. Yet just as you tinker and wrestle with your own writing, you should do the same with what you read. You should scribble, underline, question, challenge. Reading in this way, reading critically with pen or pencil in hand, will give you a fuller appreciation of what you read and a better understanding of the techniques the writer used to create the essay.

5   If you're not used to reading in this manner, it may seem foreign to you. After all, what's printed on the page should be easy enough to understand. But because words only stand for things and are not the things themselves, different readers find different meanings. If, for instance, your only memory of a beach was of nearly drowning in the Atlantic Ocean, then you would have to suspend that association when you read an essay that praises beach walking. And if your skin turns bright red at the mere mention of the sun, that adds one more obstacle to understanding why others enjoy the seashore. How then can a reader comprehend all that an author is saying? More specifically, how can a reader go about reading an essay critically?

6   ***Identifying the Purpose***   It helps to know what different kinds of writing have in common. Whether business letter, lab report, journal entry, news story, poem, or essay, all focus on a subject, address a reader, and have a point. And, too, all have a purpose and a style; they are written for specific reasons and in a certain way. These shared elements are perhaps more familiar as questions used to spark ideas for writing, the familiar journalistic *who? what? where? when? how? why?* Yet these questions can be equally useful for reading, and thinking about them will give you a general overview of what you are reading. To whom is an essay addressed? What is the writer's main point? How is the piece organized? Why is it structured that way? Where and when does the action take place? Many, many more in-

quiries can be spun off those seemingly simple questions, and they are useful tools for exploring an essay. Jotting down these questions and your answers to them in a notebook or journal can also sharpen your critical abilities and lead to a lively class discussion.

7   ***Looking for the Point***   In much of the reading we do, we are looking for information. The election coverage reported in the newspaper, the syllabus for a course, and a set of directions all exemplify this kind of reading, but reading for information and reading for comprehension are as different as a vitamin pill and a five-course dinner. To understand not only what a writer is saying but also its implications and why that writer might have chosen to say it that way isn't easy.

8   The title of an essay is a good place to start, for most titles tip you off not only about the subject of the piece but also to the author's stand. You don't need to turn to the essay titled "Sweatin' for Nothin'" to figure out it may be about exercising and that the author doesn't see much point to fitness fads. Other titles, such as "Left Sink," just imply a subject and raise your curiosity. What about a left sink? What does it mean? Some titles focus clearly on their subject, as in "Living With Cancer." Still others tip you off to the author's tone, the writer's attitude toward the subject: if an essay were called "Tube E or Not Tube E," the play on the familiar line from *Hamlet* suggests a humorous discussion of a chemistry lab course. Now and then, however, a title may announce a bald version of the thesis, such as an editorial headlined "Your Vote Counts." The editorial then would expand the idea so that a full version of the thesis becomes, "Your vote counts because a single ballot can change the outcome of an election—and it has."

9   Knowing or at least having a hint about the subject is the first step to discovering an essay's thesis, the assertion the author is making about the subject. The first paragraph or set of paragraphs that act as an introduction will also help you form a tentative thesis. Sometimes the writer will place the thesis in the first paragraph or introduction, but sometimes a bare-bones version of the thesis will appear in the title. If you see it, you should mark it. If you don't spot a thesis, you should still write down a tentative version of your own so that you have a focus for what is to follow, an idea against which you can test other ideas.

10   This last option is a bit of a challenge. You must create the thesis by identifying key sentences and then mentally composing a state-

ment that covers those ideas, a process that often takes more than one reading but is made easier if you underline the important sentences. Even then, you may well find that someone else who reads the essay comes up with a different thesis statement. And you both may be right. What's happening here? If you think about how slippery words are and the different experiences that different readers bring to an essay, you can begin to see why there's more than one "correct" thesis. If you were to give the same essay to 10 critical readers, you would find that their versions of the thesis differ but overlap. Their readings would probably cluster around two or three central ideas. If an eleventh person read the essay and came up with a thesis that contradicted the 10 other readings, that version would probably be off base.

11   Sometimes writers unwittingly set traps, making it easy to mistake a fact for a thesis. If you keep in mind that a thesis is both a sentence and an assertion—a value judgment—those traps can be avoided. "The average American watches a lot of TV" states a fact most readers would shrug off with a "So what?" On the other hand, "Television rots the minds of its viewers" takes a stand that will probably raise hackles and a "Hey, wait a minute!"

Recognizing Patterns of Development

12   Once you've nailed down a thesis, go a step further to examine how that thesis is developed. Writers depend on various patterns of thought or modes of thinking that are almost innate. To tell a joke is to narrate; to convey what a party was like is to describe and to use examples; to decide which among many courses to take is to divide and classify; to figure out which car to buy is to compare and contrast (and if you think of your old car as a peach or a lemon, you are drawing an analogy); to give directions is to use process; to consider how to improve your tennis game is to weigh cause and effect; to explain how you feel is to define. Narration, description, example, division and classification, comparison and contrast, analogy, process, cause and effect, and definition are the natural modes of thinking upon which writers rely.

13   These patterns of thought provide the structure of an essay. A piece on the ethics of using prisoners to test new medicines might open with a brief narrative that sets the scene, go on to define what kinds of medicines are involved, and then explain the effects of such experiments on the prisoners, the development of new drugs, and society's concept

of ethics. As you read, you should note each type of mode the writer uses so you can more fully understand how the thesis is developed and how the essay is organized. Though you may find an essay uses many types of modes, it's likely that one predominates.

You, the Writer

14 Central to any kind of writing is the question "Why am I doing this?" The obvious first answer for most students is "Because it's assigned." Equally obvious is that writing is hard work, involving both time and effort. While a good grade can be a reward, it rarely seems equal to the thought and struggle that went into writing an essay; however, it is also true that writing can be its own reward. By writing, you learn about yourself and your subject, you sharpen your mind, and you increase your concentration. But once you have written something you like, you will find that fear is apt to replace enthusiasm, for the only thing scarier than putting words on paper is the idea that someone is going to read them. This kind of fear is something that most writers, students or professionals, experience. Yet you will find that having someone respond to your paper with "Hey, that was really good" or "I really liked that" more than makes up for the anxiety you experienced when you first sat down to write.

15 A blank sheet of paper or an empty computer screen can be a terrifying thing, so how should you begin? Odds are, you've been thinking about what to write, so in a sense you've already started your essay even though nothing is on paper. Now you need to get those thoughts into print. Try not to think of a finished piece or how your paper will begin or end; just start writing anything— notes, a title, a list of ideas, an outline, a paragraph—whatever comes to mind. At this stage, you're brainstorming, coming up with ideas and bouncing them off each other so that you can figure out what you are trying to say. Figuring out how you want your reader to respond, shaping your ideas, organizing and then polishing them can come later. At this point you end up with scraps of paper or ideas scattered across your computer screen, and you are well on your way to writing your essay.

16 ***Thinking about Your Audience*** As you work on your notes, you'll need to decide on your purpose in writing your essay. Yes, it's because it's assigned; yes, because you want a high grade; but

more to the point, you want to inform, persuade, or entertain your reader, perhaps all three. In writing, as in speech, your purpose determines the relationship among your subject, yourself, and your reader. If you were taking a creative writing course, you would be emphasizing the text itself, a world that you have made up, and your purpose would be to entertain your reader in the best sense of the word, to engage that person with your text, to make the fictional world a real one. Most of the writing you will be doing in college, however, is intended to inform. For that reason, most of the essays included in this book are expository; their primary purpose is to explain a subject, to inform the reader. In most of your other courses, you will find that your reading fits into this category, one occupied by stacks of textbooks. As for your writing, when you write a lab or book report, a précis, or an essay exam, you focus on your subject so that you explain it to your readers.

17   Though explaining may be your primary purpose, other aims that are secondary enter in as well. In an essay exam about a historical event, you are also trying to convince your reader that you know what you are writing about. Your reader, of course, is your teacher, someone who knows more about your subject than you do, so you aren't trying to explain the subject; instead you're trying to persuade your teacher that your interpretation of it is sound.

18   If you're writing a journal or diary entry or a personal letter, however, your focus is on yourself, the writer. That's also true if you're writing an opinion piece in the newspaper or a meditative essay. If, for example, your teacher asks you to keep a journal in which you respond to what you read, your responses may range from fury over an opinion you disagree with to mild musings on what you think about the author's subject. What is important is what you feel, and your writing expresses those feelings by communicating them clearly to your reader. You, not the subject, are center stage.

19   Conveying what you feel about a subject and persuading your reader to share your opinion, however, are two different aims. Let's say you have a strong opinion about the "three strikes and you're out" policy of a mandatory sentence of life imprisonment for those convicted of a third felony. You decide to write a letter to the editor, and in it you rage on about the policy being a form of racism and claim that life imprisonment is "cruel and unusual punishment." While you may feel better for having let off some steam, few minds, if any, will have been changed; probably the only readers who fin-

ished your letter were those who agreed with you to begin with. The letter appeals to the emotions by waving the red flag of racism and the star-spangled banner of the Constitution. Think about the difference if you were to recast your ideas into the genre of an editorial or guest opinion piece, a type of writing that leans on reason for its appeal. You might start by pointing out that the definition of what is or is not a felony differs from state to state, that many more prisons would have to be built and maintained, that judges—if allowed—can weigh the severity of the offense and the punishment it deserves, that the "three strikes" presents more problems than it resolves. You are careful to address a multiple audience of readers who agree, disagree, or have no opinion. You intend to make the reader think, and, ideally, to change opinions, so the argument's appeal rests primarily on reason, not emotion.

20 ***Discovering a Thesis***   You will find that writing is a form of discovery, that writing about an idea helps clarify it. In your own experience, you have probably found that you usually don't have a clear grasp of your main point until you've written your way into it. Odds are you start with an idea, a general focus, say, on professional wrestling, but that focus becomes clearer as you rethink your choice of a particular word or reread what you've put on the page to get a sense of what should come next. Gradually, your ideas become clearer and out of them an assertion emerges: professional wrestling may not be much of a sport, but it's splendid theater. And on you go, sometimes speeding, sometimes creeping, constantly revising, working out a draft of your paper.

21   Once your thesis is clear, then you must decide where to place it for the greatest effect. You may opt for placing it at the end of your introduction, but perhaps it would be best in your conclusion, or you may decide on a more subtle solution by weaving bits and pieces of the thesis into the essay as a whole. You may find it best to hold off a decision until you've worked some more on your essay's organization.

22 ***Organizing the Essay***   Description, narration, cause and effect, and the like are modes that provide the structure of the essay, the means by which you support your major point, the thesis, and more often than not, you will draw upon several patterns of development to support your major point. Rarely does an essay rely solely on one pattern of development. In the example above, the

thesis—professional wrestling may not be much of a sport, but it's splendid theater—suggests a paper that might begin with a brief introduction that describes the cast of wrestlers and their costumes, then develop the thesis by defining what makes a sport a sport, comparing professional wrestling with that definition, and presenting examples as evidence that professional wrestling is theater. Most of the essay would concentrate on examples, which would be its primary mode of organization.

23   When you are writing, modes such as example, definition, and the like provide ways to think about your topic as well as ways to organize your essay. With practice they become as much second nature as shifting gears in a manual-transmission car. At first you might be a bit tentative about knowing when to shift from first to second, but with time you don't even think about it. Similarly, you might wonder if your point is clear without an example; in time, you automatically supply it.

24   Knowing what you want to write and having a fair idea of how it should be organized still does not necessarily help you shape individual sentences so that they convey the desired tone, so that they *sound* right. That requires draft after draft. Even the idea of finishing is a shaky notion; many writers will continue to revise right up to their deadlines. Hemingway rewrote the last page of *A Farewell to Arms* 39 times, and Katherine Anne Porter spent 20 years writing and rewriting *Ship of Fools*. Writing nonfiction doesn't make the process any easier. Wayne Booth, a distinguished essayist and scholar, speaks for most writers: "I revise many, many times, as many times as deadlines allow for. And I always feel that I would have profited from further revision." Poet, novelist, essayist, journalist, student, or professional, all continue in the tradition expressed in the eighteenth century by a fellow writer, Samuel Johnson, who said, "What is written without effort is in general read without pleasure." Pleasurable reading derives from a pleasing writing style, and though some writers strive for elegance as well as clarity, most readers will happily settle for clarity.

25   Far from following a recipe, you will find that writing an essay is like driving a car while at the same time trying to impress the passengers, read a road map, recognize occasional familiar landmarks, follow scrawled and muttered directions, and watch for and listen to all the quirks of the car. You know vaguely where you are going and how you want to get there, but the rest is risk and adventure.

With work and a number of dry runs, you can smooth out the trip
so that the passengers fully appreciate the pleasure of the drive and
the satisfaction of reaching the destination. That is the challenge the
writer faces, a challenge that demands critical reading as well as effective writing.

Reading and Writing

26   Essays can be deceptive. What you see on the printed page resembles the writer's work about as much as a portrait resembles the
real person. What you don't see when you look at printed pages
are all the beginnings and stops, the crumpled paper, the false
starts, the notes, the discarded ideas, the changed words. Instead,
you have a finished piece—the result of the writer's choices. Don't
be intimidated. The process most writers go through to produce
their essays is very like your own. The writer Andre Dubus puts it
another way: "There is something mystical [about writing] but it's
not rare and nobody should treat it as though this is something special that writers do. Anybody born physically able in the brain can
sit down and begin to write something, and discover that there are
depths in her soul or his soul that are untapped."

27   As a writer and a reader, you tap into those depths, depths that
help make meaning of the world we live in. The making of meaning is the heart of the essays contained in this book, together with
its explanations, questions, and suggestions for writing. Stated con-
cisely, this book reinforces a basic assumption: reading and writing
are highly individual processes that are active, powerful, and interrelated ways to discover meaning. To check out that statement,
think of one day within the last week when something memorable
happened to you. Isolate that incident so it's clear in your mind.
Now think of all the other details of the day, from the time your
eyes opened in the morning to the time they closed at night. That's
a lot of detail, and most of it insignificant, meaningless, bits and
pieces of information you would probably discard if you were to
write about that day. What you would be left with is that memorable thing that occurred and a few details directly related to it,
some preceding it, a few following. In writing about that day, you
would reshape events—evaluating, selecting, and recreating what
happened so that what was most meaningful comes through
clearly. As a result, someone reading your description would be

able to experience at a distance what you experienced firsthand. To write, then, is to create and structure a world; to read is to become part of someone else's. And just as reading makes a better writer, writing makes a better reader.

28   As a writer, you learn from the act of writing because of being forced to examine the subject closely, to explore it, and to communicate something of interest about it. So, too, as a reader, you learn from an interesting, well written essay, perhaps finding a fresh perspective on a familiar topic or discovering information about the unfamiliar. Both as a reader and a writer, you work to create meaning out of what is on the page. The result is not just sweat and knowledge but pleasure. Good prose delights.

➤ POINTERS FOR READING

1. **Settle in.** Gather up a good dictionary and whatever you like to write with, and then find a comfortable place to read.
2. **Think about the title.** What sort of expectations do you have about what will follow? Can you identify the subject? A thesis? Can you tell anything about the writer's tone?
3. **Look for a specific focus.** Where is the essay going? What appears to be its thesis? At what point does the introduction end and the body of the essay begin? What questions do you have about the essay so far? Is the essay directed at you? If not, who is the intended audience?
4. **Look for a predominant pattern of organization.** What are the most important ideas in the body of the essay? Note the modes the writer uses to develop those ideas. Note those you disagree with or question.
5. **Identify the conclusion.** Where does the conclusion begin? How does it end the essay? What effect does it have on you?
6. **Evaluate the essay.** Did the essay answer the questions you had about it? How effective was the support for the main ideas? Did the writer's choice of words fit the audience? What effect did the essay have on you? Why?

➤ POINTERS FOR WRITING

1. **Settle in.** Get hold of whatever you find comfortable to write with—computer, pen, pencil, legal pad, note paper, notebook—and settle into wherever you like to write. Start by jotting down words that represent a general idea of your subject. As words cross your mind, write them down so that at this point you have a vague focus.
2. **Focus.** Try writing right away and quickly. Get your ideas down on paper without worrying about organization or punctuation or whether what you

write is right. If you run out of steam, pause and read over what you have written and then summarize it in one sentence. Then start up again writing as quickly as you can. At some point you will have written your way into a tentative thesis that will help you focus as you revise what you have written.

3. **Reread.** Go over what you have written, looking for sentences that state an opinion. Mark them in some way (a highlighter is useful). These sentences can become topic sentences that lead off paragraphs and, therefore, help you organize your ideas.

4. **Organize what you have.** Go through what you have written asking yourself questions. What would make a good introduction? A good conclusion? What order best suits what's in between? What examples do you have? Where would they work best?

5. **Think about your purpose.** As you reread what you've written, think about the kind of effect you want to have on your readers. Are you explaining something to them? Arguing a cause? Telling them how you feel? Entertaining them? Some combination of purposes?

6. **Think about your readers.** What do they know about your subject? Your answer to this question may make you cut out some information; and what they don't know will guide you to what you need to include. Do they have a bias for or against what you have to say? Your answer here will tell you if you need to account for those biases and suggest how you might do that.

7. **Revise.** You've probably been revising all along, but at this point you can revise more thoroughly and deeply. You know your purpose, audience, and thesis—all of which will help you organize your paper more effectively.

8. **Proofread.** Now look for surface errors, checking for spelling and punctuation. If you're using a word-processing program, run your text through the spelling checker. As for punctuation, if you have access to a grammar checker on your word processor, try it. You may find it useful, but probably a handbook of grammar and usage will be much more helpful as the explanations are fuller and you'll find lots of examples. The easiest way to use a handbook is to look up the key word in the index.

On Using
Description

Description turns up in various guises in all types of prose, for it is the basic device a writer uses to convey sense impressions. For that reason, it is as essential to **objective**[1] writing as it is to **subjective** prose and, of course, to everything in between. A quick sketch of a family gathering that you might include in a letter to a friend draws on the same skills as a complex report on the effectiveness of a new product. Both rely on the ability to observe, to select the most important details, to create a coherent sequence for those details, and then to convey the result by appealing to the reader's senses. To describe something, then, is to recreate it in such a way that it becomes alive again, so that the reader can see and understand it. Prose that depends heavily on description invites the reader to share the writer's initial sense of vividness and perception.

The role description plays in writing will vary. Personal narratives depend heavily on description to bring scenes and actions to life, to depict an outdoor wedding, for instance, or to convey what it feels like to have a toothache. Other types of expository essays use description in a less obvious role, perhaps to clarify a step in a process or make an example vivid. And persuasion often gets its punch from description, for it enables the reader to see the prisoner on death row or the crime that led to the death sentence. While no essay relies solely on description, each of the essays that follow uses description as its primary pattern of organization. The essays' general subjects are familiar—a place, a person, a frog—but by selecting details, each author tailors description uniquely.

---

[1]Words printed in boldface are defined under "Useful Terms" at the end of each introductory section.

AUDIENCE AND PURPOSE

Most writers start with a general sense of purpose and audience. Perhaps you want to explain an event or how something works or what you think about a particular place, person, or idea, in which case your purpose is expository and what you write is **exposition.** You focus on your subject so that you can explain it clearly to your reader. That's not as dull as it sounds. Odds are that if you wrote a description of your neighborhood in such a way that your readers felt as though they could see it, you'd have an interesting expository essay. Sure, it represents your opinion, how *you* see your neighborhood, but the focus is clearly on the subject; you are in the position of narrator, telling your readers about your subject, explaining it to them.

But imagine that as you begin to think about your neighborhood your thoughts turn to ways in which your life there could be improved. Perhaps the garbage could be picked up more frequently, the sidewalks could be repaired, or the property taxes lowered. All of a sudden you're off on an argumentative tear, one that can take a number of different forms—essay, letter to the editor, or letter to your city or state representative. But no matter who you write for, you're engaging in **persuasion** and your focus is on the reader, the person whose mind you want to change.

Writers who aim their work at a definite audience, say the readers of a particular magazine, have a head start by knowing the readership. One of the essays in this chapter comes from *Sierra*, the journal of the Sierra Club, an organization devoted to the preservation of American wildlife and nature. Writing for that audience, the author can assume a definite interest in animal life of almost any variety, so the only problem that remains is how to make the particular creature real and interesting.

If your audience is a more general one, say the readers of a newspaper or your classmates, the situation is quite different. The assumptions you can make must be more general. For a newspaper it's safe to assume, for instance, that most of the readers are educated and fall into a general age group ranging from young adult to middle-aged. Knowing that can help you estimate the distance between your subject and the audience. If your subject is old age, you will know that your readers are generally knowledgeable about the topic but that their experience is indirect. That means you must fill in the gap with descriptive details so that their experience becomes more direct, so that the readers can see and feel what it's like to be old. And if your audience is your classmates, a younger group, the gap between subject and audience is even wider so your description has to be even more full.

In addition to having a firm sense of what your audience does and does not know, it helps to know how your readers may feel about your subject and how you want them to feel. How you want them to feel is a matter of **tone,** your attitude toward the subject and the audience. Many readers, for example, are understandably squeamish about the subject of war, and that creates a problem for the writer, particularly one who wants to describe a scene realistically and at the same time elicit sympathy. One solution is to pretty it up, but that does a disservice to reality; however, too realistic a description can be so revolting that no one would read it. Nor would anyone read a dry, objective account. Rudyard Kipling, who most of us know through his *Jungle Stories,* faced this problem when he wrote *The Irish Guards in the Great War,* a history of a military unit in World War I. His description of the German positions before the British attack on the Somme can be summarized objectively by removing most of the details to create an intentionally flat, dull tone:

> The Germans had been strengthening their defenses for two years. It was a defense in depth, exploiting the smooth slopes ascending to their high ground. They fortified forests and villages and dug deep underground shelters in the chalky soil. They protected their positions with copious wire, often arranged to force attackers into the fire of machine guns. (Fussell 172).

Now compare that prose with how Kipling solves the problem of tone by finding a middle yet realistic ground:

> Here the enemy had sat for two years, looking down upon France and daily strengthening himself. His trebled and quadrupled lines of defense, worked for him by his prisoners, ran below and along the flanks and on the tops of ranges of five-hundred-foot downs. Some of these were studded with close woods, deadlier even than the fortified villages between them; some cut with narrowing valleys that drew machine-gun fire as chimneys draw draughts; some opening into broad, seemingly smooth slopes, whose every haunch and hollow covered sunk forts, carefully placed mine-fields, machine-gun pits, gigantic quarries, enlarged in the chalk, connecting with systems of catacomb-like dug-outs and subterranean works at all depths, in which brigades could lie till the fitting moment. Belt upon belt of fifty-yard-deep wire protected these points, either directly or at such angles as should herd and hold up

attacking infantry to the fire of veiled guns. Nothing in the entire system had been neglected or unforeseen, except knowledge of the nature of the men who, in due time, should wear their red way through every yard of it.[2]

Kipling's description is essentially an explanation, but note the argumentative twist he puts in his last sentence, his reference to the men of the Irish Guards and their valiant attack and huge losses, the blood of their "red way." There's no question about whose side Kipling is on. And there's no question about how he wants his readers to feel.

DETAILS

No matter what the purpose or audience, descriptive essays are characterized by their use of detail. Note how many details are in the paragraph by Kipling, most of which are **concrete details.** The German defenses had not just been strengthened but "trebled and quadrupled." Nor is Kipling satisfied with **abstract words.** He tells us the quarries were "gigantic," an abstract word that has different meanings to different people, so he gives us a concrete sense of just how large those quarries are—they could hide whole brigades. We get a visual idea of their size. Visual detail also helps us see the wire defenses. Because Kipling's book, from which the passage was taken, was published in 1923, shortly after the end of World War I, a time when tanks, missiles, and bombers as we know them were unheard of, the general particulars of trench warfare were still fresh in his readers' minds; they would know, for example, that the wire he refers to is barbed wire, but Kipling makes his audience (both then and now) see it by saying that it was "belt upon belt" of wire, "fifty-yard-deep" wire.

Visual details make us see what a writer is describing, but using other appeals to the senses also bring prose to life. Once you start thinking about it, you'll find images that draw in other senses. For auditory appeal, for instance, you might think of a time when you walked in snow so dry that a snowball turns to powder and you could hear the small

---

[2]Quoted in Paul Fussell's *The Great War and Modern Memory*. New York: Oxford UP, 1977.

squeal of your footsteps; and if your climate goes to the other extreme, you might remember a blistering night and the chirps, bleeps, squeaks, and rasps put forth by a chorus of summer insects.

COMPARISON

Take any object and try to describe what it looks, feels, smells, sounds, and tastes like, and you'll quickly find yourself shifting over to comparisons. Comparisons enrich description in that they can produce an arresting image, explain the unfamiliar, make a connection with the reader's own experience, or reinforce the major point in the essay. Comparing the unfamiliar to the familiar makes what is being described more real. Even the computer-illiterate among us get the idea embedded in the term *world wide web*, immediately imagining an electronic spider web that encompasses the globe. The image is a metaphor, and often comparisons take the form of **metaphor, simile, or allusion.**

Simile and *metaphor* both draw a comparison between dissimilar things; the terms differ in that a simile uses a comparative word such as *like* or *as*. As a result, metaphor is often the more arresting because it is a direct equation. If you were writing and got stuck to the point where nothing worked—the classic writer's block—you might describe your state as "sinking in the quicksand of words." Then when you broke through and started writing again, you might think of it as being able to "open the locked door," even though the process of writing may be like the labors of Hercules, an allusion to the hero of Greek myths and his difficult and superhuman feats.

Unfortunately, the first comparisons that often come to mind can be overworked ones known as **clichés:** *green as grass, hot as hell, mad as a hornet, red as a rose,* and the like. While you can guard against them by being suspicious of any metaphor or simile that sounds familiar, clichés can sneak into your writing in less obvious ways. Watch out for descriptive words that come readily to mind—waves that pound or crash, clouds that are fluffy, bells that tinkle.

Analogy is another form of comparison. Think of it as a metaphor that is extended beyond a phrase into several sentences or a paragraph. You can understand how that can happen if you think of a metaphor for the way you write. Some may imagine a roller coaster; others might think of having to manage a busy switchboard; and for some it may be trying to build a house without having any blueprints or knowing what materials are needed. No matter which image, you can tell that it will take more than a sentence or two to develop the metaphor into an analogy.

DICTION

The words a writer chooses determine whether the description is more objective or subjective, whether its tone is factual or impressionistic. Although total objectivity is impossible, description that leans toward the objective is called for when the writer wants to focus on the subject as opposed to emotional effect, on what something is rather than how it felt. Read the paragraph below by J. Merrill-Foster in which she describes an 85-year-old woman.

> She is frightened and distressed by letters from retired military men. They write that unless she sends $35 by return mail, the Russians will land in Oregon and take over America. The arrival of the daily mail looms large in her day. Once, every few weeks, it contains a personal letter. The rest is appeals and ads. She reads every item.

That passage comes from the first part of Merrill-Foster's essay, which ends with this paragraph:

> I watch the woman—my mother—walking carefully down the frozen, snow-filled driveway to the mail box. She is a photograph in black and white, which only loving memory tints with stippled life and color.

The first description reports the unnamed woman's feelings and the facts that give rise to them and then generalizes on the importance of the daily mail, noting what it contains and the attention the woman gives it. The second description uses first person and identifies the woman as the author's mother, the words *I* and *mother* forming an emotional bond between reader and writer, overlaying with feeling the picture of the woman walking to the mailbox. On finishing the first passage, the reader understands the role an everyday event—the arrival of the mail—plays in the life of an old woman; on finishing the second, the reader knows and feels how old age has diminished a once vital person.

THESIS AND ORGANIZATION

All the details, all the comparisons are organized so that they add up to a single dominant impression. In descriptive essays, this single dominant impression may be implicit or explicit, and it stands as the **thesis.** An explicit thesis jumps off the page at you and is usually stated openly in one or two easily identifiable sentences. An implicit thesis, however, is more subtle. As reader, you come to understand what the thesis is even though you can't identify any single sentence that states it. If that process of deduction seems mysterious, think of reading a description of the ultimate pizza, a description that alluringly recounts its aroma, taste, texture. After reading about that pizza you would probably think, Wow, that's a really good pizza. And that's an implied thesis.

Whether implicit or explicit, the thesis is what the writer builds the essay on. It's the main point. The writer must select the most important details, create sentences and paragraphs around them, and then sequence the paragraphs so that everything not only contributes to but also helps create the thesis. In description, paragraphs can be arranged by **patterns of organization,** such as process and definition, and according to spatial, temporal, or dramatic relationships. The writer can describe a scene so that the reader moves from one place to another, from one point in time to another, or according to a dramatic order. If this last idea seems vague, think of how a film or novel builds to a high point, one that usually occurs just before the end.

The building block for that high point and for the essay itself is the paragraph. And just as the essay has a controlling idea, an assertion that is its thesis, so, too, does the paragraph, usually in the form of a **topic sentence.** Like the thesis, the topic sentence can be explicit or implied, and it can be found in one sentence or deduced from the statements made in several. A topic sentence often covers more than one paragraph, for paragraphs frequently cluster around a central idea, particularly in a longer essay, one over 600 words or so.

There's no magic number for how many words make up a paragraph and no magic number for how many paragraphs make up an essay. But it is safe to say that all essays have a beginning, middle, and end. The same is true of a paragraph or group of paragraphs that function under one topic sentence. As you read, ask yourself why a given paragraph ends where it does and what links it to the one that follows. You may discover that sometimes paragraph breaks are not set in cement, that they could occur in several different places and still be "right."

USEFUL TERMS

Abstract words Words that stand for something that cannot be easily visualized and, therefore, may hold different meanings for different people. A box of cereal labeled "large" may be your idea of "small."

Allusion An indirect reference to a real or fictitious person, place, or thing.

Analogy A point-by-point comparison to something seemingly unlike but more commonplace and less complex than the subject. An analogy is also an extended metaphor.

Cliché A comparison, direct or indirect, that has been used so often that it has worn out its novelty, such as *cool as a cucumber* or *ice cold*.

Concrete details Words that stand for something that can be easily visualized and have fixed meaning. If you replaced the "large" on the cereal box with "8 ounces" or "two servings for moderately hungry people," you would be replacing the abstract with more definite, concrete details.

Exposition Writing that explains; also called expository writing.

Metaphor An implied but direct comparison in which the primary term is made more vivid by associating it with a quite dissimilar term. "Life is a roller coaster" is a metaphor.

Objective prose Writing that is impersonal.

Patterns of organization Paragraphs and essays are usually organized according to the patterns illustrated in this book: description, narration, example, division and classification, comparison, process, cause and effect, and definition. Although more than one pattern may exist in a paragraph or essay, usually one predominates.

Persuasion Writing that argues a point, that attempts to convince the reader to adopt the writer's stand.

Simile A comparison in which the primary term is linked to a dissimilar one by *like* or *as* to create a vivid image. "Life is like a roller coaster" is a simile. Remove the linking word and you have a metaphor.

Subjective prose Writing that is personal.

Thesis A one-sentence statement or summary of the basic arguable point of the essay.

Tone A writer's attitude toward the subject and the audience.

Topic sentence A statement of the topic of a paragraph containing an arguable point that is supported by the rest of the paragraph.

➤ POINTERS FOR USING DESCRIPTION

Exploring the Topic

1. **What distinguishes your topic?** What characteristics, features, or actions stand out about your subject? Which are most important? Least important?
2. **What senses can you appeal to?** What can you emphasize about your subject that would appeal to sight? Smell? Touch? Taste? Motion?
3. **What concrete details can you use?** What abstract words do you associate with each of the features or events you want to emphasize? How can you make those abstractions concrete?
4. **How can you vary your narrative?** Where might you use quotations? Where might you use dialogue?
5. **What can your audience identify with?** What comparisons can you use? What similes, metaphors, or allusions come to mind?
6. **What order should you use?** Is your description best sequenced by Time? Place? Dramatic order?
7. **What is your tentative thesis?** What is the dominant impression you want to create? Do you want it to be implicit? Explicit?
8. **What is your relationship to your subject?** Given your tentative thesis, how objective or subjective should you be? Do you want to be part of the action or removed? What personal pronoun should you use?

Drafting the Paper

1. **Know your reader.** If you are writing about a familiar subject, ask yourself what your reader might not know about it. If you are writing about an unfamiliar subject, ask yourself what your reader does know that you can use for comparison.
2. **Know your purpose.** If you are writing to inform, make sure you are presenting new information and in enough detail to bring your subject to life. If you are writing to persuade, make sure your details add up so that the reader is moved to adopt your conviction. Keep in mind that your reader may not share your values and indeed may even hold opposite ones.
3. **Vary sensory details.** Emphasize important details by appealing to more than just one sense.
4. **Show, don't tell.** Avoid abstract terms such as *funny* or *beautiful*. Instead, use concrete details, quotations, and dialogue. Don't settle for vague adjectives such as *tall*; replace them with sharper details such as *6 feet 7 inches*.
5. **Use comparisons.** Make your description vivid with an occasional metaphor or simile. If you are writing about something quite unfamiliar, use literal comparison to make your description clear.

6. **Arrange your details to create a single dominant impression.** If you are writing descriptive paragraphs, check the order of your sentences to make sure they follow each other logically and support the impression you wish to create. If you are writing an essay that relies heavily on description, check for the same points from one paragraph to another. Is your topic sentence or thesis implicit or explicit? Reexamine your first paragraph. Does it establish the scene? The tone?

The Mute Sense

Diane Ackerman

As an undergraduate at Boston University and then Pennsylvania State University, Diane Ackerman studied both science and literature, twin interests she would pursue as a writer. A staff writer for The New Yorker, *Ackerman often writes on nature and its inhabitants.* The Moon by Whale Light, *a collection of her essays, was published in 1991; it is subtitled* and Other Adventures among Bats, Penguins, Crocodiles, and Whales. *Her most recent nonfiction book,* A Slender Thread *(1997), grew out of her volunteer work as a counselor at a suicide prevention and crisis center. The essay below comes from Ackerman's* A Natural History of the Senses, *which was published in 1990 and has since been translated into many languages. Ackerman is also a well-respected poet, and in "The Mute Sense" she manages to combine the vivid detail and compression characteristic of poetry with the precise detail and keen observation associated with science.*

WHAT TO LOOK FOR *Good writers have a way of listening to words so that the words talk back, one word suggesting another or a whole image that can lead both writer and reader into the prose. They use strong verbs that suggest action, not forms of the verb* to be. *Try to tune your own ear so that you pick up the comparisons implicit in your verbs. That's what might have happened when Ackerman chose* detonate *toward the end of her first paragraph, a verb from which she spins a metaphor. Notice, too, how often she uses comparisons and allusions, piling on examples so that if a reader misses one, another is sure to hit home.*

1   Nothing is more memorable than a smell. One scent can be unexpected, momentary, and fleeting, yet conjure up a childhood summer beside a lake in the Poconos, when wild blueberry bushes teemed with succulent fruit and the opposite sex was as mysterious as space travel; another, hours of passion on a moonlit beach in Florida, while the night-blooming cereus drenched the air with thick curds of perfume and high sphinx moths visited the cereus in a loud purr of wings; a third, a family dinner of pot roast, noodle pudding, and sweet potatoes, during a myrtle-mad August in a mid-

western town, when both of one's parents were alive. Smells detonate softly in our memory like poignant land mines, hidden under
the weedy mass of many years and experiences. Hit a tripwire of
smell, and memories explode all at once. A complex vision leaps
out of the undergrowth.

2   People of all cultures have always been obsessed with smell,
sometimes applying perfumes in Niagaras of extravagance. The Silk
Road opened up the Orient to the western world, but the scent
road opened up the heart of Nature. Our early ancestors strolled
among the fruits of the earth with noses vigilant and precise, following the seasons smell by smell, at home in their brimming
larder. We can detect over ten thousand different odors, so many,
in fact, that our memories would fail us if we tried to jot down
everything they represent. In "The Hound of the Baskervilles,"
Sherlock Holmes identifies a woman by the smell of her notepaper,
pointing out that "There are seventy-five perfumes, which it is very
necessary that a criminal expert should be able to distinguish from
each other." A low number, surely. After all, anyone "with a nose
for" crime should be able to sniff out culprits from their tweed,
Indian ink, talcum powder, Italian leather shoes, and countless
other scented paraphernalia. Not to mention the odors, radiant and
nameless, which we decipher without even knowing it. The brain is
a good stagehand. It gets on with its work while we're busy acting
out our scenes. Though most people will swear they couldn't possibly do such a thing, studies show that both children and adults, just
by smelling, are able to determine whether a piece of clothing was
worn by a male or a female.

3   Our sense of smell can be extraordinarily precise, yet it's almost
impossible to describe how something smells to someone who
hasn't smelled it. The smell of the glossy pages of a new book, for
example, or the first solvent-damp sheets from a mimeograph machine, or a dead body, or the subtle differences in odors given off
by flowers like bee balm, dogwood, or lilac. Smell is the mute
sense, the one without words. Lacking a vocabulary, we are left
tongue-tied, groping for words in a sea of inarticulate pleasure and
exaltation. We see only when there is light enough, taste only when
we put things into our mouths, touch only when we make contact
with someone or something, hear only sounds that are loud
enough. But we smell always and with every breath. Cover your
eyes and you will stop seeing, cover your ears and you will stop

hearing, but if you cover your nose and try to stop smelling, you will die. Etymologically speaking, a breath is not neutral or bland— it's *cooked air;* we live in a constant simmering. There is a furnace in our cells, and when we breathe we pass the world through our bodies, brew it lightly, and turn it loose again, gently altered for having known us.

THESIS AND ORGANIZATION

1. Ideally, a first paragraph can do many jobs: introduce the topic, suggest or state the thesis, snag the reader's interest, set the tone of the essay. Rereading Ackerman's first paragraph, you can understand more fully how it functions in relation to the rest of the essay. Explain what you have discovered and give examples to support your ideas.
2. Does paragraph 2 have a topic sentence? If so, what is it? If not, what topic sentence would you supply?
3. Try out paragraph 3 as the introductory paragraph. Explain why it doesn't work well in that position.
4. To what extent is the last paragraph a satisfactory ending for the essay?
5. In your own words, without looking at the essay, state what you find to be its thesis. Then look at the essay. What sentence, if any, comes closest to your statement?

TECHNIQUE AND STYLE

1. Take a highlighter and mark all the active verbs you find in one paragraph. Choose one and explain how it is or is not effective.
2. Ackerman's essay alludes to both people and places: "a lake in the Poconos," "a moonlit beach in Florida," "a midwestern town," "Niagaras," "The Silk Road," Sherlock Holmes, and "The Hound of the Baskervilles." Explain how these allusions relate to Ackerman's sense of her audience.
3. Do you think the tone of Ackerman's essay is more objective than subjective or the other way around? Explain your answer by citing examples from the text.
4. When you write an essay that uses a central term, you risk ineffective repetition. Reread Ackerman's essay, keeping track of the number of times she uses the word *smell.* In what ways do you find the repetition effective or ineffective?
5. Poets rely on sound as well as sense to carry meaning, and Ackerman is well aware of the sound of her language. Look, for example, at the *s* sounds in Ackerman's second sentence. Try this device in your own writing by taking one of your longer sentences and revising it in such a way that you emphasize its sound.

SUGGESTIONS FOR WRITING

Journal

1. Try out Ackerman's idea that "Nothing is more memorable than a smell" by describing a particular smell you have experienced and its associations for you.

2. Think of a smell that would be familiar to almost everyone in the class, one that has neutral to pleasant associations, and describe it without naming it. You may want to try out your description on the class to see if anyone recognizes your subject.

Essay

With the word choice *conjure up* in Ackerman's second sentence, she implies that the sense of smell has an almost magical effect on memory. Assuming she is correct, think of a smell that triggered (or triggers) your memory of a place, person, or event. Once you have a topic, write down as many details as you can, then examine your list to find out what order would be best to present them in. Consider your readers' general attitude toward your subject; if it is neutral or hostile, try to counter it. Suggestions:

the indoor smell of cut flowers
the smell of leather, bread baking, or brakes burning
the smell of a parents' or relatives' aftershave or perfume
the smell of a particular hospital, school, or church

The Bridge

Jason Holland

Almost everyone has a special place, either in the present or past, that represents any number of emotions, pleasure being first among them. For Jason Holland, that place was a bridge and the time was when he was in high school. He is now a student at Valley City State University in Valley City, North Dakota, having decided on attending VCSU because of the academic and athletic opportunities the university provided. When he began his first semester composition course, he says that he was "somewhat skeptical of my writing skills, but began finding it was easy to write about memorable moments," particularly those spent with his friends in high school. He used "writing about these incidents as an outlet as well as a coping device" to accommodate himself to the difficulties of college life. One of the results is what he characterizes "a short, descriptive essay," "The Bridge." Noreen Braun, his instructor, reprinted the essay on a web page devoted to what she titled as "Some Fine Student Writing from Composition I, Fall Semester, 1997."

WHAT TO LOOK FOR   *If you are having a difficult time giving your reader a vivid picture of your scene, you might try writing down as many adjectives and adverbs about various objects or people that you associate with the place. After you have done this, then you can choose the most appropriate ones. That is what Jason Holland did when he was coming up with his descriptive essay about his adventures with his friends on a condemned bridge. As you read the essay look specifically at the detail he uses to enhance his essay.*

1   I can see it now. The four of us sitting out on the wood bridge puffing on our cheap, Swisher cigars. The smoke rising above the rusty, cast iron sides and filtering up to the full moon above. As the moon reflects off the Goose River my friends and I sit and talk about everything from girls to UFO theories. We sit without a worry on our minds.

2   The bridge looks like it's something from a surreal movie with a midnight atmosphere. Located two miles out of town, it's hidden on a winding, gravel road that sometimes gets washed out if it

rains heavily. Because of the lack of maintenance the bridge has old oak and maple trees leaning against it. The wood tiling on the bottom is spaced far apart, almost to the point where our feet could fall through.

3   When we were at the bridge we felt as though nothing could go wrong. We thought that all our problems and fears would go away if we stayed out there long enough. We felt as though our parents, teachers, and coaches had no control over us. We could talk about anything and anyone without even thinking about the consequences. No one could touch us. We were like 1920 bootleg gangsters that the law couldn't catch up with. We were almost invincible as we smoked our cigars and talked about our dreams and aspirations.

4   As we sat and smoked it felt as though we were the only people on earth. The world revolved around us. It was like we could control the world while we were out at the bridge. It was a rickety, old bridge, but it seemed to empower us to the point where we felt as though we could control our own destiny. My friend who didn't do well in school was a smarter and more insightful person when he was at the bridge. My friend who wasn't good at athletics felt like he was as good an athlete as any professional. My friend who didn't have a girlfriend seemed like he was a savvy, babe magnet. The bridge had the power to give us confidence.

5   The bridge was county property, but my friends and I felt like ~~we~~ were the owners. It was a mutual relationship. We owned the ~~bridge and it~~ owned us. On the long, cool summer nights ~~we n~~eeded company so we would get our ~~cars o~~n the long, windy road and leave our ~~cars ou~~t at the bridge for hours basking in the ~~habit~~at of a mosquito, the cooing of an owl ~~the splashin~~g of a fish in the river, with the cool yet ~~humid air abou~~t.

~~There was no pla~~ce where I could be so much in my own ~~environm~~ent as I could when I was at the bridge. ~~Our laughter a~~nd cheap cigars made me enjoy it even

1. Paragraph 1 tells you where the scene takes place and who is there. What else does it do?

2. Examine paragraphs 2–5 and in one or two words list a subject or main idea for each one. What progression do you find?
3. Considering the ideas you identified in question 2, what does the bridge represent to the writer?
4. State the thesis of the essay in your own words. Where in the essay does the writer place the thesis? How effective do you find that placement?
5. Reread the last paragraph. What relationship does it bear to the rest of the essay?

TECHNIQUE AND STYLE

1. In a handbook of grammar and style, look up *sentence fragment* and then reexamine Holland's second and third sentences. What are they missing? Explain whether the two sentences are acceptable fragments.
2. If you vary the length of your sentences, you'll find that your prose moves more smoothly and is apt to be of greater interest to the reader. What evidence can you find that Holland uses this technique?
3. Reread paragraph 2. Which sentence functions as a topic sentence? What words in the other sentences are related to it?
4. Repetition can be effective or ineffective. Explain how you judge Holland's similar sentence beginnings in paragraph 3.
5. Reread paragraph 5 looking for details that appeal to the senses. What are they?

SUGGESTIONS FOR WRITING

Journal

1. Imagine that you are the narrator of "The Bridge." What "problems and fears" would you be leaving behind?
2. Holland describes the bridge as looking like "something from a surreal movie with a midnight atmosphere." Think about places you know about that match that description and describe one of them.

Essay

Almost everyone has at least one "special place" that represents a particular mood or feeling, either positive or negative. To write an essay about such a place that holds meaning for you, think first about an emotion and then about the place you associate with it. Here's one list to consider, but other ideas will probably occur to you as well:

comfort
fear
happiness
excitement
curiosity

Once you've decided on a topic, then you can start accumulating details that will make your scene and the way you feel about it come alive for the reader.

El Hoyo

Mario Suarez

*When Mario Suarez returned from four years in the Navy, he enrolled
at the University of Arizona and found himself taking freshman
English. The essay that follows was written for that class and so impressed his teacher, Ruth Keenan, that she not only encouraged him
to take other writing courses but also to submit "El Hoyo" to the*
Arizona Quarterly, *where it was published. That was a long time ago
(1947), but it started Suarez on a successful writing career; it is a
rare anthology of Chicano literature that doesn't include at least one
of Suarez's works.*

WHAT TO LOOK FOR   *Like many writers, Suarez faces the
problem of explaining the unfamiliar, but for Suarez the problem is
compounded. Many of his readers do not know the meaning of*
barrio, *nor are they familiar with Latino culture. Those who do know
the terms may have negative associations with them. As you read his
essay, note the techniques he uses to combat these problems. Also note
how Suarez uses repetition effectively to lend emphasis to his
description. Read Suarez's second paragraph out loud so you can
hear the repetition more clearly.*

1   From the center of downtown Tucson the ground slopes gently
away to Main Street, drops a few feet, and then rolls to the banks of
the Santa Cruz River. Here lies the section of the city known as El
Hoyo. Why it is called El Hoyo is not very clear. In no sense is it a
hole as its name would imply; it is simply the river's immediate valley. Its inhabitants are chicanos who raise hell on Saturday night
and listen to Padre Estanislao on Sunday morning. While the term
chicano is the short way of saying Mexicano, it is not restricted to
the paisanos who came from old Mexico with the territory or the
last famine to work for the railroad, labor, sing, and go on relief.
Chicano is the easy way of referring to everybody. Pablo Gutíerrez
married the Chinese grocer's daughter and now runs a meat department; his sons are chicanos. So are the sons of Killer Jones who
threw a fight in Harlem and fled to El Hoyo to marry Cristina
Mendez. And so are all of them. However, it is doubtful that all
these spiritual sons of Mexico live in El Hoyo because they love

each other—many fight and bicker constantly. It is doubtful they live in El Hoyo because of its scenic beauty—it is everything but beautiful. Its houses are simple affairs of unplastered adobe, wood, and abandoned car parts. Its narrow streets are mostly clearings which have, in time, acquired names. Except for some tall trees which nobody has ever cared to identify, nurse, or destroy, the main things known to grow in the general area are weeds, garbage piles, dark-eyed chavalos, and dogs. And it is doubtful that the chicanos live in El Hoyo because it is safe—many times the Santa Cruz has risen and inundated the area.

2   In other respects living in El Hoyo has its advantages. If one is born with weakness for acquiring bills, El Hoyo is where the collectors are less likely to find you. If one has acquired the habit of listening to Octavio Perea's Mexican Hour in the wee hours of the morning with the radio on at full blast, El Hoyo is where you are less likely to be reported to the authorities. Besides, Perea is very popular and sooner or later to everyone "Smoke in the Eyes" is dedicated between the pinto beans and white flour commercials. If one, for any reason whatever, comes on an extended period of hard times, where, if not in El Hoyo, are the neighbors more willing to offer solace? When Teofila Malacara's house burned to the ground with all her belongings and two children, a benevolent gentleman carried through the gesture that made tolerable her burden. He made a list of 500 names and solicited from each a dollar. At the end of a month he turned over to the tearful but grateful señora $100 in cold cash and then accompanied her on a short vacation. When the new manager of a local store decided that no more chicanas were to work behind the counters, it was the chicanos of El Hoyo who, on taking their individually small but collectively great buying power elsewhere, drove the manager out and the girls returned to their jobs. When the Mexican Army was en route to Baja California and the chicanos found out that the enlisted men ate only at infrequent intervals, it was El Hoyo's chicanos who crusaded across town with pots of beans and trays of tortillas to meet the train. When someone gets married, celebrating is not restricted to the immediate friends of the couple. Everybody is invited. Anything calls for a celebration and a celebration calls for anything. On Memorial Day there are no less than half a dozen good fights at the Riverside Dance Hall. On Mexican Independence Day more than one flag is sworn allegiance to amid cheers for the queen.

3   And El Hoyo is something more. It is this something more which brought Felipe Suarez back from the wars after having killed a score of Japanese with his body resembling a patchwork quilt to marry Julia Armijo. It brought Joe Zepeda, a gunner, . . . back to compose boleros. He has a metal plate for a skull. Perhaps El Hoyo is proof that those people exist, and perhaps exist best, who have as yet failed to observe the more popular modes of human conduct. Perhaps the humble appearance of El Hoyo justifies the indifferent shrug of those made aware of its existence. Perhaps El Hoyo's simplicity motivates an occasional chicano to move away from its narrow streets, babbling comadres and shrieking children to deny the bloodwell from which he springs and to claim the blood of a conquistador while his hair is straight and his face beardless. Yet El Hoyo is not an outpost of a few families against the world. It fights for no causes except those which soothe its immediate angers. It laughs and cries with the same amount of passion in times of plenty and of want.

4   Perhaps El Hoyo, its inhabitants, and its essence can best be explained by telling a bit about a dish called capirotada. Its origin is uncertain. But, according to the time and the circumstance, it is made of old, new or hard bread. It is softened with water and then cooked with peanuts, raisins, onions, cheese, and panocha. It is fired with sherry wine. Then it is served hot, cold, or just "on the weather" as they say in El Hoyo. The Sermeños like it one way, the Garcias another, and the Ortegas still another. While it might differ greatly from one home to another, nevertheless it is still capirotada. And so it is with El Hoyo's chicanos. While being divided from within and from without, like the capirotada, they remain chicanos.

THESIS AND ORGANIZATION

1. Examine the essay using the standard journalistic questions. Which paragraph describes *where* El Hoyo is? What paragraphs describe *who* lives there? What paragraph or paragraphs describe *how* they live? *Why* they live there?
2. All of the questions above lead to a larger one: *What* is El Hoyo? Given the people and place, and how and why they live there, what statement is the author making about El Hoyo?
3. The essay ends with an analogy, and toward the end of paragraph 4, Suarez spells out some details of the analogy. What other characteristics of

capirotada correspond to those of chicanos? Where in the essay do you find evidence for your opinion?

4. How would you describe the movement in the essay? Does it move from the general to the particular? From the particular to the general? What reasons can you give for the author's choice of direction?

5. In one sentence, state Suarez's opinion of El Hoyo.

TECHNIQUE AND STYLE

1. The introductory paragraph achieves coherence and cohesion through the author's use of subtle unifying phrases. Trace Suarez's use of "it is doubtful." How often does the phrase occur? Rewrite the sentences to avoid using the phrase. What is lost? Gained?

2. What key words are repeated in paragraph 2? Why does he repeat them?

3. Paragraph 2 gives many examples of the advantages of living in El Hoyo. List the examples in the order in which they appear. The first two can be grouped together under the idea of El Hoyo as a sanctuary, a place where people aren't bothered. What other groupings does the list of examples suggest? What principle appears to have guided the ordering of the examples?

4. Why might the author have chosen not to use either first or second person? What is gained by using "one"?

SUGGESTIONS FOR WRITING

Journal

1. Write a journal entry explaining why you would or would not like to live in El Hoyo. Use examples from the essay to flesh out your reasons.

2. Suarez compares the dish capirotada to El Hoyo, developing it as a metaphor. Think of a metaphor that would work for your neighborhood or for one of your classes. Write a paragraph or two developing your comparison and you will probably discover that using metaphor may also make you see the familiar in a new way.

Essay

If you live in an ethnic neighborhood, you can use the essay as a close model. If you do not, you can still use the essay as a general model by choosing a topic that combines people and place. Suggestions:

family ritual at Christmas or Hanukkah
family ritual at Thanksgiving
dinner at a neighborhood restaurant
busy time at the university student center

Frightened by Loss

J. Merrill-Foster

*By combining the objective with the subjective, the particular with the
general, and the past with the present, the author presents a compelling picture of old age. The essay was published in the* New York
Times *in 1988.*

WHAT TO LOOK FOR   *When you use description in your essays,
you may find yourself in the position of a narrator who stands
outside of the scene. If you find that this position becomes tiresome
and gives more of an impression of distance from your subject than
you want, you might try two of the techniques Merrill-Foster uses—
dialogue and metaphor. By quoting a person you are describing, you
bring the reader into the scene directly, as Merrill-Foster does when
she lists a string of statements made by the old woman she depicts.
Note that the dialogue doesn't have to be a continuous chunk; a few
pertinent, though not consecutive, sentences will do the job. Metaphor
also changes the pace of an essay, slowing the reader slightly by
presenting a vivid image; that vividness also brings the reader closer
to the subject.*

1   Her walk is slow, hesitant, leaning slightly forward from the
waist. Her hands, swollen and misshapen with arthritis, have trac-
eries of blue veins across the back. They are never still.

2   She often interrupts to ask what we are talking about. The telephone seems to confuse her; she thinks the ringing is on the television. She calls us to report that she has lost her Christmas card list.
It turns up on her desk, hidden under a pile of appeals. She is on
every mailing list there is, and is constantly importuned to "Save the
whales" and "Stop the Japanese slaughter of dolphins."

3   She is frightened and distressed by letters from retired military
men. They write that unless she sends $35 by return mail, the
Russians will land in Oregon and take over America. The arrival of
the daily mail looms large in her day. Once, every few weeks, it
contains a personal letter. The rest is appeals and ads. She reads
every item.

4   Her checkbook is a constant puzzle of missing entries and double deposits of retirement checks. She goes out to do an errand and

cannot find the place—a place she's frequented for years. She telephones to say the furnace door has exploded open; the kindly repair man arrives at 10 P.M. to check and assure her that all is well. She tells you about it, not because there is anything needing to be done. She tells you in order to make you understand that life is out of control—that there is a conspiracy of inanimate objects afoot.

5   Often, if you suggest this or that solution, she is annoyed. She wasn't asking for a solution. She was merely reporting disaster. She sits down to read and falls asleep.

6   America's life style prepares us well for our first day at school, for adolescence, for college, for matrimony, for parenthood, for middle age, for retirement. But it prepares us not at all for old age. Busy and active until her seventy-eighth year, the woman, now 85, is frightened by her own loss of power.

7   "Why am I so tired all the time?" she asks.

8   "I couldn't figure out how to turn on the dashboard lights."

9   "I look at the snow and wonder how I'll live through the winter."

10   "I think I must light the wood stove. I'm so cold."

11   I do not see the woman as she is today. I look at her familiar face and see her on a stage, floating up a flight of stairs in *Arsenic and Old Lace,* with that skilled power in her knees that made her seem to glide from one step to another. I hear her speak and remember her light but lovely contralto singing Katisha in *The Mikado.*

12   I watch her sleeping in her chair, her head on her chest, and remember her pacing up and down an English classroom, reading aloud from Beowulf, bringing to life the monster Grendel for a class of 16-year-olds. I remember late winter afternoons, fortified with hot cocoa, sitting on the floor at her feet, listening to "The Ballad of the White Horse," *Don Quixote* and *King Lear.*

13   I remember her as a young widow, coming home from school and pulling three children through the snow on a sled. I remember always the summer jobs when school was let out, selling life insurance or encyclopedias, or studying remedial reading at New York University. I remember her as a bride the second time, and the second time a widow. Hers was the home the family came to, a place of books, a big, old house where civility was spoken.

14   There is some rage in aging—a disbelief that one's life has rounded its last curve and this stretch of road leads to death. She has always been a woman of strong faith, and it seems that faith at last has failed her. She quotes Claudius in *Hamlet:*

15   "My words fly up, my thoughts remain below;
16   Words without thoughts never to heaven go."
17   Widowed, alone, children and grandchildren flung wide from California to New England, she fills her days with little things. Socializing fatigues her. She withdraws from the intense conversational jousting that used to delight her.
18   I watch the woman—my mother—walking carefully down the frozen, snow-filled driveway to the mail box. She is a photograph in black and white, which only loving memory tints with stippled life and color.

THESIS AND ORGANIZATION

1. Paragraph 1 describes the woman physically, and paragraphs 2–5 describe her psychologically, both leading up to the concluding sentence of paragraph 6. What details in paragraphs 1–5 relate to the idea of being "frightened by her own loss of power"?
2. Test the assertions in the first two sentences of paragraph 6. To what extent do they hold true in the experience of you and your family? Are the assertions valid?
3. Paragraphs 7–10 use quotations from the present to illustrate the generalization that ends paragraph 6 and to set up the shift to the past that takes place in paragraphs 11–13, while paragraphs 14–18 return to the present. Do you find the essay's chronology effective or ineffective? How so?
4. How would you characterize the author's feelings for the old woman? What evidence can you cite to support your ideas?
5. Where in the essay do you find the author generalizing on old age? What generalization is being made about the author's mother? About old age? Putting the two generalizations together, how would you express the thesis of the essay?

TECHNIQUE AND STYLE

1. The author alludes to a play and an operetta (paragraph 11) and to an epic, a poem, a novel, and a play (paragraph 12). What do these allusions imply about the author's mother? What do they contribute to her characterization—the person she was then and the person she is now?
2. In a standard dictionary, look up *pity* and *empathy*. Which does the author feel for the old woman? Which does the writer evoke in you? Cite examples to support your opinion.

3. Throughout the essay the author never refers to the old woman by name. What is the effect of using a pronoun instead? What effect is achieved by holding off identifying her as "my mother"?

4. Examine paragraph 13 for details. What do they imply about the author's mother? How do those characteristics compare with those you can deduce from paragraphs 7–10? What does this contrast achieve?

5. The essay concludes with a metaphor. Rephrase the metaphor in your own words and explain how that statement supports the thesis of the essay.

Suggestions for Writing

Journal

1. Merrill-Foster says "There is some rage in aging—a disbelief that one's life has rounded its last curve and this stretch of road leads to death." Does that statement hold up to what you have observed in your experience? If so, describe a person to whom it applies; if not, describe a person who refutes the idea.

2. Write a journal entry that describes someone performing an everyday repetitive action such as walking, reading, or eating. It's easiest to write such a description if you do it as you observe the person. That way you note each movement. You may want to use some of this description in the essay assignment that follows.

Essay

Think of someone you know who would make a good subject for a character sketch, a short essay in which you describe a person so that you report the qualities that make up the individual. Like Merrill-Foster, you may also want to generalize about the larger category that the person represents. Rely on quotation as well as description to create the overall impression you wish to make. That impression, implicit or explicit, is your thesis. For subjects to write about, think of someone who typifies a certain

manner

age

occupation

Left Sink

Ellery Akers

Ellery Akers is a writer, naturalist, and poet who lives near San Francisco. Knocking on the Earth, her first book of poems, was published in 1989 by Wesleyan University Press. As you read the essay, you'll discover that her prose reflects a number of characteristics of poetry—imagery, concise language, and an acute eye for detail. You'll also see that the line between description and narration is a fine one. The essay won the 1990 Sierra Club Award for nature writing and was published the same year in Sierra. While the essay is longer than most in this book, you'll find its length is deceptive. You'll read it quickly.

WHAT TO LOOK FOR   *Writers who deal with familiar subjects face the challenge of making the familiar new or unusual, and to do that they rely on concrete detail. Ellery Akers knows her readers are familiar with bathrooms and frogs, but she goes on to individualize this particular bathroom and the frog she names Left Sink. Some writers might be content to state "The frog was small." Akers, however, takes the word* small *and gives it substance, "no bigger than a penny, and his round, salmon-colored toes stuck out like tiny soupspoons." Remember as you write that one person's idea of a general term, such as* small, *may not be the same as another's, so it's best to use concrete details to show just what you mean.*

1   The first time I saw Left Sink, I was brushing my teeth and almost spit on him by mistake. I wasn't expecting to find a frog in a Park Service bathroom, but there he was, hopping out of the drain and squatting on the porcelain as casually as if he were sitting beside a pond.

2   He was a small green tree frog, no bigger than a penny, and his round, salmon-colored toes stuck out like tiny soupspoons. For a few minutes I stared into his gold eyes, each pupil floating in the middle like a dark seed.

3   I was so close I could see his throat pulse, but I was probably too close, for he looked at me fearfully and leaped onto the silver "C" of the cold-water faucet.

4   Then he must have thought better of it, for he jumped down again, and sat, hunched over, by the soap. He kept making nervous

little hops toward the safety of the drain, but my looming face was obviously in the way, so I ducked below the basin for a moment, and when I looked again he was descending into the hole, head first.

5   Feeling I'd disturbed his evening hunt, I decided to make amends. I grubbed around the floor for a dead moth, found one (though it was a little dried up), and offered it to the hole. The wing slanted into the drain, but nothing happened. I thought perhaps he'd hopped back down into the pipe. Trying to find something a little more appealing, I picked around the window sills until I discovered a really decent-looking moth, pushed it up to the drain, and waited. After a few minutes, I got discouraged and walked away. When I turned back to sneak one last look, I found both moths had vanished.

6   The next day was so hot I forgot Left Sink completely. It is always hot in the California chaparral in September, especially in the Gabilan Mountains. I spent the afternoon in the shade, lying on the cool pebbles of a dry wash and looking over my field notes. I had been camping for weeks, studying birds, and by now I had gotten used to the feeling of expectation in the landscape.

7   Everything seemed to be waiting for rain. The streambeds were dry, the fields were dry, and when the buckeye leaves hissed in the wind they sounded like rattlesnakes. Ravens flew overhead, croaking, their wings flapping loudly in the air, and the rocks baked. Once in a while a few thirsty finches fluttered up to a seep in a cliff and sipped from a damp clump of algae.

8   I leaned against the cool flank of a boulder and fanned myself with my hat. From far away I could hear the staccato drill of a Nuttall's woodpecker.

9   All the animals had some way of coping with the heat. The wrentits could last for several weeks without drinking. The deer found beds of shade and waited patiently until evening. Even the trees adapted. Though I couldn't see it, I knew that somewhere beneath my boots, 100 feet down, the root of a digger pine was twisting along a crevice in the bedrock, reaching far below the surface to tap into the permanent water.

10   And the frogs—the normal ones—were sleeping away the summer and fall, huddled in some moist spot in the ground in a kind of hot-weather hibernation.

11   That night, when I went back to the bathroom, I discovered Left Sink had a neighbor. Even before I turned on the water in the right-hand basin, I noticed a second frog, and when I stepped back to

look at both of them in their respective sinks, I started to laugh: They reminded me of a couple of sober, philosophical old monks peering out of their cells.

12   Overhead was a third frog, puffy and well-fed, squatting on top of the fluorescent lights, surrounded by tattered moths. Light Buddha, I would call him.

13   In the world of the bathroom the light shelf was a delicatessen of the highest order. Light Buddha sat there night after glorious night, lazily snapping up moths as they fluttered past. The other two frogs seemed content to stake out the sinks, which weren't quite as dependable a food source, though they weren't bad. Almost every night I found a damp moth thrashing around in one of the basins, one little flopping death after another, leaving a trail of scales behind.

14   Right Sink was extremely shy, and spent most of his time crouched far back in the pipe. Usually I saw his gold eyes shining in the darkness, but that was all. Left Sink was more of an adventurer, and explored the whole bathroom, darting behind the mirror, splatting onto the porcelain, hopping on the window sills, leaping on the toilet, and climbing the slippery painted walls toe pad by toe pad.

15   From time to time I was tempted to pick him up as he was climbing. But I didn't think it would be fair; I knew this geometrical universe, and he didn't. Besides, there was no place for him to hide on those smooth, painted bricks, so I let him be.

16   I was amazed at how few people noticed Left Sink, even when he was sitting on top of the faucet. Kids saw him right away, though, and I worried sometimes that one night a little girl would pop him into a jar and take him home to some confining terrarium.

17   Also, he stood out. Even though tree frogs can change color in ten minutes, there was nothing in Left Sink's repertoire that could possibly match white paint; the best he could do was a sickly pink.

18   I could always tell if he had just emerged from the drain because he would still be a murky gray-green. As the evening wore on he got paler and paler. Once I couldn't find him for half an hour. Finally I caught sight of him over my head. Plopped on a narrow ledge, he looked like a pale pebble in all that metal and paint. I climbed onto the toilet for a better look. To my horror he began hopping along the ledge, which was no wider than half an inch. It was a ten-foot fall to the floor—for a frog that small, an abyss. He bounded past me, his grainy throat quivering.

19   He headed toward a swarm of moths and flies that circled the fluorescent lights. A fly drifted down from the glare; Left Sink, his pink mouth flashing, snapped it up.

20   I was never quite sure just how skittish he really was. Sometimes he tolerated my watching him, sometimes he didn't. I got in the habit of sidling up to the plumbing, bent over so as not to be seen, and I must have looked pretty peculiar. One night a woman came into the bathroom and caught me hunched over like Quasimodo, staring intently at the drains, my hands full of dead moths.

21   "Left Sink! Right Sink!" I was saying. "Got a little treat for you guys!"

22   The woman bolted out the door.

23   For the next few weeks I checked on the frogs every morning and evening. Sometimes when I saw Left Sink skidding down a length of plastic, unable to hold on in spite of his adhesive toe pads, I worried. I couldn't help thinking there was something unnatural about a frog in a bathroom.

24   Of course, I knew there were a few oddballs that *had* managed to live with us in our artificial world, but they were mostly insects. One year in school I had learned about the larvae of petroleum flies: They lived in the gunk of oil fields, so numerous at times that, according to my textbook, they imparted "a shimmering effect to the surface of the oil." Their world was oil; if you deprived them of it, took them out and cleaned them off, they'd curl up and die in less than a day.

25   In that same class I'd learned that furniture beetles live in our table legs, and occasionally, in wooden spoons; drugstore beetles float happily in bottles of belladonna, mating, pupating, dying. We have cheese mites in our cheese, and flour mites in our flour.

26   As far as I knew no one had ever done any research on frogs and plumbing. Luckily, I always carried a trunkful of books and field guides in my car, and one night I flipped through every book I had to see if I could find any instances where humans and animals—wild ones—had actually gotten along. Arthur Cleveland Bent said that wrens nested in old clothes in barns, and swallows on moving trains. Edwin Way Teale said he had once read about a pigeon using rubber bands and paper clips in her nest on a window ledge off Times Square. One year, he wrote, a thrush spent the entire winter in a florist's shop on Madison Avenue, flitted about between the iced gladiolas and roses, and flew away in spring.

27   But no one mentioned anything about frogs.

28   Actually, considering the drought, Left Sink had a pretty good set-up. It was already October and still no rain. Once in a while a few drops would plop into the dirt and gravel, and I would catch a whiff of wet dust, soaked cheat grass, and buckwheat. But that was all.

29   All the other frogs were holed up in the dirt, huddled in a moist crack or an abandoned gopher hole, waiting for the first rains of winter to wake them up. There were probably a few hiding in the field next to Left Sink's bathroom, their eyelids closed, their toes pulled under them to conserve moisture, unmoving, barely breathing, their heartbeats almost completely stilled. If I dug them up they would look like small stones.

30   One night just before I was about to leave, I had a nightmare. It was a dream I had had many times, a dream of a city so polluted the air rose in black plumes above the granite and cement. I was at the entrance of a tunnel. Inside I could hear a whoosh of air: Millions of butterflies were flashing in the dark, thousands of ducks, eagles, sparrows, their wings making a vast rustling as they flew off and vanished.

31   I heard a low shuffling. After a while I realized it was the sound of feet: the slow trudge of bears, the pad of badgers, the pattering of foxes, the rasp of a hundred million beetles, rabbits, ants, mice. I looked around, panicked, to see if any animals were left. There were still cockroaches scuttling over the window sills. There were pigeons, flies, starlings. I named them over and over in a kind of chant: the adaptable, the drab, the ones who could live with us, who had always lived with us.

32   A fox coughed close to my camp in the middle of the nightmare and woke me up. I unzipped the tent and looked out at the stars: Rigel, Algol, clear, cold, and changeless. A golden-crowned sparrow chirped from a nearby branch, then sputtered off into silence. For a while I tried to stay awake, but soon drifted off.

33   The next morning huge bluish clouds rolled across the sky. A couple of ravens sailed past the cliff in front of me. One of them jackknifed its wings, plummeted straight down, and then, at the last minute, unfolded them and flapped away. It was still early, but when I reached the bathroom it had already been cleaned. It reeked of ammonia, and a mop and bucket leaned against the door.

34   I rinsed off my face, brushed my hair, and looked sleepily into the drains. As usual, Right Sink was huddled far back into the dark pipe; he retreated still further when I bent over.

35   Left Sink, however, was gone. I wondered if he had slipped behind the mirror, or had come up in the world and was squatting
above with Light Buddha. The shelf was empty. I looked on the
window sill—not there either.

36   It was not until I opened the door to the toilet that I found him.
There, in the center of the ammonia-filled bowl, his green bloated
body turning gray, was Left Sink, splayed out in the milky liquid,
dead. Floating in front of him was a dead damselfly. I suppose he
must have jumped in after his prey, convinced he was at the edge
of a strange-looking pond, his toe pads gripping the cold, perfectly
smooth surface of the porcelain.

37   His skin looked curdled, and it occurred to me he might have
been there all morning waiting to die. Then I remembered that
frogs breathe through their skin; it must have been a hard, stinging
death, but a quick one.

38   I flushed him down, wishing I could think of something to say as
he made his way through the pipes and rolled out to the septic
tank, some acknowledgment of the link between my kind and his,
but I couldn't think of anything except that I would miss him,
which was true.

39   When I opened the door, a couple of nervous towhees blun-
dered into the bushes. It was beginning to rain.

THESIS AND ORGANIZATION

1. The story of Left Sink unfolds slowly. Which paragraphs provide the introduction? What reasons can you give for your choice?
2. An essay of this length tends to group paragraphs around a topic sentence or main idea rather than have a topic sentence for each paragraph. What groupings can you identify? What ideas tie those paragraphs together?
3. Paragraphs 30 and 31 stand out because they strike a very different note
from the rest of the essay. What function do they serve?
4. Akers says "there was something unnatural about a frog in a bathroom"
(paragraph 23). What does she imply in that paragraph and elsewhere
about the relationship between humans and nature?
5. Many essays have an explicit thesis, one that you can spot in a complete
sentence. Others, however, have an implied thesis, one that the writer
suggests and the reader must deduce. That is the case with Akers' essay.
What do you find to be its thesis?

Technique and Style

1. What does Akers think and feel about Left Sink? What details can you find to support your opinion?
2. What details can you find that lead to the conclusion that Akers is a naturalist?
3. Unlike many more formal essays, Akers uses lots of short paragraphs. Look up types of paragraphs in your handbook. What justification can you find for short paragraphs?
4. Akers' choice of verbs helps create the fast pace of the essay and its readability. Find a sentence that uses unusual verbs and rewrite it, substituting other verbs. What is gained? lost?
5. At various places in the essay, Akers refers to rain or the lack of it. What does that contribute to the essay?

Suggestions for Writing

Journal

1. The tone of an essay can be tricky, particularly if it appeals to emotion. To pinpoint Akers' tone, explain how you feel about the frog at the start of the essay, in the middle, and at the end.
2. Take a moment to jot down all the words you associate with the word *frog*. Looking at your list, mark the associations according to whether they are positive, negative, or neutral. Then make another list of the adjectives you think Akers would use for Left Sink. What differences do you find between your list and Akers'?

Essay

Day-to-day life is apt to be full of contrasts, though not usually so striking as a frog in a bathroom. See how many contrasts you can spot in the course of a day when you're looking for them. Jot down what you see, and then choose from your notes to work the contrast into a descriptive essay. Like Akers' essay, yours should have a thesis, either implied or explicit. Suggestions:

at a beach, look for a fully dressed person
in a library, look for someone who is nervous or loud
at a film, look for someone who has brought a baby
in a cafeteria, look for someone who is studying

On Using Narration

2

Whether prompted by the child's "Tell me a story" or the adult's "What happened?" **narration** supplies much of our entertainment and information. But anyone who has asked "What happened?" only to be overwhelmed with every detail knows that telling everything can blunt the point and bore the listener. Effective narration takes more than telling a story; it calls for compressing and reshaping experience so that the listener or reader relives it with you and is left with a particular point. Shaping narrative draws on some of the same skills used in description: keen observation, careful selection of details, and coherent sequencing. But with a narrative you must go a step further: you must present a conflict and its resolution. A story with no point is indeed pointless; one with no conflict is no kind of story at all.

Often the narrative and the subject are the same: if you are writing about what happened to you when lightning struck your house, what happened is the subject of your narrative. Frequently, however, a writer chooses narrative to introduce or to conclude an essay or perhaps to do both, thus building a narrative framework. Or perhaps you would opt for narrative to emphasize a particular point. An essay that explains the dangers of toxic waste may be made more effective if it starts with a brief narrative of what happens at a place where pollution threatens the area and its residents; an essay on Los Angeles and its smog, for example, might begin with the story of an asthma attack. A paper on the same subject that argues for stricter federal and state controls may end by predicting what might happen without tougher regulation. The essays in this chapter, however, rely on narration for their primary structure. All present conflicts, build to a point, and spring from personal experience—from the something that happened.

AUDIENCE AND PURPOSE

No one tells a story for the sake of telling a story, at least no one who wants to be listened to. Most of us will use a narrative to explain something, or to argue a point, or perhaps to entertain. If you think of a journal, the concepts of narration, audience, and purpose may become clearer. If you've ever kept a journal, then you realize that even though *you* are the audience, much of what you write may not make much sense later. It does, of course, right after you finish the journal entry, but two months or two years down the line, you can no longer supply the details from your memory. "Had a terrible argument," you might write, but unless you explain what the argument was about, you may be mystified when you reread that entry. And had you told the whole story behind the quarrel, you might have found that you could muster even more ammunition to support your side than you did in the heat of battle. In that case, you would not only have written about an argument, you would also have written one.

Much of what people write in journals, however, has explanation and entertainment as the goals. Writing in a journal helps many of us think through problems or events. Essentially, we are reliving the incident or situation so that we may examine and comprehend it more clearly: we retell our stories to understand them. A seemingly simple question (such as "Why did I feel so _____?"), calls for a narrative that provides the context. Often, however, we record an event simply because it gave us pleasure, pleasure that we want to be able to relive, once as it is written and again and again as you reread it.

The need for details increases as the distance between the reader and the subject grows. Yet there are always general experiences held in common. Say, for example, you are writing an essay based on something that happened to you in high school. And say you went to a small, all-male Catholic high school in Chicago. You might well wonder how you can make your narrative speak to a general readership, people who attended public, private, or religious schools, schools large and small, rural and urban, some single sex but most coed. Big differences, yes, but when you start thinking about details, you may find yourself turning to description to tap into shared experience—the blurred hum and jangle of students gathered together before a bell rings, the stale, dusty smell of chalk, the squeal of rubber-soled shoes on a waxed floor.

Emotion also speaks across differences. Anyone who has ever been to school knows the panic of being called on by a teacher when you don't even know the question, much less the answer. Moments of praise are equally memorable, whether it be for a point scored on a test or on a basketball court. Joy, despair, fear, elation, anguish, frustration, boredom, laughter, embarrassment—all these and an almost infinite number of other emotions are interwoven in narratives, no matter what the topic, making the topic more interesting because the reader has experienced the same feeling.

WHO, WHAT, WHERE, WHEN, HOW, WHY

These are the standard questions used in journalism, and they are important in narrative essays as well. *What happened?* That's the essential question for narrative, and you'll probably find that the greater part of your essay supplies the answer. *How* and *why* will probably figure in as well, and *who* is obviously essential. But it's easy to neglect *where* and *when*.

If you think of both *where* and *when* as the **setting,** as ways to set the scene, you can remember them more easily and perhaps put them to good use. An essay that relates the tale of a job interview that began as a disaster and ended as a success, for example, might begin by describing the writer as a night person, barely human before 11 A.M. The time of the interview? Nine o'clock. Sharp. The office is impersonal to the point of being cell-like, and the interviewer is so buttoned into his three-piece suit that it looks like armor. Add to those descriptions so that the reader gets the impression that the interview itself will make the Spanish Inquisition look like the first Woodstock, and the writer will have set the tone for the essay as well as built up the readers' interest in what will happen next, the meat of the essay.

CONFLICT

Narratives are structured around a **conflict.** In its simplest form, conflict is *x* versus *y*, Superman versus the Penguin, the Roadrunner versus Wily Coyote. But rarely does conflict exist in such a clear-cut way. Put real people in place of any of those terms, and you begin to understand that what seemed so simple is not; the defense versus the prosecution, a

Republican candidate versus a Democrat—these conflicts are complex. The issues become even more complex when you substitute ideas, such as reality versus illusion, a distinction that even a postcard can blur (how many of us have been disappointed when a scene didn't live up to its photograph?). Even distinguishing good from evil isn't always clear, as the debates over capital punishment and abortion constantly remind us. When a writer explores the complexity involved in a conflict, the essay gains depth and substance, making the reader think. That exploration can be direct, such as naming the opposing forces, or indirect, implying them.

The conflict that occurs in narrative essays is of two kinds and many layers. If, for instance, you were to write about leaving home for the first time—whether you were headed off to college, to the army, or just off—your initial conflict might have been **internal:** Should you go or should you stay? But it might have been **external** as well—what your parents wanted you to do versus what *you* wanted to do. And the conflict was probably also one of ideas—of freedom versus constraints, independence versus dependence.

POINT OF VIEW

A not-so-obvious question about any narrative you're about to write is "Who tells it?" This question identifies the **point of view,** the perspective from which the narrative is related. Probably the first pronoun that comes to mind is *I,* first-person singular, and that's a good choice if you want your readers to identify with you and your angle on the narrative you're relating. When a reader sees first person, an automatic psychological identification takes place, one that allows the reader to look through the writer's eyes. That sort of identification is strongest if you, as narrator, are part of the action. Obviously, there's a huge difference between "I was there" and "I heard about it."

At some point in some classroom, you have probably been warned off *I.* There are at least three reasons: it's easy to overuse the pronoun; it can modify your purpose in a way you hadn't intended; and it can lead to an overly informal tone. If you were to take a look at your first draft for an essay you wrote using *I,* odds are you used it too frequently. The result is apt to be short, choppy sentences that are similar in structure—subject (*I*) followed by a verb and its complement (the word or words that complete the sense of the verb). That's fine for a first draft, and you can revise your way out of the problem. You *need* to revise because too many *I*'s can shift the aim of your essay away from exposition or argument to self-expression; what becomes important is you, not your subject. Your tone may also change, becoming more informal than the assignment calls for, which is why you don't see many research papers that use first person.

Choosing to relate the narrative from the position of *he* or *she* (rarely *they*) puts more distance between the subject and the reader. Think of the difference between "I fell out of the window" and "He fell out of the window." With the latter, the reader's sympathies are at one remove. That's not the case with the second person, *you*. *You* is direct and that's what makes it a somewhat slippery choice. If you're going to use a second-person point of view, make sure the reader understands exactly who is meant by *you*. Many a teacher has been stopped short when reading an essay that has a sentence such as "When you graduate, you'll start looking for a job that can turn into a career"; if that sentence occurred in an essay on surviving an important job interview, its author had too narrow an audience in mind, one composed only of classmates and ignoring everyone else interested in the topic—including the teacher. One way around that problem is to specify the audience in your paper. "All of us who are now in college worry about jobs" tells the reader just who the audience is, and the teacher then reads the essay from the perspective of a college student.

THESIS AND ORGANIZATION

Narratives often begin with the setting, which is the context for the conflict, then establish the nature of the conflict and move toward its resolution. Setting, conflict, and resolution all reinforce the essay's thesis, one that can be explicit or implicit. If the thesis is explicit, it's apt to occur in the introduction; sometimes, however, the writer will reserve it for the conclusion. That kind of placement puts an extra burden on the writer, in that everything in the essay must build to the conclusion. If the organization isn't tight, the reader wonders where the story is going; with a delayed thesis, the reader needs to have the feeling that the story is going somewhere, even though the final destination isn't apparent till the very end.

With narrative essays, as with short stories, the thesis is often implied and the reader must deduce it. If you opt for an implied thesis, make sure that the reader can easily identify your subject and then, without too much effort, move on to infer your thesis. The question that reader needs to ask is "What is the writer saying about the subject?" The answer, phrased as a complete sentence, is the thesis.

One way to control what the reader infers is to work with the narrative's chronology. The sequence of events can be shaped to emphasize different elements. It may help to list the most important incidents in the narrative on a scrap of paper; then you can review them to check that each one is essential and to figure out the best order in which to present them. Writers often disrupt exact chronology, opting for dramatic placement over actual time sequence. The **flashback** is a technique that allows the writer to drop from the present into the past and bring in an event that occurred prior to the narrative's action. You may be most familiar with this device from seeing it in films, the moment when the camera fades out on a scene and then fades into a past event.

You can also reinforce your thesis, implicit or explicit, by underscoring the relationship between what happens and where it happens. If the two are incongruous, for example, then the resulting irony will probably emphasize your main point. A narrative of the job interview that began badly but ended well, for example, may use the turn from bad to good to imply that "all's well that ends well."

Useful Terms

Conflict An element essential to narrative. Conflict involves pitting one force, a force that may be represented by a person or a physical object or abstract concept, against another.

External conflict Conflict that is outside of a person in the narrative though it may involve that person, as in St. George versus the Dragon.

Internal conflict Conflict that takes place within a person, as in "Should I or should I not."

Flashback A break in the narrative that takes the reader to a scene or event that occurred earlier.

Narration Narration tells a story, emphasizing what happened.

Point of view In essays, point of view usually refers to the writer's use of personal pronouns. These pronouns control the perspective flow from which the work is written. For example, if the writer uses *I* or *we* (first-person pronouns), the essay will have a somewhat subjective tone because the reader will tend to identify with the writer. If the writer depends primarily on *he, she, it,* or *they* (third-person pronouns), the essay will have a somewhat objective tone because the reader will be distanced from the writer. Opting for *you* (second person) can be a bit tricky in that *you* can mean you the reader, quite particular, or you a member of a larger group, fairly general. In both cases, *you* brings the reader into the text.

Setting The *where* and *when* in the narrative, its physical context.

➤ POINTERS FOR USING NARRATION

Exploring the Topic

1. **What point do you want to make?** What is the subject of your narrative? What assertion do you want your narrative to make about the subject? Is your primary purpose to inform, to persuade, or to entertain?
2. **What happened?** What are the events involved in the narrative? When does the action start? Stop? Which events are crucial?
3. **Why and how did it happen?** What caused the events? How did it cause them?
4. **Who or what was involved?** What does the reader need to know about the characters? What do the characters look like? Talk like? How do they think? How do others respond to them?
5. **What is the setting for your story?** What does the reader need to know about the setting? What features are particularly noteworthy? How can they best be described?
6. **When did the story occur?** What tense will be most effective in relating the narrative?
7. **What was the sequence of events?** What happened when? Within that chronology, what is most important: time, place, attitude?
8. **What conflicts were involved?** What levels of conflict exist? Is there any internal conflict?
9. **What is the relationship between the narrator and the action?** Is the narrator a participant or an observer? What is the attitude of the narrator toward the story? What feelings should the narrator evoke from the reader? What should be the attitude of the reader toward the narrative? What can be gained by using first person? Second person? Third person?

Drafting the Paper

1. **Know your reader.** Try to second-guess your reader's initial attitude toward your narrative so that if it is not what you want it to be, you can

choose your details to elicit the desired reaction. A reader can be easily bored, so keep your details to the point and your action moving. Play on similar experiences your reader may have had or on information you can assume is widely known.

2. **Know your purpose.** If you are writing to inform, make sure you provide enough information to carry your point. If you are writing to persuade, work on how you present yourself and your thesis so that the reader will be favorably inclined to adopt your viewpoint. If you are writing to entertain, keep your tone in mind. A humorous piece, for instance, can and probably will vary from chuckle to guffaw to belly laugh. Make sure you're getting the right kind of laugh in the right place.

3. **Establish the setting and time of the action.** Use descriptive details to make the setting vivid and concrete. Keep in mind the reaction you want to get from your reader, and choose your details accordingly. If, for instance, you are writing a narrative that depicts your first experience with fear, describe the setting in such a way that you prepare the reader for that emotion. If the time the story took place is important, bring it out early.

4. **Set out the characters.** When you introduce a character, immediately identify the person with a short phrase such as "Anne, my sister." If a character doesn't enter the narrative until midpoint or so, make sure the reader is prepared for the entrance so that the person doesn't appear to be merely plopped in. If characterization is important to the narrative, use a variety of techniques to portray the character, but make sure whatever you use is consistent with the impression you want to create. You can depict a person directly—through appearance, dialogue and actions—as well as indirectly—through what others say and think and how they act toward the person.

5. **Clarify the action.** Narration is set within strict time limits. Make sure the time frame of your story is set out clearly. Within that time limit, much more action occurred than you will want to use in your narrative. Pick only the high points so that every action directly supports your thesis. Feel free to tinker with the action, sacrificing a bit of reality for the sake of your point.

6. **Sharpen the plot.** Conflict is essential to narration, so be sure your lines of conflict are clearly drawn. Keeping conflict in mind, review the action you have decided to include so that the plot and action support each other.

7. **Determine the principle behind the sequence of events.** Given the action and plot you have worked out, determine what principle should guide the reader through the events. Perhaps time is the element you want to stress, perhaps place, perhaps gradual change. No matter what you choose, make sure that the sequence has dramatic tension so that it builds to the point you want to make.

8. **Choose an appropriate point of view.** Your choice of grammatical point of view will depend on what attitude you wish to take toward your narrative and your audience. If you can make your point more effectively by distancing yourself from the story, you will want to use *he, she,* or *they.* On the other hand, if you can make your point most effectively by being in the story, use first person and then decide whether you want to be *I* the narrator only or *I* the narrator who is also directly involved in the story.

9. **Make a point.** The action of the narrative should lead to a conclusion, an implicit or explicit point that serves as the thesis of the piece. If explicit, the thesis can appear in a single sentence or it can be inferred from several sentences, either in the introduction or conclusion of the essay. Ask yourself if everything in the narrative ties into the thesis.

Designer of Audio CD Packaging Enters Hell

Steve Martin

Anyone who has watched television or been to the movies in the last few years is familiar with the wacky world of Steve Martin. Best known as a comedian, he is also becoming a familiar name to the readers of The New Yorker, *where his writing often appears in the "Shouts & Murmurs" slot. Martin got his start in television as a writer, turning out material for Sonny and Cher and the Smothers Brothers, among many others. From there, he went on to stand up comedy and made frequent and memorable appearances on* Saturday Night Live *as well as various talk shows. More recently, he starred in dramatic as well as comic films and is also the author of* Picasso at the Lapin Agile, *a play that opened off-Broadway in 1995. Firmly grounded in the absurd, his comic sense runs from slapstick to sophistication, both of which can be found in the essay that follows, one published in the April 19, 1999, issue of the* New Yorker.

WHAT TO LOOK FOR *Dialogue is often used in narrative writing because it adds a sense of realism and also provides variety. As you read Martin's essay, keep track of who is speaking and note how the dialogue matches the speaker. Also keep track of how Martin breaks up a quoted sentence so that the emphasis is right where he wants it. That's a technique that can work well any time you use dialogue.*

1   The burning gates of Hell were opened and the designer of CD packaging entered to the Devil's fanfare. "We've been wanting him down here for a long time," The One of Pure Evil said to his infernal minions, "but we decided to wait, because he was doing such good work above, wrapping the CDs with cellophane and that sticky tape strip. Ask him to dinner and be sure to invite the computer-manual people too."

2   The Devil vanished, missing the warm display of affection offered the inventor. "Beelzebub himself opened a nasty cut on his finger trying to unwrap a Streisand best-of," whispered an imp. A thick snake nuzzled closer, and wrapped itself around the inven-

tor's leg. "He used to be enamored of the remote-control people, with their tiny little buttons jammed together, and their enigmatic abbreviations," the snake said, "but now all he ever talks about is you, you, you. Come on, let's get you ready for dinner. We can talk about your assignment later."

3   As the snake led the way to the dressing halls of Hell, a yearning, searching look came over its face. "How did you do it?" the snake asked. "You know, invent the packaging? Everyone wants to know."

4   The inventor, his feet comfortably aflame, and flattered by all the recognition, relaxed into his surroundings. "The original plastic CD 'jewel box' was just too damn easy to get into," he explained. "I mean, if we're going to prevent consumer access, for God's sake, let's prevent it! I wanted a packaging where the consumer would run to the kitchen for a knife, so there was a chance to at least slice open his hand."

5   "Is that when you got the idea for shrink-wrap?" said the snake.

6   "Shrink-wrap was nice for a while. I liked that there was absolutely no place to tear into it with a fingernail, but I knew there was further to go. That's when I hit on cellophane, cellophane with the illusion of an opening strip, where really none exists."

7   That night, at the celebratory dinner held once an aeon to honor new arrivals, the inventor sat to the Devil's right. On his left sat Cerberus, the watchdog of Hades and noted designer of the pineapple. The Devil chatted with the inventor all night long, then requested that he open another bottle of wine, this time with a two-pronged, side-slip corkscrew. The inventor perspired, and an hour later the bottle was uncorked.

8   At first, no one noticed the muffled disturbance from above, which soon grew into a sustained clamor. Eventually, the entire gathering looked toward the ceiling, and finally the Devil himself noticed that their attention had shifted. He raised his head.

9   Hovering in the ether were three angels, each holding an object. The inventor knew clearly what the objects were: the milk carton, the Ziploc bag, and the banana, all three perfectly designed packages. He remembered how he used to admire them before he fell into evil. The three angels glided toward the dais. One held the Ziploc bag over the aspirin-bottle people, and bathed them in an otherworldly light. A yellow glow from the banana washed over the hellhound Cerberus, designer of the pineapple, and the milk carton

poured its white luminosity in the direction of the CD packager. The Devil stood up abruptly, roared something in Latin while succubae flew out of his mouth, and then angrily excused himself.

10   After the fiasco, the inventor went back to his room and fiddled with the five remotes it took to operate his VCR. Frustrated, he closed his eyes and contemplated the eternity to come in the bleakness of Hell, and how he would probably never again see a snowflake or a Fudgsicle. But then he thought of the nice meal he'd just had, and his new friends, and decided that snowflakes and Fudgsicles weren't that great anyway. He thought how the upcoming eternity might not be so bad after all. There was a knock at the door, and the snake entered.

11   "The Devil asked me to give you your assignment," the snake said. "Sometimes he gets powerful headaches. He wants you to be there to open the aspirin bottle."

12   "I think I could do that," the inventor replied.

13   "Just so you know, he likes a fresh aspirin every time, so you'll have to remove the tamper-resistant collar, the childproof cap, *and* the aluminum sealer," said the snake.

14   The inventor breathed easily. "No problem."

15   "Good," the snake said, and turned to go.

16   Just then a shudder rippled through the inventor's body. "Say"— his voice quavered with nervousness—"who will remove the cotton wad from the inside of the bottle?"

17   The snake turned slowly, its face contorted into the mask of Beelzebub. Then its voice deepened and transformed itself, as though it were coming from the bowels of Hell:

18   "Why, *you* will," he said. "HA HA HA HA HA!"

THESIS AND ORGANIZATION

1. What paragraph or paragraphs introduce the essay? What reasons do you have for your choice?
2. Trace the essay's organization. What paragraphs mention articles that can be grouped with CD packaging? What articles are contrasted with it?
3. What paragraph or paragraphs make up the essay's conclusion? How effective do you find the conclusion?
4. Reread the essay keeping track of the various conflicts in it. What are they?
5. Unlike many essays, Martin's has an implied thesis. Think about the various conflicts in the essay and state his implied thesis in your own words.

TECHNIQUE AND STYLE

1. Jot down the various items Martin mentions. Why might he have presented them in the sequence he does?

2. The main person in the essay is never named but instead referred to as "the inventor." What does the essay gain by not naming him?

3. "Hot as Hell" is a common expression, so common that it has lost any freshness it might have had. How does Martin breathe life into what has become a cliché?

4. For a narrative as short as this one is, it has a surprisingly large cast of characters. How does Martin make them easy to keep track of?

5. Often, humor arises from the linking of unlikely objects. Where do you find Martin using this technique? How else does he create a comic effect?

SUGGESTIONS FOR WRITING

Journal

1. Write an entry in which you describe your own battle with a product or machine.

2. Think of a time when you expected one thing but got another. Perhaps you were dreading a particular event and then found it was fun, or perhaps you thought you had done badly on a test only to find you did well. The difference between expectation and reality can become the central conflict for a narrative in your journal.

Essay

Write your own narrative of Hell, either serious or comic, replacing "the inventor" with a choice of your own. The list below gives you some categories to think about:

former friend
political figure
music group
historical figure
celebrity

You can use Martin's essay as a fairly close model if you like, incorporating dialogue and using much the same devilish cast.

The Night of Oranges

Flavius Stan

Flavius Stan was 17 years old when this piece was published on Christmas Eve day, 1995, in the New York Times. *At the time, he was an exchange student at the Fieldston School in the Bronx, one of New York City's five boroughs. The time and place he writes about, however, is Christmas Eve in the city of Timisoara in the Romania of 1989, when the country was emerging from Communist rule. It had been an incredible December. On December 16, government forces opened fire on antigovernment demonstrators in Timisoara, killing hundreds. The President, Nicolae Ceausescu, immediately declared a state of emergency, but that did not stop antigovernment protests in other cities. Finally, on December 22, army units also rebelled, the President was overthrown, and civil war raged. The new government quickly won out, and Ceausescu was tried and found guilty of genocide. He was executed on December 25.*

WHAT TO LOOK FOR   *Few of us reading this essay have had firsthand experience of a revolution, nor have many of us lived under Communism or a dictatorship, much less a government whose leader was not only overthrown but also executed. But all of us know oranges. What is familiar to us was strange to Stan, and what is strange to us was his everyday world. The resulting gap between Stan's society and ours is huge, yet in this essay he is able to bring his readers into the cold, postrevolution world of a city in Romania and make us see our familiar orange in a new way. Read the essay once for pleasure and then read it again, looking for the ways in which he makes the unfamiliar familiar and vice versa.*

1   It is Christmas Eve in 1989 in Timisoara and the ice is still dirty from the boots of the Romanian revolution. The dictator Nicolae Ceausescu had been deposed a few days before, and on Christmas Day he would be executed by firing squad. I am in the center of the city with my friends, empty now of the crowds that prayed outside the cathedral during the worst of the fighting. My friends and I still hear shots here and there. Our cold hands are gray like the sky above us, and we want to see a movie.

2　　There is a rumor that there will be oranges for sale tonight. Hundreds of people are already waiting in line. We were used to such lines under the former Communist Government—lines for bread, lines for meat, lines for everything. Families would wait much of the day for rationed items. As children, we would take turns for an hour or more, holding our family's place in line.

3　　But this line is different. There are children in Romania who don't know what an orange looks like. It is a special treat. Having the chance to eat a single orange will keep a child happy for a week. It will also make him a hero in the eyes of his friends. For the first time, someone is selling oranges by the kilo.

4　　Suddenly I want to do something important: I want to give my brother a big surprise. He is only 8 years old, and I want him to celebrate Christmas with lots of oranges at the table. I also want my parents to be proud of me.

5　　So I call home and tell my parents that I'm going to be late. I forget about going to the movie, leave my friends and join the line.

6　　People aren't silent, upset, frustrated, as they were before the revolution; they are talking to one another about life, politics and the new situation in the country.

7　　The oranges are sold out of the back doorway of a food shop. The clerk has gone from anonymity to unexpected importance. As he handles the oranges, he acts like a movie star in front of his fans.

8　　He moves his arms in an exaggerated manner as he tells the other workers where to go and what to do. All I can do is stare at the stack of cardboard boxes, piled higher than me. I have never seen so many oranges in my life.

9　　Finally, it is my turn. It is 8 o'clock, and I have been waiting for six hours. It doesn't seem like a long time because my mind has been flying from the oranges in front of me to my brother and then back to the oranges. I hand over the money I was going to spend on the movie and watch each orange being thrown into my bag. I try to count them, but I lose their number.

10　　I am drunk with the idea of oranges. I put the bag inside my coat as if I want to absorb their warmth. They aren't heavy at all, and I feel that is going to be the best Christmas of my life. I begin thinking of how I am going to present my gift.

11　　I get home and my father opens the door. He is amazed when he sees the oranges, and we decide to hide them until dinner. At dessert that night, I gave my brother the present. Everyone is silent. They can't believe it.

12   My brother doesn't touch them. He is afraid even to look at them. Maybe they aren't real. Maybe they are an illusion, like everything else these days. We have to tell him he can eat them before he has the courage to touch one of the oranges.

13   I stare at my brother eating the oranges. They are my oranges. My parents are proud of me.

THESIS AND ORGANIZATION

1. Paragraphs 1–3 introduce the essay. Explain how they do or do not fit the journalistic questions establishing *who, what, where, why, when, how.*

2. The central part of the essay takes the reader from the time Stan decides to buy the oranges to his presenting them to his brother. What is the effect of presenting the narrative chronologically?

3. The last paragraph functions as the essay's one-paragraph conclusion, a conclusion presented in three short sentences. Explain whether you find the ending effective.

4. On the surface, Stan's essay has a simple thesis—that finding the rare and perfect gift for his brother fills him with pride, pride also reflected by his family. If you dig a bit, however, you may also discover other less obvious theses. What, for instance, might Stan be implying about Christmas? About Romania's future?

5. How would you characterize the conflict or conflicts in this essay?

TECHNIQUE AND STYLE

1. Although the essay was written in 1995, it is set at an earlier time, 1989. Many writers would, therefore, opt for the past tense, but Stan relates his narrative in the present. What does he gain by this choice?

2. Trace the number of contrasts Stan has in his essay. What do you discover? How do they relate to the thesis?

3. Paragraphs 7 and 8 describe the clerk in charge of selling the oranges in some detail. What does this description add to the essay?

4. Why is it important that the money Stan spends on the oranges is the money he was going to spend on the movies?

5. Reread the first paragraph, one that sets not only the scene but also the atmosphere, the emotional impression arising from the scene. In your own words, describe that atmosphere.

SUGGESTIONS FOR WRITING

Journal

1. Choose a common object and describe it as though you were seeing it for the first time.

2. In a sense, Stan's essay is written from the perspective of an 11-year-old, the age he was at the time of the narrative. Leaf through your journal to find a short narrative and then try rewriting it from the perspective of a much younger person.

Essay

Sift through your memory to find several times when you felt proud. Choose one to turn into a narrative essay. Perhaps, like Stan, you may want to retell the event in the present tense, placing yourself in the position of reliving it. If you do, check your draft to see if you have an implied thesis that is larger than the apparent one, for you want your essay to have some depth to it. For ideas of what might have made you feel proud, consider something you

did

didn't do

saw

owned

said

The Good Daughter

Caroline Hwang

You'll learn much about Caroline Hwang in her essay that follows, for there she describes the kind of life she had led before she dropped out of graduate school. She is now an editor at Redbook *and is also fulfilling her dream of writing by working on a novel. The essay was published in the September 21, 1998, issue of* Newsweek, *where it appeared in the regular feature called "My Turn." That feature is an ideal place for short essays, and the magazine welcomes submissions. To find out more, look in a recent issue.*

WHAT TO LOOK FOR   *Writing about yourself may present an interesting problem in tone as you need to be aware of your attitude toward your audience and your subject. It's easy, for example, to fall into a "poor me" trap when you're writing about something that affected you negatively. That is precisely the problem Hwang faced in writing her essay. When you read it, be on the lookout for the ways in which she solves the problem and achieves a balanced tone.*

1   The moment I walked into the dry-cleaning store, I knew the woman behind the counter was from Korea, like my parents. To show her that we shared a heritage, and possibly get a fellow countryman's discount, I tilted my head forward, in shy imitation of a traditional bow.

2   "Name?" she asked, not noticing my attempted obeisance.

3   "Hwang," I answered.

4   "Hwang? Are you Chinese?"

5   Her question caught me off-guard. I was used to hearing such queries from non-Asians who think Asians all look alike, but never from one of my own people. Of course, the only Koreans I knew were my parents and their friends, people who've never asked me where I came from, since they knew better than I.

6   I ransacked my mind for the Korean words that would tell her who I was. It's always struck me as funny (in a mirthless sort of way) that I can more readily say "I am Korean" in Spanish, German and even Latin than I can in the language of my ancestry. In the end, I told her in English.

7   The dry-cleaning woman squinted as though trying to see past the glare of my strangeness, repeating my surname under her breath. "Oh, *Fxuang*," she said, doubling over with laughter. "You don't know how to speak your name."

8   I flinched. Perhaps I was particularly sensitive at the time, having just dropped out of graduate school. I had torn up my map for the future, the one that said not only where I was going but who I was. My sense of identity was already disintegrating.

9   When I got home, I called my parents to ask why they had never bothered to correct me. "Big deal," my mother said, sounding more flippant than I knew she intended. (Like many people who learn English in a classroom, she uses idioms that don't always fit the occasion.) "So what if you can't pronounce your name? You are American," she said.

10   Though I didn't challenge her explanation, it left me unsatisfied. The fact is, my cultural identity is hardly that clear-cut.

11   My parents immigrated to this country 30 years ago, two years before I was born. They told me often, while I was growing up, that, if I wanted to, I could be president someday, that here my grasp would be as long as my reach.

12   To ensure that I reaped all the advantages of this country, my parents saw to it that I became fully assimilated. So, like any American of my generation, I whiled away my youth strolling malls and talking on the phone, rhapsodizing over Andrew McCarthy's blue eyes or analyzing the meaning of a certain upperclassman's offer of a ride to the Homecoming football game.

13   To my parents, I am all American, and the sacrifices they made in leaving Korea—including my mispronounced name—pale in comparison to the opportunities those sacrifices gave me. They do not see that I straddle two cultures, nor that I feel displaced in the only country I know. I identify with Americans, but Americans do not identify with me. I've never known what it's like to belong to a community—neither one at large, nor of an extended family. I know more about Europe than the continent my ancestors unmistakably come from. I sometimes wonder, as I did that day in the dry cleaner's, if I would be a happier person had my parents stayed in Korea.

14   I first began to consider this thought around the time I decided to go to graduate school. It had been a compromise: my parents wanted me to go to law school; I wanted to skip the starched-collar

track and be a writer—the hungrier the better. But after 20-some years of following their wishes and meeting all of their expectations, I couldn't bring myself to disobey or disappoint. A writing career is riskier than law, I remember thinking. If I'm a failure and my life is a washout, then what does that make my parents' lives?

15   I know that many of my friends had to choose between pleasing their parents and being true to themselves. But for the children of immigrants, the choice seems more complicated, a happy outcome impossible. By making the biggest move of their lives for me, my parents indentured me to the largest debt imaginable—I owe them the fulfillment of their hopes for me.

16   It tore me up inside to suppress my dream, but I went to school for a Ph.D. in English literature, thinking I had found the perfect compromise. I would be able to write at least about books while pursuing a graduate degree. Predictably, it didn't work out. How could I labor for five years in a program I had no passion for? When I finally left school, my parents were disappointed, but since it wasn't what they wanted me to do, they weren't devastated. I, on the other hand, felt I was staring at the bottom of the abyss. I had seen the flaw in my life of halfwayness, in my planned life of compromises.

17   I hadn't thought about my love life, but I had a vague plan to make concessions there, too. Though they raised me as an American, my parents expect me to marry someone Korean and give them grandchildren who look like them. This didn't seem like such a huge request when I was 14, but now I don't know what I'm going to do. I've never been in love with someone I dated, or dated someone I loved. (Since I can't bring myself even to entertain the thought of marrying the non-Korean men I'm attracted to, I've been dating only those I know I can stay clearheaded about.) And as I near that age when the question of marriage stalks every relationship, I can't help but wonder if my parents' expectations are responsible for the lack of passion in my life.

18   My parents didn't want their daughter to be Korean, but they don't want her fully American, either. Children of immigrants are living paradoxes. We are the first generation and the last. We are in this country for its opportunities, yet filial duty binds us. When my parents boarded the plane, they knew they were embarking on a rough trip. I don't think they imagined the rocks in the path of their daughter who can't even pronounce her own name.

THESIS AND ORGANIZATION

1. What paragraph or paragraphs provide the essay's introduction? Explain your choice.
2. In what ways is Hwang tied to American culture? Which paragraphs bring that out?
3. In what ways is Hwang tied to Korean culture? Which paragraphs bring that out?
4. One of the main conflicts in the essay is between Korean and American cultures. What other conflicts do you find?
5. Considering the conflicts Hwang depicts, what is her thesis? Where in the essay does she present it?

TECHNIQUE AND STYLE

1. Explain whether the title of the essay is appropriate.
2. Paragraph 10 is an intentionally short one. Explain what is gained by making it short.
3. It is a paradox that Hwang does not know how to pronounce her name correctly. What other examples of paradox do you find in the essay?
4. It's not very likely that many of the readers of the essay are of Korean descent, which creates a gap between Hwang's experience and that of her readers. How does she generalize about her experience so that she solves that problem?
5. What technique does Hwang use that ties her last paragraph to her introduction?

SUGGESTIONS FOR WRITING

Journal

1. Hwang's essay depicts the conflict between her own wishes and what she calls her "filial duty." Think about similar conflicts in your own experience and select one to write about in your journal.
2. In a sense, Hwang's life had been one of compromise, a balancing act between what she wanted and what her parents wanted for her. Consider some of the compromises you have made and choose one to write about. You may well find that this journal entry and the one above can be turned into solid essays.

Essay

"Know thyself" was a basic belief of the ancient Greeks, and it is as difficult to do today as it was then. You can define yourself, for example, in any number of ways by associating yourself with a group or belief or heritage, to name just a few. Think about the various ways in which you define yourself and write an essay in which you explain who you are. To generate some ideas, try thinking about who you are in relation to

    family
    ethnic heritage
    friends
    religion
    political beliefs

Choose one of these ideas, or any other, and consider the conflicts you encountered in becoming who you are. The danger here is taking on too much so that you have the first chapter of your autobiography instead of an essay, so be sure you narrow down your topic.

The Pie

Gary Soto

Gary Soto grew up in the San Joaquin Valley, and as he describes it, "We had our own culture which was more like the culture of poverty." Thinking he couldn't get into the University of California system, he applied to California State University, Fresno, where he soon changed his major from geography to English after being particularly struck by a poem by Edward Field, "Unwanted," that depicted the alienation Soto himself felt. Since then, he has earned an MFA at the University of California, Irvine, and taught at a number of universities, including Berkeley. Now, he devotes himself full-time to writing. The results are apparent in Books in Print, *where you will find that Soto has a very long list indeed. In 1996 alone, three of his books were published, all children's fiction. Soto is also well known for his poetry, as numerous awards attest. The essay that follows was first published in his collection* A Summer Life *(1990). Though the essay is hardly "poetic" in the stereotypical sense, you'll find he uses a number of techniques that also characterize his poetry: precise diction, strong verbs, and imagery that appeals to the senses.*

WHAT TO LOOK FOR   *To make writing memorable, the first draft of an essay will frequently depend more on adverbs and adjectives than on verbs, yet it is verbs that have muscle and can best get the job done—but not just any verb. All too often that same first draft is sprinkled with various forms of the verb* to be, *usually in its most simple form* is. *Soto shows you how to avoid that trap by using action verbs that convey far more precisely exactly what he is feeling.*

1   I knew enough about hell to stop me from stealing. I was holy in almost every bone. Some days I recognized the shadows of angels flopping on the backyard grass, and other days I heard faraway messages in the plumbing that howled underneath the house when I crawled there looking for something to do.

2   But boredom made me sin. Once, at the German Market, I stood before a rack of pies, my sweet tooth gleaming and the juice of guilt wetting my underarms. I gazed at the nine kinds of pie, pecan and apple being my favorites, although cherry looked good, and

my dear, fat-faced chocolate was always a good bet. I nearly wept trying to decide which to steal and, forgetting the flowery dust priests give off, the shadow of angels and the proximity of God howling in the plumbing underneath the house, sneaked a pie behind my coffee-lid frisbee and walked to the door, grinning to the bald grocer whose forehead shone with a window of light.

3   "No one saw," I muttered to myself, the pie like a discus in my hand, and hurried across the street, where I sat on someone's lawn. The sun wavered between the branches of a yellowish sycamore. A squirrel nailed itself high on the trunk, where it forked into two large bark-scabbed limbs. Just as I was going to work my cleanest finger into the pie, a neighbor came out to the porch for his mail. He looked at me, and I got up and headed for home. I raced on skinny legs to my block, but slowed to a quick walk when I couldn't wait any longer. I held the pie to my nose and breathed in its sweetness. I licked some of the crust and closed my eyes as I took a small bite.

4   In my front yard, I leaned against a car fender and panicked about stealing the apple pie. I knew an apple got Eve in deep trouble with snakes because Sister Marie had shown us a film about Adam and Eve being cast into the desert, and what scared me more than falling from grace was being thirsty for the rest of my life. But even that didn't stop me from clawing a chunk from the pie tin and pushing it into the cavern of my mouth. The slop was sweet and gold-colored in the afternoon sun. I laid more pieces on my tongue, wet finger-dripping pieces, until I was finished and felt like crying because it was about the best thing I had ever tasted. I realized right there and then, in my sixth year, in my tiny body of two hundred bones and three or four sins, that the best things in life came stolen. I wiped my sticky fingers on the grass and rolled my tongue over the corners of my mouth. A burp perfumed the air.

5   I felt bad not sharing with Cross-Eyed Johnny, a neighbor kid. He stood over my shoulder and asked, "Can I have some?" Crust fell from my mouth, and my teeth were bathed with the jam-like filling. Tears blurred my eyes as I remembered the grocer's forehead. I remembered the other pies on the rack, the warm air of the fan above the door and the car that honked as I crossed the street without looking.

6   "Get away," I had answered Cross-Eyed Johnny. He watched my fingers greedily push big chunks of pie down my throat. He swal-

lowed and said in a whisper, "Your hands are dirty," then returned home to climb his roof and sit watching me eat the pie by myself. After a while, he jumped off and hobbled away because the fall had hurt him.

7   I sat on the curb. The pie tin glared at me and rolled away when the wind picked up. My face was sticky with guilt. A car honked, and the driver knew. Mrs. Hancock stood on her lawn, hands on hip, and she knew. My mom, peeling a mountain of potatoes at the Redi-Spud factory, knew. I got to my feet, stomach taut, mouth tired of chewing, and flung my frisbee across the street, its shadow like the shadow of an angel fleeing bad deeds. I retrieved it, jogging slowly. I flung it again until I was bored and thirsty.

8   I returned home to drink water and help my sister glue bottle caps onto cardboard, a project for summer school. But the bottle caps bored me, and the water soon filled me up more than the pie. With the kitchen stifling with heat and lunatic flies, I decided to crawl underneath our house and lie in the cool shadows listening to the howling sound of plumbing. Was it God? Was it Father, speaking from death, or Uncle with his last shiny dime? I listened, ear pressed to a cold pipe, and heard a howl like the sea. I lay until I was cold and then crawled back to the light, rising from one knee, then another, to dust off my pants and squint in the harsh light. I looked and saw the glare of a pie tin on a hot day. I knew sin was what you take and didn't give back.

THESIS AND ORGANIZATION

1. What does the first paragraph lead you to expect in the rest of the essay?
2. The time sequence traces Soto's guilt. What stages can you identify?
3. How would you describe the nature of the conflict in the essay?
4. What emotions does Soto feel in the course of his narrative?
5. What does Soto learn?

TECHNIQUE AND STYLE

1. Soto relates his narrative from the perspective of his six-year-old self. What is the first clue about his age?
2. Reread paragraph 4. What images appeal to what senses?

3. Paragraphs 5 and 6 bring in Cross-Eyed Johnny. What does that incident add to the narrative?
4. What other titles can you think of for the essay? What is gained? Lost?
5. Choose two sentences from paragraph 3 and rewrite them, using different verbs. Which versions do you prefer and why?

SUGGESTIONS FOR WRITING

Journal

1. Place yourself in the position of Cross-Eyed Johnny and retell the scene (paragraphs 5 and 6) from his perspective.
2. The area under the house and its howling plumbing holds special significance for Soto. Think of a place that holds similar significance for you and describe it. Like Soto, you may want to use that place to frame a narrative.

Essay

Soto's experience probably reminds you of a similar one of your own or of a friend's. Recall a time when, directly or indirectly, you lived though such an event and use your memory of it as the basis of a narrative. Like Soto, you will want to describe not only what you or your friend did but also how it made you feel. Suggestions:

being embarrassed
feeling guilty
getting caught
getting away with "it"

I Have a Gun

Tania Nyman

Sometimes being able to defend yourself can be as frightening as being defenseless, a paradox sharply felt by Tania Nyman, who wrote this essay her sophomore year at the University of New Orleans. At the time, 1989, New Orleans was fast becoming the murder capital of the United States, a fact of which the editors of the local newspaper, the Times-Picayune, *were well aware. Urban violence makes many people feel the way Tania Nyman does, which is one reason the* Times-Picayune *published her essay as an opinion piece.*

WHAT TO LOOK FOR   *Pace, the speed at which the story unfolds, is crucial to the impact of a narrative, and one way to quicken the pace is to use present tense. Notice how Nyman relies on the present tense to make her story immediate. Note, too, how she uses flashbacks to interrupt her narrative but still maintains its pace and supports her thesis.*

1   I have a gun, a .38 caliber that holds five bullets. It is black with a brown handle and it stays by my bed.

2   I don't want a gun. I don't even like guns. But it seems I need one.

3   I've always believed in gun control, and the funny thing is I still do. But my gun is loaded next to my bed.

4   It wasn't ignorance of crime statistics that previously kept me from owning a gun. Nor was it the belief that I was immune to violence.

5   I thought that because I didn't believe in violence, that because I wasn't violent, I wouldn't be touched by violence. I believed that my belief in the best of human nature could make it real.

6   I want to believe in a world where people do not need to protect themselves from one another. But I have a gun, and it stays by my bed.

7   I should carry the gun from my house to my car, but I don't. What the gun is capable of, what the gun is for, still frightens me more than what it is supposed to prevent.

8   If I carry my gun and I am attacked, I must use it. I cannot shoot to injure. I must shoot to kill.

9   I have confronted an attacker not in reality but in my imagination. The man is walking down the street. To prove I am not paranoid, I lock my car and walk to my door with my house key ready.

10   Before I reach the steps, I think I hear a voice. "Money." Before I open the door I hear a voice. "Money." I turn to see the man with the gun.

11   He is frightened. I am frightened. I am frightened that I will scare him and he will shoot. I am frightened that I will give him my money and he will shoot.

12   I am frightened, but I am angry. I am angry because there is a gun pointed at me by someone I've never met and never hurt.

13   There is something that bothers me about this robbery I have created in my head. It is something that makes me uncomfortable with myself. It is something I don't want to admit, something I almost intentionally omitted because I am ashamed.

14   I guess I understand why I imagine being robbed by a man. They're physically more intimidating and I've never heard of anyone being robbed by a woman, though I'm sure it happens. But I'm being robbed by a man.

15   But why is he a black man? Why is he a black man with a worn T-shirt and glassy eyes? Why do I not imagine being robbed by a white man?

16   I am standing in a gas station on Claiborne and Jackson waiting to pay the cashier when a black man walks up behind me. I do not turn around. I stare in front of me waiting to pay. I try not to admit that I am nervous because a black man has walked up behind me in a gas station in a bad neighborhood and he does not have a car.

17   There is another scenario I imagine. I am walking to my door with my gun in my hand and I hear the voice. The man mustn't have seen my gun. I get angry because I am threatened, because someone is endangering my life for the money in my pocket.

18   I turn and without really thinking, angry and frightened, I shoot. I kill a man for $50. Or it could be $100. It does not matter that he was trying to rob me. A man has died for money. Not my money or his money, just money. Who put the price on his life, he or I?

19   I remember driving one night with my friend in her parents' car. We stop at a red light at Carollton and Tulane and a black man is crossing the street in front of us. My friend quickly but nonchalantly locks the doors with the power lock.

20   I am disgusted that she sees the man as a reminder to lock her doors. I wonder if he noticed the two girls nonchalantly lock their doors. I wonder how it feels to have people lock their doors at the sight of you.

21   I imagine again a confrontation in front of my house. I have my gun when the man asks for money. I am angry and scared, but I do not use the gun. I am afraid of what may happen to me if I don't use it, but I am more afraid of killing another human being, more afraid of trying to live with the guilt of murdering another person. I bet my life that he will take my money and leave, and I hope I win.

22   I am in a gas station on St. Charles and South Carollton near my house and there is a black man waiting to pay the cashier. I walk up behind him to wait in line and he jumps and turns around.

23   When he sees me, he relaxes and says I scared him because of the way things have gotten in this neighborhood.

24   "Sorry," I say and smile. I realize I am not the only one who is frightened.

THESIS AND ORGANIZATION

1. As in the Merrill-Foster essay (p. 34), the paragraphs here conform to newspaper columns. If you were reparagraphing for a regular page, what paragraphs would you use to make up an introduction? What reasons do you have for your decision?
2. List the three imaginary incidents. What do they have in common? How are they different?
3. List the real incidents. What do they have in common? How are they different?
4. What is the point of the last narrative?
5. What is the author's attitude toward violence? Toward having a gun? Toward race? Combine your answers into a thesis statement.

TECHNIQUE AND STYLE

1. How would you describe the *I* in this essay? Is this the kind of person you would like to know? Why or why not?
2. The author uses repetition intentionally. Find an example and describe its effect.
3. What effects are achieved by mixing real and imagined situations?

4. How would you describe the various conflicts in the narrative? Which is the most important and why?

5. The author depends heavily on the first-person singular, *I*. Explain whether she overuses the pronoun.

SUGGESTIONS FOR WRITING

Journal

1. Turn to a blank page and get set to do a timed entry, say five minutes or so. Think of the word *gun* and write down all the associations that come to mind. The result will be a list that may make sense only to you, but if you select one of your associations, you can probably build a narrative around it if you want to turn your ideas into an essay.

2. These days, it's almost impossible to find a person who has not been confronted by violence. Write a journal entry that briefly relates a violent incident and your response to it. You may want to return to this entry later and use it in an essay.

Essay

Think of a time when your action or actions contradicted your values. What were your values? What situation or action conflicted with those values? Perhaps you will want to develop how the conflict made you feel, how it affected others, and how you either resolved the conflict or learned to live with it. To come up with ideas for a topic, you might try to remember times when you

were forced to lie to protect a friend

kept silent when you should have spoken

spoke when you should have kept quiet

were pressured to do something you knew you shouldn't do

On Using Definition

3

"When I use a word," said Humpty Dumpty, "it means just what I choose it to mean—neither more nor less." To that Alice replied, "The question is whether you can make words mean so many different things." Humpty Dumpty then pronounced, "The question is which is to be the master—that's all." Writers are the masters of their words, although not to the extent that Humpty Dumpty would like, and often a discussion or argument boils down to the meaning of a crucial word. *Liberty, justice, civil rights, freedom,* and other similar concepts, for example, are all abstractions until they are defined.

If you had to write a paper on what *freedom* means to you, you might be tempted first off to look up the word in a dictionary, but you will discover more to say if you put aside the dictionary and first think about some basic questions, such as "Whose freedom?" If it's your freedom you are writing about, who or what sets limits on your freedom? The law? The church? Parents? Family responsibilities? After you mull over questions such as these, you are in a better position to make use of a dictionary definition. The dictionary is the most obvious place to find what the word means, but what you find there is only explicit meaning, the word's **denotation.** Look up *freedom* in a collegiate dictionary, and you'll see the different ways in which the word can be used, and also its etymology, but that won't convey the rich layers of meaning that the word has accumulated through the years.

What the dictionary does not reveal is the word's associative or emotional meanings, its **connotation.** One way to discover connotation is to ask yourself questions about the word, questions similar to those above that get at how the concept of freedom touches your life. The more specific your examples, the more concrete your definition can be, and the less the danger of slipping into clichés. Unless the word you are defining is quite unusual, most readers will be familiar with its dictionary definition; your own definition and your speculations on the word's connotation are of much greater interest.

A paper that defines a familiar word can hold just as much interest as one that examines an unfamiliar word or a word that is particularly powerful. "What does boredom mean?" "Why is synergism a useful concept?" "What does it mean to be called handicapped?" Questions such as these can be explored through almost any mode of thinking and writing. You can use those that you have already studied both to probe your subject as you think about it and to develop your ideas as you write.

Description   What details best describe it? What senses can you appeal to?

Narration   What story might best illustrate it? What kind of conflict might the word involve?

And even though you may not have read essays that use the other modes discussed in this book, they are already familiar to you as ways of thinking and can, therefore, also be useful to you as you think and write about your central term.

Example   What sorts of examples illustrate it? What different times and sources can you use to find examples?

Comparison and contrast   What is it similar to? What is it different from?

Analogy   What metaphor would make it vivid? What might the reader be familiar with that you can draw an analogy to?

Division and classification   How can it be divided? What types or categories can it be broken into?

Process   What steps or stages are involved in it? Which are crucial?

Cause and effect   What are the conditions that cause it? What effect does it have?

When questions such as these are tailored to the particular word or concept under scrutiny, they will help you develop your ideas.

AUDIENCE AND PURPOSE

Unless your subject is unusual, you can assume that your audience has a general understanding of the word or phrase to be defined. The nature of that general understanding, however, differs. For instance, the word *spinster* most often raises an image of "little old lady," a picture possibly fleshed out with a cat or two and fussy furnishings. Short of those associations, a spinster is an unmarried woman of a certain age, but that age varies from one decade to another. Forty years ago, a single woman who was 26 might well have been considered a spinster. These days, the term—when used at all—would be applied to someone considerably older. Even so, the negative image remains, and those who use the word probably assume that the spinster leads a lonely, narrow life. Such an image, however, is a far cry from the likes of Katharine Hepburn, who never married but who, at the age of 80 plus, was still being asked about her long-term love affair with her married Hollywood costar, Spencer Tracy. Were you to write an essay arguing against the stereotype and focusing on the Katharine Hepburns of our time, you might introduce your subject by reminding your readers of the word's usual connotations.

Sometimes you not only want to change the reader's understanding but also want to make the reader aware of how the meaning of a word has changed, a change that has an effect on our society. In that case you may choose to argue for a redefinition of the word or go a step further and attack the effects of the term's changed meaning. Words such as *amateur, dilettante,* and *gay* have all undergone major shifts in meaning within a relatively short period of time, at least short in the linguistic sense. *Amateur* used to refer to someone engaged in an activity for pleasure, not pay, but it now has the common meaning of inexperienced, unskilled. *Dilettante* also had a positive connotation, someone who was a lover of the arts; now it is more likely associated with someone who dabbles at them. As for *gay*, today it is associated with the word *homosexual*, which puts a very different spin on the nineteenth century and its Gay Nineties.

Definition can also be used to explore what people know and don't know about a place. If you were to write an essay that explains what your neighborhood means to you, you would essentially be presenting a personal definition of it. The same would be true if you were to write about any favorite spot, whether it be a tree house from your childhood or a park bench. To some, a park bench may be an eyesore or a necessity or a plain park bench, whereas to you it may hold particular meaning as the place where you find peace and quiet.

Perhaps you merely want your readers to reexamine a term and consider its importance. *Education* is a word familiar to all, and you and your classmates have had years of experience with it, but it may well mean different things to different people. Were you to write about the word within the context of your college education, you might begin by chasing down its etymology, which would bring you to the Latin *educatus*, meaning brought up, taught. From there you might speculate on how the meaning of education has shifted, slipping from the general—conveying general knowledge and developing reason and judgment—to the particular—emphasizing skills and preparation for a profession. At that point, you would have the makings of a good argument against or in favor of the change.

USING OTHER MODES

Definition, perhaps more than any other rhetorical pattern, depends on other modes to serve its purpose. Were you to write an essay on *honesty,* for example, you might begin your discussion with a narrative, a brief story about a friend who bought a magazine at a newsstand and received too much change for a 20-dollar bill. The narrative can then lead to comparison and contrast, making a distinction between honest and dishonest. And if the friend kept the money but feels guilty about it, then you would be dealing with cause and effect. Make your reader feel that guilt, and you'll be using description.

While an essay that depends primarily on definition can be developed as a personal narrative, one that is organized as straight-forward exposition will also involve other patterns of organization. If you were writing a short research paper on the common cold, comparison would help you distinguish it from the flu and process would enable you to trace its progress from first sore throat to last sniffle. In between you might discuss possible ways to relieve symptoms, which would bring in classification. Although you may use many different modes, your primary one would still be definition.

To flesh out the definition of a term, you can draw upon a number of sources. You might make a quick connection with your reader's experience, for instance, by drawing examples from the world of athletics. An essay defining *grace* can cite Michael Jordan's drive to a basket, just as one on *bizarre* might well put Dennis Rodman at the head of the list for his habit of dying his hair different colors and cross-dressing. Citing examples of well-known figures from film, television, the arts, and politics is also a quick way to remind your readers of what they know and to make use of that to explain the unfamiliar. While contemporary figures are probably the first to come to mind, historical ones will serve just as well with the additional advantage of broadening the base of your information and adding to your credibility, your **persona,** the image of self that you create that then you present through the prose in your essay. A brief mention of the grace of a Donatello bronze or the bizarre world of Hieronymus Bosch extends the range of your definition while also revealing the depth of your knowledge, portraying you as someone who knows the fine arts. Combining those references with a formal vocabulary, varied sentence structure, and wit, you will create a sophisticated, informed persona.

THESIS AND ORGANIZATION

Although a definition can play a key role in an essay, it is not the essay's thesis. The thesis rises from the author's assertion about the definition. Sometimes your title can serve as your thesis or at least hint at it, as in "Honesty Isn't Easy" or "No Cure for the Common Cold." The explicit thesis is also obvious, usually found in one sentence in the introduction. Sometimes, however, you want the reader to infer the thesis by combining the ideas in two or more sentences. Far more subtle is the implied thesis, which is what you have here:

> Pile on onions, lettuce, tomato, cheese, even mushrooms and jalapeño peppers, douse it with ketchup, mustard, mayonnaise, and still you can't hide the classic American hamburger—a quarter pound or so of relatively lean grilled beef snuggled into a soft but not spongy round roll. If the meat's too lean, the hamburger's too dry, but if it's not lean enough, the juice soaks the bun and the whole creation falls apart.

The thesis? Several are possible but two come quickly to mind, variations on "You can't spoil the classic American hamburger" and "The classic American hamburger is a splendid creation." Either way, what you have is a definition and an assertion about it.

Like the thesis, an essay's organization can be straightforward or somewhat complex. At times, you may want to use a roughly chronological pattern of organization, starting at one point in time and moving forward to another. Structuring an essay so that it moves from the least to the most important point is another obvious pattern, one used by several of the writers in this chapter. You might also consider organizing your paper by question/answer, the introduction posing a question and the body of the essay answering it. A variation on that pattern is one in which one part of the essay poses a problem that is then discussed and analyzed in terms of possible solutions. Both those ways of organizing an essay are relatively uncomplicated. Perhaps the hardest to handle successfully is the organization that goes from the particular to the general. Were you to write a paper on the American flag, for example, you might start with the particular—a description of the modern flag—and then discuss the general—what it means as a symbol.

Useful Terms

Connotation   The associations suggested by a word that add to its literal meaning. *Home* and *domicile* have similar dictionary meanings, but they differ radically in their connotation.

Denotation   The literal meaning of a word, its dictionary definition.

Persona   The character of the writer that comes through from the prose.

➤ Pointers for Using Definition

Exploring the Topic

1. **What are the denotations of your term?** You should consult an unabridged dictionary and perhaps a more complete or specialized one, such as the *Oxford English Dictionary* or a dictionary of slang.
2. **What are the connotations of your term?** What emotional reactions or associations does it elicit from people? What situations evoke what responses and why?
3. **What other words can be used for your term?** Which are similar?
4. **What are the characteristics, qualities, or components of your term?** Which are most important? Are some not worth mentioning?
5. **What other modes are appropriate?** What modes can you draw on to help support your definition and the organization of the essay? Where can you use description? Narration? What examples can you use to illustrate your term?
6. **Has your word been used or misused?** If so, might that misuse be turned into an introductory narrative? A closing one?

Drafting the Paper

1. **Know your reader.** Review your lists of denotations and connotations together with the characteristics related to your term to see how familiar they are to your reader. Check to see if your reader may have particular

associations that you need to redirect or change. Or if your reader is directly affected by your topic, make sure your definition does not offend.

2. **Know your purpose.** Unless your term is unusual, one of your biggest problems is to tell the reader something new about it. Work on your first paragraph so that it will engage the reader from the start. From that point on, keep your primary purpose in mind. If you are writing a paper that is basically self-expressive or persuasive, make sure you have an audience other than yourself. If your aim is informative, consider narration, example, cause and effect, and analogy as possible ways of presenting familiar material in a fresh light.

3. **Use evidence.** Provide examples as evidence to illustrate what your key term means. Also consider using negative examples and setting out distinctions between the meaning of your word and other, similar words.

4. **Draw on a variety of sources.** Define your term from several perspectives. Perhaps a brief history of the word would be helpful, or maybe some statistical information is in order. See if a brief narrative might provide additional meaning for the term.

5. **Make a point.** Don't mistake your definition for your thesis. The two are certainly related, but one is an assertion; the other is not. Perhaps your definition is a jumping-off place for a larger point you wish to make or a key part of that point. Or perhaps your term evokes a single dominant impression you want to convey. Whatever purpose your definition serves, it needs to support your thesis.

In All Ways a Woman

Maya Angelou

Known to all who watched the inauguration of President William Jefferson Clinton on January 20, 1993, for her reading of her poem "On the Pulse of Morning," Maya Angelou has long been a celebrated writer and speaker. She is as apt to begin a speaking engagement with an acappela blues song as with a narrative from her childhood, a childhood many readers are familiar with through her book I Know Why the Caged Bird Sings. *Author of a large body of poetry, essays, children's books, and memoirs, Angelou is currently Reynolds Professor in the English Department at Wake Forest University. Her published poetry has been collected in* The Complete Collected Poems of Maya Angelou *(1994), and the essay that follows comes from* Wouldn't Take Nothing for My Journey Now *(1993), a collection dedicated to her good friend Oprah Winfrey.*

WHAT TO LOOK FOR   *Changing from the particular to the general or from the personal to the impersonal is often difficult. One choice many writers make involves writing a draft in first person and then shifting out of first person in the next version. Maya Angelou takes a different approach, starting with first person and her own experience, then generalizing about that experience by using one of the categories she belongs to, that of woman. All of us belong to any number of larger groups. Like Angelou, you can generalize based on gender, or you can use any other category that fits—age, occupation, family relationship (father or mother or child), voter, citizen. The list is almost endless.*

1   In my young years I took pride in the fact that luck was called a lady. In fact, there were so few public acknowledgments of the female presence that I felt personally honored whenever nature and large ships were referred to as feminine. But as I matured, I began to resent being considered a sister to a changeling as fickle as luck, as aloof as an ocean, and as frivolous as nature.

2   The phrase "A woman always has the right to change her mind" played so aptly into the negative image of the female that I made myself a victim to an unwavering decision. Even if I made an inane and stupid choice, I stuck by it rather than "be like a woman and change my mind."

3   Being a woman is hard work. Not without joy and even ecstasy, but still relentless, unending work. Becoming an old female may require only being born with certain genitalia, inheriting long-living genes and the fortune not to be run over by an out-of-control truck, but to become and remain a woman command the existence and employment of genius.

4   The woman who survives intact and happy must be at once tender and tough. She must have convinced herself, or be in the unending process of convincing herself, that she, her values, and her choices are important. In a time and world where males hold sway and control, the pressure upon women to yield their rights-of-way is tremendous. And it is under those very circumstances that the woman's toughness must be in evidence.

5   She must resist considering herself a lesser version of her male counterpart. She is not a sculptress, poetess, authoress, Jewess, Negress, or even (now rare) in university parlance a rectoress. If she is the thing, then for her own sense of self and for the education of the ill-informed she must insist with rectitude in being the thing and in being called the thing.

6   A rose by any other name may smell as sweet, but a woman called by a devaluing name will only be weakened by the misnomer.

7   She will need to prize her tenderness and be able to display it at appropriate times in order to prevent toughness from gaining total authority and to avoid becoming a mirror image of those men who value power above life, and control over love.

8   It is imperative that a woman keep her sense of humor intact and at the ready. She must see, even if only in secret, that she is the funniest, looniest woman in her world, which she should also see as being the most absurd world of all times.

9   It has been said that laughter is therapeutic and amiability lengthens the life span.

10   Women should be tough, tender, laugh as much as possible, and live long lives. The struggle for equality continues unabated, and the woman warrior who is armed with wit and courage will be among the first to celebrate victory.

THESIS AND ORGANIZATION

1. What paragraph or paragraphs introduce the essay? What reasons do you have for your choice?

2. Where and what is the essay's thesis? What reasons can you find for its placement? Explain whether you find that placement effective.
3. Where in the essay does Angelou use comparisons? What do they contribute to the thesis?
4. What do paragraphs 2 and 9 have in common? How do they relate to the thesis?
5. Given that essays can be organized in a number of ways—such as chronological, particular/general (or vice versa), dramatic, problem/solution—how would you characterize Angelou's sequencing of paragraphs?

TECHNIQUE AND STYLE

1. Explain the ways in which the title fits the essay's thesis and content.
2. What reasons can you find for Angelou's use of sayings and associations in paragraphs 1 and 2?
3. To what extent, if any, does Angelou make use of race in the essay? What purpose does it or the lack of it serve?
4. Angelou alludes to Shakespeare's *Romeo and Juliet* in paragraph 6 and to Maxine Hong Kingston, author of *Woman Warrior*, in paragraph 10. What do these allusions contribute to the essay?
5. Although the audience for the essay is a general one, the piece focuses almost exclusively on women. Discuss the degree to which that focus limits the essay. What is in it for men?

SUGGESTIONS FOR WRITING

Journal

1. Use your journal to explore what Angelou means by *tender*. What examples can you find in your own experience that fit the definition?
2. If you prefer, explore what Angelou means by *tough*. Again, flesh out her definition with examples from your own experience.

Essay

Write your own "in all ways" essay, drawing on a category or group to which you belong. The tone of your essay may be serious, like Angelou's, or humorous. Either tone would work, for instance, if you were to write "In All Ways a Student" or "In All Ways Underpaid." Other suggestions:

a parent (or child or sibling)
a winner (or loser)
a reader (or writer)
a fan

I Was a Member of the Kung Fu Crew

Henry Han Xi Lau

New York City is still in many ways a city of neighborhoods, many of which are ethnic ones. The Chinatown that Henry Han Xi Lau writes about is one of the oldest, and it's where you can still walk down the street and not hear a word of English. To Lau, it's also home, even though he and his family have moved to Brooklyn. A sophomore at Yale University at the time he wrote this essay, he describes the people and places of Chinatown, defining it as "ghetto." The piece was published in the New York Times Magazine *on October 19, 1997.*

WHAT TO LOOK FOR   *Lau relies heavily upon definition to convey what it's like to be a member of the Kung Fu Crew and to be "ghetto." Many of the techniques he uses are ones that can carry over to your own writing, so be on the look out for the details that define the Crew's physical prowess, hair, pants, attitudes, accessories, and language, all of which add up to being "cool."*

1   Chinatown is ghetto, my friends are ghetto, I am ghetto. I went away to college last year, but I still have a long strand of hair that reaches past my chin. I need it when I go back home to hang with the K.F.C.— for Kung Fu Crew, not Kentucky Fried Chicken. We all met in a Northern Shaolin kung fu class years ago. Our *si-fu* was Rocky. He told us: "In the early 1900's in China, your grand master was walking in the streets when a foreigner riding on a horse disrespected him. So then he felt the belly of the horse with his palms and left. Shortly thereafter, the horse buckled and died because our grand master had used *qi-gong* to mess up the horse's internal organs." Everyone said, "Cool, I would like to do that." Rocky emphasized, "You've got to practice really hard for a long time to reach that level."

2   By the time my friends and I were in the eighth grade, we were able to do 20-plus pushups on our knuckles and fingers. When we practiced our crescent, roundhouse and tornado kicks, we had 10-pound weights strapped to our legs. Someone once remarked,

"Goddamn—that's a freaking mountain!" when he saw my thigh muscles in gym class.

3   Most Chinatown kids fall into a few general categories. There are pale-faced nerds who study all the time to get into the Ivies. There are the recent immigrants with uncombed hair and crooked teeth who sing karaoke in bars. There are the punks with highlighted hair who cut school, and the gangsters, whom everyone else avoids.

4   Then there is the K.F.C. We work hard like the nerds, but we identify with the punks. Now we are reunited, and just as in the old days we amble onto Canal Street, where we stick out above the older folks, elderly women bearing leaden bags of bok choy and oranges. As an opposing crew nears us, I assess them to determine whether to grill them or not. Grilling is the fine art of staring others down and trying to emerge victorious.

5   How the hair is worn is important in determining one's order on the streets. In the 80's, the dominant style was the mushroom cut, combed neatly or left wild in the front so that a person can appear menacing as he peers through his bangs. To gain an edge in grilling now, some kids have asymmetrical cuts, with long random strands sprouting in the front, sides or back. Some dye their hair blue or green, while blood red is usually reserved for gang members.

6   Only a few years ago, examination of the hair was sufficient. But now there is a second step: assessing pants. A couple of years ago, wide legs first appeared in New York City, and my friends and I switched from baggy pants. In the good old days, Merry-Go-Round in the Village sold wide legs for only $15 a pair. When Merry-Go-Round went bankrupt, Chinatown kids despaired. Wide-leg prices at other stores increased drastically as they became more popular. There are different ways of wearing wide legs. Some fold their pant legs inward and staple them at the hem. Some clip the back ends of their pants to their shoes with safety pins. Others simply cut the bottoms so that fuzzy strings hang out.

7   We grill the opposing punks. I untuck my long strand of hair so that it swings in front of my face. Nel used to have a strand, but he chewed it off one day in class by accident. Chu and Tom cut their strands off because it scared people at college. Jack has a patch of blond hair, while Tone's head is a ball of orange flame. Chi has gelled short hair, while Ken's head is a black mop. As a group, we have better hair than our rivals. But they beat us with their wide legs. In our year away at college, wide legs have gone beyond our

24-inch leg openings. Twenty-six- to 30-inch jeans are becoming the norm. If wide legs get any bigger, they will start flying up like a skirt in an updraft.

8   We have better accessories, though. Chi sports a red North Face that gives him a rugged mountain-climber look because of the jungle of straps sprouting in the back. Someone once asked Chi, "Why is the school bag so important to one's cool?" He responded, "Cuz it's the last thing others see when you walk away from them or when they turn back to look at you after you walk past them." But the other crew has female members, which augments their points. The encounter between us ends in a stalemate. But at least the K.F.C. members are in college and are not true punks.

9   In the afternoon, we decide to eat at the Chinatown McDonald's for a change instead of the Chinese bakery Maria's, our dear old hangout spot. "Mickey D's is good sit," Nel says. I answer: "But the Whopper gots more fat and meat. It's even got more bun." Nel agrees. "True that," he says. I want the Big Mac, but I buy the two-cheeseburger meal because it has the same amount of meat but costs less.

10   We sit and talk about ghettoness again. We can never exactly articulate what being ghetto entails, but we know the spirit of it. In Chinatown toilet facilities we sometimes find footprints on the seats because F.O.B.'s (fresh off the boats) squat on them as they do over the holes in China. We see alternative brand names in stores like Dolo instead of Polo, and Mike instead of Nike.

11   We live by ghettoness. My friends and I walk from 80-something Street in Manhattan to the tip of the island to save a token. We gorge ourselves at Gray's Papaya because the hot dogs are 50 cents each. But one cannot be stingy all the time. We leave good tips at Chinese restaurants because our parents are waiters and waitresses, too.

12   We sit for a long time in McDonald's, making sure that there is at least a half-inch of soda in our cups so that when the staff wants to kick us out, we can claim that we are not finished yet. Jack positions a mouse bite of cheeseburger in the center of a wrapper to support our claim.

13   After a few hours, the K.F.C. prepares to disband. I get in one of the no-license commuter vans on Canal Street that will take me to Sunset Park in Brooklyn, where my family lives now. All of my friends will leave Chinatown, for the Upper East Side and the Lower East Side, Forest Hills in Queens and Bensonhurst in Brooklyn. We

live far apart, but we always come back together in Chinatown. For most of us, our homes used to be here and our world was here.

THESIS AND ORGANIZATION

1. The essay is set out in chronological order. What paragraphs cover what times?
2. What categories of kids does Lau describe? Where does the Crew fit?
3. Lau describes "grilling" in paragraphs 4–8. What is his point?
4. Paragraphs 9–11 are set at McDonald's. What information can you infer from that scene?
5. Is Lau's thesis explicit or implicit? How can you phrase it in your own words?

TECHNIQUE AND STYLE

1. Look up the term *comma splice* in a handbook of grammar and usage, and check what you find against Lau's first sentence. Why is it a legitimate comma splice?
2. Lau uses dialogue in paragraphs 8 and 9. What does it add to the essay?
3. The essay piles on details and information that lead up to a definition of *ghetto*. State that definition in your own words.
4. *Ghetto* usually has a negative connotation. How does Lau make it positive?
5. The essay is written in standard American English. Why might Lau have chosen to write it that way instead of in "ghetto"?

SUGGESTIONS FOR WRITING

Journal

1. If you met the Kung Fu Crew on the street, you might find yourself ignoring them, "grilling" them, admiring them, but no matter what, you'd have some sort of reaction. Describe how you would react.
2. Look up the word *intimidation* in an unabridged dictionary, and think about times in your experience when you were intimidated or intimidated someone. Use your journal to define how you felt.

Essay

People spend a lot of time analyzing what's in and what's out. For some, those in advertising or fashion, for instance, it's a business, but all of us are affected by it. Perhaps you would find a lot to say in an essay about what it means to be "in" or "cool" or the opposite. Think about a category (some suggestions are listed below), choose a subject, and then start jotting down details such as the particulars of language (spoken and body), appearance, attitudes, and likes and dislikes that define your central term.

music
films or television shows
dates
schools
cars

As you draft your essay, try to keep your focus on definition. It's natural to lean toward comparisons, but, like Lau, make sure you use them to support what you are defining.

The Handicap of Definition

William Raspberry

Although William Raspberry is the urban affairs columnist for the
Washington Post, *he is better known as the author of a syndicated
column that runs in more than 200 newspapers. His commentary on
issues such as rap music, crime, and AIDS earned him a Pulitzer
Prize in 1994. In the essay that follows, he writes about the terms*
black *and* white, *words that have connotations we don't often think
about. Raspberry shows us that if we stop to think about* black, *we'll
see that it has so narrow a definition that it is "one of the heaviest
burdens black Americans—and black children in particular—have
to bear." Not much has changed since 1982, when this essay first appeared in Raspberry's syndicated column.*

WHAT TO LOOK FOR   *Somewhere along the line, we've all been
warned never to begin a sentence with a conjunction such as* and,
but, *and the like. But as long as you know how to avoid the trap of a
sentence fragment, beginning a sentence with a conjunction can
lend a conversational tone to your essay. As you read Raspberry's
essay, notice how often he uses this technique.*

1   I know all about bad schools, mean politicians, economic depri-
vation and racism. Still, it occurs to me that one of the heaviest burdens black Americans—and black children in particular—have to
bear is the handicap of definition: the question of what it means to
be black.

2   Let me explain quickly what I mean. If a basketball fan says that
the Boston Celtics' Larry Bird plays "black," the fan intends it—and
Bird probably accepts it—as a compliment. Tell pop singer Tom
Jones he moves "black" and he might grin in appreciation. Say to
Teena Marie or The Average White Band that they sound "black"
and they'll thank you.

3   But name one pursuit, aside from athletics, entertainment or sexual performance in which a white practitioner will feel compli-
mented to be told he does it "black." Tell a white broadcaster he
talks "black," and he'll sign up for diction lessons. Tell a white reporter he writes "black" and he'll take a writing course. Tell a white
lawyer he reasons "black" and he might sue you for slander.

4   What we have here is a tragically limited definition of blackness, and it isn't only white people who buy it.

5   Think of all the ways black children can put one another down with charges of "whiteness." For many of these children, hard study and hard work are "white." Trying to please a teacher might be criticized as acting "white." Speaking correct English is "white." Scrimping today in the interest of tomorrow's goals is "white." Educational toys and games are "white."

6   An incredible array of habits and attitudes that are conducive to success in business, in academia, in the nonentertainment professions are likely to be thought of as somehow "white." Even economic success, unless it involves such "black" undertakings as numbers banking, is defined as "white."

7   And the results are devastating. I wouldn't deny that blacks often are better entertainers and athletes. My point is the harm that comes from too narrow a definition of what is black.

8   One reason black youngsters tend to do better at basketball, for instance, is that they assume they can learn to do it well, and so they practice constantly to prove themselves right.

9   Wouldn't it be wonderful if we could infect black children with the notion that excellence in math is "black" rather than white, or possibly Chinese? Wouldn't it be of enormous value if we could create the myth that morality, strong families, determination, courage and love of learning are traits brought by slaves from Mother Africa and therefore quintessentially black?

10   There is no doubt in my mind that most black youngsters could develop their mathematical reasoning, their elocution and their attitudes the way they develop their jump shots and their dance steps: by the combination of sustained, enthusiastic practice and the unquestioned belief that they can do it.

11   In one sense, what I am talking about is the importance of developing positive ethnic traditions. Maybe Jews have an innate talent for communication; maybe Chinese are born with a gift for mathematical reasoning; maybe blacks are naturally blessed with athletic grace. I doubt it. What is at work, I suspect, is assumption, inculcated early in their lives, that this is a thing our people do well.

12   Unfortunately, many of the things about which blacks make this assumption are things that do not contribute to their career success—except for that handful of the truly gifted who can make it as

entertainers and athletes. And many of the things we concede to whites are the things that are essential to economic security.

13   So it is with a number of assumptions black youngsters make about what it is to be a "man": physical aggressiveness, sexual prowess, the refusal to submit to authority. The prisons are full of people who, by this perverted definition, are unmistakably men.

14   But the real problem is not so much that the things defined as "black" are negative. The problem is that the definition is much too narrow.

15   Somehow, we have to make our children understand that they are intelligent, competent people, capable of doing whatever they put their minds to and making it in the American mainstream, not just in a black subculture.

16   What we seem to be doing, instead, is raising up yet another generation of young blacks who will be failures—by definition.

THESIS AND ORGANIZATION

1. Examine paragraphs 1–4 as a unit. What sentence functions as the major assertion for this group of paragraphs?
2. Take paragraphs 5–7 as a unit and analyze it also, looking for the controlling assertion.
3. Paragraphs 8–11 form another paragraph block. What is its controlling assertion?
4. Examine paragraphs 12–16 as a concluding paragraph block. What is the relationship between paragraph 12 and the preceding paragraphs?
5. Consider the controlling ideas that guide the paragraph blocks and the conclusions Raspberry draws from the examples that support those assertions. Stated fully, what is Raspberry's thesis?

TECHNIQUE AND STYLE

1. This essay was one of Raspberry's syndicated columns; as a result, it appeared in a large number of newspapers with equally large readerships, mostly white. What evidence can you find that Raspberry is trying to inform his white audience and persuade his black readers?
2. How and where does Raspberry establish his credibility as a writer on this subject? What grammatical point of view does he use?
3. Where in the essay does he qualify or modulate his statements? What is the effect of that technique?

4. Many techniques can be used to give a paragraph coherence, but an often neglected one is syntax. Examine paragraphs 2, 3, 5, and 9 to discover the similar sentence structure at work. What do you find?

5. Paragraphs 3, 7, 13, and 14 all begin with a conjunction. What effect does this technique achieve? Consult a handbook of grammar and usage for a discussion of this device. To what extent does Raspberry's usage conform to the handbook's advice?

6. Paragraph 16 is an example of a rhetorical paragraph, a one-sentence paragraph that gives dramatic emphasis to a point. If you eliminate the dash or substitute a comma for it, what happens to the dramatic effect? What does the pun add?

7. A militant who read this essay would argue that Raspberry is trying to make blacks "better" by making them white. Is there any evidence to support this view? Explain.

8. A feminist who read the essay would argue that it is sexist. Is there any evidence to support this view? Explain.

Suggestions for Writing

Journal

1. Raspberry's essay was published in 1982. Write a journal entry explaining whether his point holds true today.

2. Write down any examples you can think of that can substitute for those Raspberry uses, but focus on women. In a paragraph or two, explain how the substitutions would add to or detract from his point.

Essay

Find a word that has accumulated broad connotations and then see what definitions have evolved and their effect. Like Raspberry, you may want to consider two terms but emphasize only one. Possibilities:

man
hero
student
woman
worker
lover
politician

The Myth of the Matriarch

Gloria Naylor

Best known for her novels, Gloria Naylor was born in Queens, a borough of New York City, and received her first library card at the age of four. After graduating from Brooklyn College and earning a master's degree at Yale, she began her career as a writer. Her first novel, The Women of Brewster Place, *was published in 1982 and received the American Book Award for best first novel. Her most recent,* Bailey's Café, *rounds off what Naylor calls her "novel quartet." A winner of the National Book Award for her fiction, Naylor is also noted for editing* Children of the Night: The Best Short Stories by Black Writers, 1967 to the Present *(1996). The essay that follows was published in* Life *in the spring of 1988. The neighborhood she grew up in and her travels have given Naylor lots of opportunity to observe both the myth and the reality of the matriarch.*

WHAT TO LOOK FOR   *When you think of the term* paragraph, *you probably imagine a fairly large chunk of prose that illustrates and develops a particular point that's stated or implied as a topic sentence. But paragraphs serve other functions as well, as Naylor's essay shows. Her essay is complex, which makes the need for clear transitions between paragraphs important, but providing a transition from one major part of the essay to another is more difficult. Naylor does it by using a short paragraph in which she poses a question that she then answers in the paragraphs that follow.*

1   The strong black woman. All my life I've seen her. In books she is Faulkner's impervious Dilsey, using her huge dark arms to hold together the crumbling spirits and household of the Compsons. In the movies she is the quintessential Mammy, chasing after Scarlett O'Hara with forgotten sunbonnets and shrill tongue-lashings about etiquette. On television she is Sapphire of *Amos 'n Andy* or a dozen variations of her—henpecking black men, herding white children, protecting her brood from the onslaughts of the world. She is the supreme matriarch—alone, self-sufficient and liking it that way. I've seen how this female image has permeated the American consciousness to the point of influencing everything from the selling of pancakes to the structuring of welfare benefits. But the strangest thing is that when

I walked around my neighborhood or went into the homes of family and friends, this matriarch was nowhere to be found.

2   I know the statistics: They say that when my grandmother was born at the turn of the century as few as 10 percent of black households were headed by females; when I was born at mid-century it had crept to 17 percent; and now it is almost 60 percent. No longer a widow or a divorcée as in times past, the single woman with children today probably has never married—and increasingly she is getting younger. By the time she is 18, one out of every four black unmarried women has become a mother.

3   But it is a long leap from a matrifocal home, where the father is absent, to a matriarchal one, in which the females take total charge from the males. Though I have known black women heading households in different parts of the country and in different social circumstances—poor, working class or professional—none of them has gloried in the conditions that left them with the emotional and financial responsibility for their families. Often they had to take domestic work because of the flexible hours or stay in menial factory or office jobs because of the steady pay. And leaving the job was only to go home to the other job of raising children alone. These women understood the importance of input from black men in sustaining their families. Their advice and, sometimes, financial assistance were sought and accepted. But if such were not forthcoming, she would continue to deal with her situation alone.

4   This is a far cry from the heartwarming image of the two-fisted black woman I watched striding across the public imagination. A myth always arises to serve a need. And so it must be asked, what is it in the relationship of black women to American society that has called for them to be seen as independent Amazons?

5   The black woman was brought to America for the same reason as the black man—to provide slave labor. But she had what seemed to be contradictory roles: She did the woman's work of bearing children and keeping house while doing a man's work at the side of the black male in the fields. She worked regardless of the advanced stages of pregnancy. In the 19th century the ideal of the true woman was one of piety, purity, domesticity and submissiveness; the female lived as a wife sheltered at home or went abroad as a virgin doing good works. But if the prevailing belief was that the natural state of women was one of frailty, how could the black female be explained? Out in the fields laboring with their muscled bodies and during rest

periods suckling infants at their breasts, the slave women had to be seen as different from white women. They were stronger creatures: they didn't feel pain in childbirth; they didn't have tear ducts. Ironically, one of the arguments for enslaving blacks in the first place was that as a race they were inferior to whites—but black women, well, they were a little *more* than women.

6   The need to view slavery as benign accounted for the larger-than-life mammy of the plantation legends. As a house servant, she was always pictured in close proximity to her white masters because there was nothing about her that was threatening to white ideas about black women. Her unstinting devotion assuaged any worries that slaves were discontented or harbored any potential for revolt. Her very dark skin belied any suspicions of past interracial liaisons, while her obesity and advanced age removed any sexual threat. Earth mother, nursemaid and cook, the mammy existed without a history or a future.

7   In reality, slave women in the house or the field were part of a kinship network and with their men tried to hold together their own precarious families. Marriages between slaves were not legally recognized, but this did not stop them from entering into living arrangements and acting as husbands and wives. After emancipation a deluge of black couples registered their unions under the law, and ex-slaves were known to travel hundreds of miles in search of lost partners and children.

8   No longer bound, but hardly equal citizens, black men and women had access to only the most menial jobs in society, the largest number being reserved solely for female domestics. Richard Wright wrote a terribly funny and satirical short story about the situation, "Man of All Work." His protagonist is unable to find a job to support his family and save his house from foreclosure, so he puts on his wife's clothes and secures a position as a housekeeper. "Don't stop me. I've found a solution to our problem. I'm an army-trained cook. I can clean a house as good as anybody. Get my point? I put on your dress. I looked in the mirror. I can pass. I want that job."

9   Pushed to the economic forefront of her home, the 19th century mammy became 20th century Sapphire. Fiery, younger, more aggressive, she just couldn't wait to take the lead away from the man of the house. Whatever he did was never enough. Not that he wanted to do anything, of course, except hang out on street cor-

ners, gamble and run around with women. From vaudeville of the 1880s to the advent of *Amos 'n Andy,* it was easier to make black men the brunt of jokes than to address the inequities that kept decent employment from those who wanted to work. Society had not failed black women—their men had.

10   The truth is that throughout our history black women could depend upon their men even when they were unemployed or underemployed. But in the impoverished inner cities today we are seeing the rise of the *unemployable.* These young men are not equipped to take responsibility for themselves, much less the children they are creating. And with the increasing youth of unwed mothers, we have grandmothers and grandfathers in their early thirties. How can a grandmother give her daughter's family the traditional wisdom and support when she herself has barely lived? And on the other side of town, where the professional black woman is heading a household, usually because she is divorced, the lack of a traditional kinship network—the core community of parents, uncles, aunts— makes her especially alone.

11   What is surprising to me is that the myth of the matriarch lives on—even among black women. I've talked to so many who believe that they are supposed to be superhuman and bear up under all things. When they don't, they all too readily look for the fault within themselves. Somehow they failed their history. But it is a grave mistake for black women to believe that they have a natural ability to be stronger than other women. Fifty-seven percent of black homes being headed by females is not natural. A 40 percent pregnancy rate among our young girls is not natural. It is heartbreaking. The myth of the matriarch robs a woman caught in such circumstances of her individuality and her humanity. She should feel that she has the *right* at least to break down—once the kids are put to bed—and do something so simple as cry.

THESIS AND ORGANIZATION

1. Paragraphs 1–3 introduce the essay. In what ways do they set the stage for what follows?

2. Paragraph 3 introduces the concepts of matrifocal and kinship relationships, and Naylor refers to these concepts again in paragraphs 7 and 10. What is her point?

3. Naylor states that "A myth always arises to serve a need" (paragraph 4). Reread paragraphs 5–9 and explain the needs served by the myth of the matriarch.
4. How does Naylor's description of the present situation relate to the idea of the myth of the matriarch?
5. The essay concludes with the negative effects of the myth. What are they? Given those negative effects and the history of the myth explained in paragraphs 4–9, what is Naylor's thesis?

TECHNIQUE AND STYLE

1. The essay opens with allusions to fiction and television shows. How would you update them?
2. Paragraphs 2 and 11 introduce statistics into the essay. What do they contribute?
3. Naylor describes the role of black women in the days of slavery and the attitudes of whites toward them. Explain whether you find her tone more objective than subjective or the opposite.
4. What does the irony in paragraph 5 add to the idea of myth?
5. How would you describe Naylor's audience?

SUGGESTIONS FOR WRITING

Journal

1. Test your own experience against Naylor's myth of the strong black woman. Does the myth exist or not? Write a journal entry in which you describe what you discovered.
2. In what ways have you been affected by a myth? List those that may apply to you, choose one, and write down your response to it.

Essay

The myth of the matriarch is just one of the many myths in our culture that have given rise to stereotypes similar to the mammies and Sapphires that Naylor points out. These stereotypes show up frequently in popular culture—in films, books, television shows—thus furthering the myth. Mull over recent movies or television shows you've seen or popular fiction you've read. Once you've focused on a myth, search your memory for other examples of it and for how it may show up in real life. Your paper may turn out like Naylor's, defining the myth and showing its harmful and false side, or you may prefer a simpler route, exploring only the myth. Suggested myths:

the hero
the "Wild West"
the supermom
the adorable child
the nightmare slasher
the happy homemaker

Waiting

Edna O'Brien

Born in Ireland, Edna O'Brien has lived in London and the United States, as the essay that follows will reveal. Although her most recent book is an appreciation of the writer James Joyce, she is best known for her novels and short stories, many of which have been published in this country and most of which are available in paperback. The list is a long one, covering 13 novels and 5 short story collections. Her most recent novel, Down by the River, *(1997), deals with the conflict between personal freedom and the limits placed by society as she explores the plight of a victim of rape and incest. O'Brien also writes nonfiction, as the essay that follows attests. You'll find in it what novelist Mary Gordon notes as O'Brien's "deftness and precision of language." It was published in the* Los Angeles Times Magazine *in 1994 and reprinted in* The Best American Essays 1995, *edited by Jamaica Kincaid.*

WHAT TO LOOK FOR *When you read O'Brien's essay, note how she draws on other modes to help define her central term. In defining* waiting, *she not only uses her own experience, that of others, and literary allusions, she also relies on examples, compares and contrast, analyzes cause and effect, and categorizes various types of waiting. Though full discussions of example, comparison and contrast, cause and effect, and division and classification follow later in this text, you won't have any trouble recognizing them and you'll find them equally useful in your own writing, particularly when you define essential terms.*

1   "Just you wait, Henry Higgins, just you wait," Eliza Doolittle says, advancing the threat of equality, or maybe even superiority, over her cranky mentor, Professor Higgins. Everyone I know is waiting, and almost everyone I know would like to rebut it, since it is slightly demeaning, reeks of helplessness, and shows we are not fully in command of ourselves. Of course, we are not. In his book on Jean Genet, Sartre says, "To Be is to belong to someone." He was speaking in particular about Genet the orphan child, who felt he had never belonged and therefore never was. Orphans or not, the pain and seeming endlessness of waiting begins at the cradle, goes through many permutations, assumes various disguises, but is

as native to us as our breathing. Some do it discreetly, some do it actively, some keep so abreast of things that their determination not to wait is in itself a kind of fidgety waiting. One thing is sure, nobody is proud of it except perhaps Job.

2   There is the angry waiting, the plaintive waiting, the almost cheerful waiting in which we believe for certain that the phone call or the revelation will occur presently. All these states, of course, overlap and can bafflingly succeed and re-succeed each other in a matter of minutes. For sheer brutality, the telephone waiting, in my opinion, takes precedence, insofar as it can (and does) ring at any moment. I think with no small degree of apprehension of the promised future when, thanks to the optic fiber in our computers, we will be able to see and, worse, be seen by the recalcitrant caller, and imagine how hard it will be to explain away the puffy eyes, the umbrage, the piled-up dishes, in short, the depression and inertia that attends waiting.

3   Is there anything good about it? Well, there are some fine moments of literature founded on excruciation. There is, toward the end of *Godot*, that wonderful exchange between the two characters:
"He didn't come?"
"No."
"And now it's too late."
"Yes, now it's night."

4   And there are hordes of fictional heroines—I am thinking at this moment of those of Patrick White and Karen Blixen in outbacks waiting for the arrival of the promised one, and there is a scene in Zola's *Nana* that to my mind surpasses all others in its depiction of that malady. A philandering count who suspects his wife of adultery stations himself outside the paramour's window at two in the morning to watch the room, a room he has once visited so he knows every detail: furniture, hangings, the water jug, and so on. With what tension Zola depicts it—the man waiting for a shadow to appear keeps thinking of the couple in bed, determining that at the first sight of a clue he will ring the bell, go upstairs despite the concierge's protest, break down the door, and strangle them. Then, in his musing, he sees a silhouette spring to life in the dimly lit room and wonders if it is his wife's neck or a slightly thicker neck but cannot tell. Darkness again. Two o'clock, three o'clock, four o'clock, and guess what happens. In the end he grows weary and decides to go home and sleep for a while and, in fact, misses the moment of verification that he had so achingly and so ardently

longed for. We mortals weary of our vigils, unlike the animals who wait in the most concentrated and flexed way until the prey is caught. They seem unperturbed, possibly because they know they are going to succeed, and therein lies the secret of the sickness or the nonsickness of waiting—the wait that is founded on hope and the wait that is founded on despair.

5   Do women wait more than men? I think women wait for men more than men wait for women and this despite the sisterly enjoinders that suppose that you can suppress instinct with statement. You cannot. We learn a few things as we go along, but we do not learn to love, to hate, or to quarrel very differently. Men wait, too: they wait for the promotion, they wait for the kill, they wait for the prize, and one has only to watch the antics in Parliament or in the Senate to see with what libido each is waiting for his moment to rise and strike a blow that will vanquish his opponent. Very often this seems to me more impassioned than the very principle about which they are debating. Men wait for women, too, once they have decided this one is the one, but they wait more busily, and so the little atoms of dread are likely to be diffused and tossed up and down so that they scatter. Activity always leavens waiting, but now, of course, with a beeper connecting us to our own abodes, we can in some restaurant or gymnasium, as longing strikes, call our own number to discover whether or not our prayer has been answered.

6   Prayer itself is a form of waiting but fortified with a glimmer of faith—or do I mean hope? For those who pray or chant with great perseverance, there is the suggestion that their waiting has been converted into purposefulness.

7   Of course, we do not just wait for love; we wait for money, we wait for the weather to get warmer, colder, we wait for the plumber to come and fix the washing machine (he doesn't), we wait for a friend to give us the name of another plumber (she doesn't), we wait for our hair to grow, we wait for our children outside school, we wait for their exam results, we wait for the letter that will undo all desolation, we wait for Sunday, when we sleep in or have the extra piece of toast, we wait for the crocuses to come up, then the daffodils, we wait for the estranged friend to ring or write and say, "I have forgiven you," we wait for our parents to love us even though they may be long since dead, we wait for the result of this or that medical test, we wait for the pain in the shoulder to ease, we

wait for that sense of excitement that has gone underground but is not quite quenched, we wait for the novel that enthralls the way it happened when we first read *Jane Eyre* or *War and Peace*, we wait for the invitation to the country, and often when we are there, we wait for the bus or the car that will ferry us home to the city and our props, our own chairs, our own bed, our own habits. We wait for the parties we once gave and that somehow had a luster that parties we now give completely lack. We wait (at least I do) for new potatoes, failing to concede that there are new potatoes all the time, but the ones I am waiting for were the ones dug on the twenty-ninth of June in Ireland that tasted (or was it imagination?) like no others. We wait to go to sleep and maybe fog ourselves with pills or soothing tapes to lull us thither. We wait for dreams, then we wait to be hauled out of our dreams and wait for dawn, the postman, tea, coffee, the first ring of the telephone, the advancing day.

8   Waiting in a theater bar in a London interval to secure a drink is galling, convinced as I am that the ladies behind the counter are congenital teetotalers. Waiting in the post office in any city large or small sends me into a tizz. Waiting in one's place in the hairdresser's is another scenario devised to oust any semblance of grace or good manners, and hairdressers, if they are good at all, tend to cultivate suspense. How many times has one not sat on a stool along with other enraged victims fuming while the stylist lingered over a long head of hair as if discovering its aura?

9   While indoors, waiting has a touch of masochism, outdoors it takes on a martial turn. Out in the street we join the army of waiting people, to cross the road or not to cross the road, to catch the bus, to skewer some obstreperous mortal with the ferrule of an umbrella! Waiting for a taxi shows us in splendid pugilistic style. In New York one evening lately, I waited and waited—it was that fallow hour between five and six—and eventually sighted a free taxi and hopped in, only to find three gentlemen had got in by the other door, claiming they were first, refusing to get out, giving me, as it seemed, threatening Gallic looks—they were Spanish—while a driver with a vexing combination of ennui and insolence asked where it was we wished him to go. I refused to leave the taxi, they refused, and as we set out for a destinationless spot, it occurred to me that this somewhat risk to my person was preferable to having to get out onto the street and wait again.

10   Logic and waiting, at least to our Western sensibilities, are not great bedfellows. It ended happily; they dropped me on East Sixty-fourth Street, refused money, and even suggested a drink later on.

11   To wait for a taxi is one thing, but to wait for a friend is quite another, and as we know, there are those friends who are always late, because they cannot help it, or because they are so busy, or because time is not a factor that matters to them. One wonders what does matter. I used to endure it, but I no longer can. Ten minutes and I feel the implosion, twenty minutes and it's an explosion. One thinks of things that one could do. Knitting. Crocheting. One can neither knit nor crochet in the street. Tai-chi. Except that I have not learned tai-chi. Memorizing a poem or passage from Shakespeare. Except that I have not brought Shakespeare with me. No. The exasperation mounts, and by the time the friend arrives, the lurking umbrage for each and every wrong is unleashed and a happy evening kiboshed.

12   It may be my race or my trade or it may be my childhood, but I seem to think that writers are worse at waiting than other breeds. As an aside, I think that fishermen are best. You see them on riverbanks, perched on their little stools, rod and line apparently motionless in the water, and they have the contemplativeness of cows chewing the cud. Not so writers, who, from their diaries, their confessions, their essays about their crackups, have less aptitude for it than others, which seems a contradiction, since to write and rewrite requires infinite patience. I think it may be that unlike actors, brain surgeons, or animal tamers, writers never really feel that they matter. The book is finished, it is sent away, the publication day is nine months hence, and on publication day one may or one may not receive a telegram or a bunch of flowers. Reviews trickle in, but there is no palpable connection between the doer and the doing. The writer in that sense is a kind of perpetual exile from himself or herself.

13   To train myself in the art of waiting, I sometimes think of insufferable situations—I think of people in prison having to fill up the hours, I think of people in hospitals or in asylums. I think of the Portuguese nun, writing her dirges or that other nun, Heloise, who, after her lover, Peter Abelard, was castrated, went to a convent, where, indeed, she still hoped that he might come for her, and I think of the last empress of China as described by Sterling Seagrave in *Dragon Lady*, this woman who had been chosen as a concubine at a very young age, left a widow, still at a very young age, spend-

ing the rest of her life inside the walls of the Forbidden City, her day starting with her toilet and then being dressed, flowers put in her hair, her breakfast of porridge and lotus leaves, gift baskets arriving, bolts of silks sent by courtiers, playing with her dogs, twisting blades of grass into the shapes of rabbits or birds, tending her flowers, a eunuch reading perhaps a piece of history or lore to her, playing a board game or painting onto silk, meals, the tiny dishes on little saucers that she mostly declined, and thinking of it I thank my stars that I was born in the west of Ireland in relative hardship and not in imperial China.

14   This brings me to either the value or the futility of waiting, and I think one must distinguish between the two. The telephone waiting, the waiting for the miracle—these seem in their way to be both crushing and ridiculous, because we all know that things do not happen when we wait too keenly. They happen when we least expect it. There is, however, a fertile kind of waiting that was brought to my attention by a piece written by Václav Havel that was called "Planting Watering and Waiting." He spoke of his own impatience while he was president of Czechoslovakia. He had wanted to achieve something visible and tangible, and it was hard for him to resign himself to the idea that politics, like history, is an emerging process. He was succumbing to a kind of impatience, thinking that he alone could find a solution to the problem. He thought he could but saw with enforced patience that the world and history are ruled by a time of their own, as are our lives, in which we can creatively intervene but never achieve complete control. He ended his piece with the beautiful image of planting something, of putting the seed in, of watering the earth, and of giving the plant the time that is essential to it. One cannot fool a plant any more than one can fool history, was how he put it. I suppose the same is true for ourselves. One cannot force the hearts or minds of other people, or get them to do what we want them to do at the precise moment we want it: We can only wait and, perhaps like the Portuguese nun, convert our tribulations into lasting prose.

THESIS AND ORGANIZATION

1. What paragraph or paragraphs introduce the essay? What reasons do you have for your choice?

2. Which paragraphs use multiple examples? What do they contribute to her definition?
3. Which paragraphs focus on one extended example? What do they contribute to her definition?
4. Where in the essay does O'Brien use comparisons? How do they support her definition?
5. Reread paragraphs 1 and 14 and consider the examples and comparisons O'Brien uses. What do you conclude is her thesis?

TECHNIQUE AND STYLE

1. Where in the essay does O'Brien use literary allusions? What do they contribute to the essay?
2. The essay is a complex one in which most of the paragraphs develop a main idea in some depth. Writing this kind of essay, you may find it difficult to move smoothly from the idea in one paragraph to that in the next. Examine several of O'Brien's paragraphs to see how she does it. What do you find?
3. Varying both the length of sentences and the type affects the pace and style of an essay, but it's not often that you run into a sentence the length of the one that begins paragraph 7. Take another look at that sentence and see where you might break it into two or more sentences. What is gained or lost by your changes?
4. In paragraph 11, you'll see that O'Brien uses sentences that are one or two words long. To test them out to see if they are really sentences, read them out loud. Do they work? Why or why not?
5. If an essay this length were written with sentences all the same length and if the author's tone remained the same throughout, the result would be flat, boring prose. But you'll find that O'Brien varies her tone as much as her sentences. How would you describe the tone? What examples can you find where the tone differs?

SUGGESTIONS FOR WRITING

Journal

1. O'Brien is quite correct in assuming that waiting is a common affliction. Think of all the recent times when you have had to wait: in grocery lines, bank lines; for good or bad news; for an important telephone call; for a friend who is always late—the list is almost endless. Choose one of those times to write about in your journal so that you define the primary emotion you felt while you were waiting.

2. Not all waiting is frustrating, and O'Brien is careful to point out that there is a "fertile kind of waiting" (paragraph 14). Describe a time in your experience that fits that definition.

Essay

One advantage in writing about a common activity is that it is just that—familiar. But familiarity also presents a challenge, for to make that activity come alive you will need to present it so that it seems new. To do that, you can draw on the same techniques O'Brien uses: extended and multiple examples, comparisons, causal analysis, allusions, and sentence variety. If you also draw upon the experience of others as well as your own, you'll find yourself balancing the personal with the general in such a way that your essay will engage the reader. To come up with a subject to write about, consider some common activities such as

> reading
> studying
> arguing
> playing
> making a decision

When you start your draft, keep in mind that you are defining the activity so that you don't go off in another direction. Examples, for instance, must support and expand your definition.

On Using
Example

4

Any time you encounter *for instance, such as,* or *for example,* you know what will follow: an **example** that explains and supports the generalization. Used with general statements, examples fill in the gaps. If you are writing on the subject of violent crime and want to show that the facts contradict what many people believe, you might write "Many people believe most crime is violent and that crime is increasing." Then you might continue by citing statistics as examples that show the rate of crime peaked in the seventies but then ceased to rise in the eighties and actually fell in the nineties. You would have supported the idea that crime rates have fallen, but you would still need to provide evidence for the idea that many people believe the opposite. Readers also need to know what evidence supports your claim that crime, to many people, means violent crime. That evidence is apt to come in the form of an example, an illustration that clarifies or develops a point. The most basic building block of all, examples pin down generalizations, supporting them with specifics.

To use examples well, you first need to know when to use them, then which ones to select, and finally, how to incorporate them. If you read actively, responding to the words on the page as you would to a person talking to you, odds are you will spot where examples are needed. On reading the sentence above about crime, you might think to yourself, "Hey, wait a minute! How about that violent crime statement?" Often it helps to read your own work belligerently, ready to shoot down any generalization with a "Says who?" The response to "Says who" will vary according to your audience. A sociology paper will call for statistics; a personal narrative will draw on your own experience. Other good sources are the experiences of others and those of authorities whose work you can quote. The skill here is to match the example not only to the generalization it supports but also to the readers to whom it is addressed.

After you have found good examples, you need to sequence them logically, while at the same time you avoid overusing terms such as "for example." Where you use multiple examples, you can use **transitions** that signal addition (*and, also, again, besides, moreover, next, finally*, etc.); where you use examples that compare, opt for transitions that indicate a turn (*but, yet, however, instead, in contrast*, etc.). Occasionally you may find yourself introducing an example that serves as a concession, calling for *of course, certainly*, or *granted*. Other times you may want a transition that indicates result—*therefore, thus, as a result, so.* More obvious are transitions setting up a summary, as in *finally, in conclusion, hence*, or *in brief*. Less obvious and, therefore, apt to be more effective are transitions that don't call attention to themselves, such as the repetition of a key word from the previous sentence or the use of a personal or demonstrative pronoun. If you use pronouns, however, make sure that what they refer to is clear. The demonstrative pronoun *this*, for instance, should usually be followed by a noun, as in *this sentence* or *this idea*. A *this* standing by itself may force your reader to go back to the previous sentence to understand exactly what it refers to.

AUDIENCE AND PURPOSE

In general, the less familiar your audience is with your subject, the more important it is to have examples, and lots of them. If you find yourself writing about a sport, for instance, you would do well to think about what your audience may or may not know about it. If the sport is ice hockey and your readers are your classmates most of whom live in Mississippi, you'll know that most of your readers won't know much about your topic, so you will have to use lots of examples. And if you are arguing that ice hockey is an underrated sport, you can draw on your readers' experience with more familiar games such as basketball. You might use the example of the pace of a basketball game to make the point that ice hockey is even faster, so fast that at times the crowd can't even see the puck.

If your readers are relatively familiar with your topic, then your job is to make that familiarity come to life and shape it to your purpose. If you are writing an essay that explores the various levels of anxiety experienced by a first-year college student, you will probably cite a number of instances. You might start with the example of registering by telephone and the mild concern that the machine on the other end of the line will send your course requests to electronic heaven, then the fear of not finding the right classroom and turning up, if at all, late for class; next the uneasiness that occurs with the first look at the course syllabus, followed by the apprehension over the speed of a lecture; and then you might end with the sheer terror of the first test. If you provide enough examples, at least one is bound to remind a reader of a similar response.

The examples get harder to come by if your subject is a controversial or sensitive one. On familiar topics such as abortion, capital punishment, and prayer in public schools, your readers are not only apt to have opinions but very set ones, so set that you might do well to steer clear of the topic. Even less touchy subjects are difficult to write about because you have to be sensitive to views that differ from yours so that you don't alienate those readers. When dealing with a topic on which there has been much debate, it often helps to list the opposing arguments so you can find examples to support your points and to defeat the opposite ones.

Now and then, you may also find yourself writing an essay that tackles a subject that isn't controversial but still requires some caution on your part. You might, for example, want to write about what you find to be our culture's "throwaway" mentality and how it is adversely affecting the environment. When you start listing the more obvious throwaway items you can think of, you find you have fast-food wrappings and boxes, ballpoint pens, paper napkins and towels, and plastic coverings for CDs, all items your readers probably use and throw away without thinking. Your problem then becomes one of educating your readers without insulting or blaming them, which isn't easy. Recognizing the problem, however, is halfway to solving it, and you'll read essays in this chapter that do just that.

TYPES OF EXAMPLES

Examples generally fall into two categories, extended and multiple. An essay that rests its assertion on only one example is relatively rare, but you will run across one now and then. When you do, the example often takes the form of a narrative in support of the author's thesis. To show that a minimum-wage job can be a fulfilling one (or a demeaning one—take your pick), you might support your thesis by telling about a typical day on the job. While you are relying on only one example, you will have developed it in considerable depth, and you probably will have included a sentence or two to indicate that other experiences may contradict yours, so your readers will accept your extended example as valid. Far more frequent, however, are multiple examples. They add clarity, support, and emphasis, and save you from having to make the kind of disclaimer mentioned above. Sometimes the examples will be drawn from your own experience and the experiences of others, but often you will find you want more generalized sources, so you consult books, magazines, interviews, reports, and so on. You may well find that examples drawn from outside sources give your essay a more objective, reasoned **tone.** If you think of that term as similar to tone of voice, you will realize that it means the writer's attitude toward the subject and audience. Examples drawn from personal experience are apt to create an informal, conversational tone; those drawn from outside sources often provide a cooler, more formal tone. No matter where you find your examples, however, you can present them with some variety, summarizing some, quoting others.

Examples not only illustrate generalizations, they expand and develop them. After you have written a draft of an essay, you may find it useful to double-check each of your examples by asking several questions: How does the example support the generalization? Is the source of the example clear? How does it connect to the readers' experiences? If the example is an extended one, is it sufficiently developed so that it can support the thesis by itself? Then you might think about the examples as a whole: Do they draw on a variety of sources? Do they incorporate both summary and quotation?

DETAILS

In presenting an example, the writer uses many of the same techniques that come into play in description. Descriptive details can come from unlikely places, such as the pushers and products Michiko Kakutani cites as examples to support her claim that advertising has saturated our lives.

> The dead, including Marilyn Monroe (Chanel No. 5), Gene Kelly (Gap khakis) and Fred Astaire (Dirt Devil vacuum cleaners), have been hired as pitchmen, and so have New Delhi paraplegics, who now hawk Coca-Cola under bright red-and-white umbrellas. Even bananas have been colonized as

billboard space, with stickers promoting the video release of "Space Jam" and the "Got Milk?" campaign turning up on the fruit. (130)

Drawing on the familiar and unfamiliar, Kakutani's examples catch our attention.

As with description, details are used to make the abstract concrete. If you were writing about an abstract principle such as freedom, for example, you might find yourself writing about one kind of freedom that you particularly value, the freedom that your parents allowed you to make mistakes. You would probably provide a number of examples, and each one might be in the form of a short narrative, but the effectiveness of those narratives will lie in the details you use. Your parents might not have wanted you to go out with a particular person, for instance, but merely stated their reasons and left the decision up to you. You decided not to take their advice, and the result was a "disaster." Spell out the details so that the reader concludes it was a disaster, and you will have made your point effectively.

THESIS AND ORGANIZATION

Whether an essay is developed by multiple examples or a single extended example, it has a major assertion. In your first draft, you may want to state your thesis in one sentence and in an obvious place, such as the end of your introduction. When you revise, however, you may want to play with the placement of the thesis, delaying it until the conclusion. If that's where you decide you want it, check to make sure that everything that precedes the conclusion leads up to it and that the reader has a clear focus on your subject all the way.

You might also try weaving your thesis into the introduction in a subtle way, taking the thesis apart so that it is in bits and pieces, each in its own sentence. If you try that idea, check to make sure that someone reading your introduction will come up with a thesis that closely matches the one-sentence assertion you had in your first draft.

Delaying your thesis or weaving it into your introduction are subtle ways of treating your major assertion. If you are worried that they are so subtle that the reader may miss your point, consider getting some mileage out of a title. An imaginative title can serve several purposes: arouse the reader's curiosity, set the tone, highlight the subject, reveal the essay's organization, or pave the way for the thesis. Good titles serve more than one purpose.

When examples are used as the primary mode for an essay, they are usually arranged in chronological or dramatic order, moving from what came first and ending with what came last or beginning with the least dramatic and finishing with the most. To decide which example is the most dramatic, all you need to do is ask some obvious questions: Which is the most important? Which is most likely to affect the reader? Which carries the most impact? Odds are you'll come up with the same answer for each question. That's the example you should use to cap your essay, the one that all the others should lead up to.

Although all the essays in this chapter have a thesis developed by examples, the examples themselves often cross over into other categories. You will discover that is also the case with your own writing. You may well find yourself using an example that is also a narrative, or, to put it more precisely, a narrative that functions as an example. Other patterns of organization such as a description, an analysis of causal relationships, a comparison, a definition, or an analysis of a process can also serve as examples. The function—to support and develop an assertion—is more important than the label.

USEFUL TERMS

Example An illustration that supports a generalization, usually an assertion, by providing evidence that develops or clarifies it.
Transition A word, phrase, sentence, or paragraph that carries the reader smoothly from point A to point B. Some transitions, such as time markers (*first, next,* and the like) are obvious; others are more subtle, such as a repeated word or phrase or a synonym for a key term.
Tone A writer's attitude toward the subject and the audience. An author's tone can be contemplative, intense, tongue-in-cheek, aloof, matter of fact—as many kinds as there are tones of voice.

➤ POINTERS FOR USING EXAMPLE

Exploring the Topic

1. **What examples can you think of to illustrate your topic?** Are all of them from your own experience? What examples can you find from other sources?
2. **Are your examples pertinent and representative?** Do they fit? Do they illustrate?

3. **Are your examples of equal weight?** Which are relatively unimportant?
4. **How familiar is your audience with each of your examples?**
5. **Which examples best lend themselves to your topic?** In what order would they best be presented?
6. **What point do you want to make?** Do your examples all support that point? Do they lead the reader to your major assertion?
7. **What is your purpose behind your point?** Is your primary aim to express your own feelings, to inform, to persuade, or to entertain?

Drafting the Paper

1. **Know your reader.** Figure out where your reader may stand in relation to your topic and thesis. It may be that your audience knows little about your subject or that the reader simply hasn't thought much about it; on the other hand, maybe the reader knows a great deal and holds a definite opinion. Once you have made an informed guess about your audience's attitude toward your topic and thesis, reexamine your examples in light of that information. Some may have to be explained in greater detail than others, and the more familiar ones will need to be presented in a new or different light. Use the techniques you would employ in writing descriptive papers.

2. **Know your purpose.** Self-expressive papers are often difficult to write because you are so close to being your own audience. If you are writing with this aim in mind, try making yourself conscious of the personality you project as a writer. Jot down the characteristics you wish to convey about yourself and refer to this list as you revise your paper. While this is a highly self-conscious way to revise, when it is done well, the result appears natural. You will also need to double-check your examples, making sure that you present them in sufficient detail to communicate fully to your audience. That warning serves as well for informative and persuasive papers. Again, use description to make your examples hit the mark: use sensory detail, compare the unfamiliar to the familiar, be concrete. If you are writing a persuasive paper, use these techniques to develop your emotional appeal.

3. **Consider extended example.** If an essay rests on one example, you must choose and develop that illustration with great care. Make sure your example is representative of its class and that you provide all relevant information. Make as many unobtrusive connections as you can between your example and the class it represents. During revision, you may want to eliminate some of these references, but at first it's best to have too many. If you are writing a persuasive paper, you don't want to be found guilty of a lapse in logic.

4. **Consider multiple examples.** Most essays rely on multiple examples to support their points; nevertheless, some examples will be more developed

than others. Figure out which examples are particularly striking and develop them, reserving the others for mere mention. Show how your examples fit your point and stress what is noteworthy about them. To lend breadth and credibility to your point, consider citing statistics, quotations, authorities, and the experience of others. Comment on what you take from other sources in order to make it more your own.

5. **Arrange your examples effectively.** The most frequent pattern of organization moves from the less dramatic, less important to the most, but examples can also be arranged chronologically or in terms of frequency (from the least to the most frequent). Like the essay itself, each paragraph should be developed around a central assertion, either stated or implied. In longer papers, groups of paragraphs will form a section in support of a unifying statement. These statements guide the reader through your examples and prevent the paper from turning into a mere list.

6. **Make a point.** Examples so obviously need to lead up to something that it's not hard to make a point in this kind of paper. The only real pitfall is that your point may not be an assertion. Test your thesis by asking whether your point carries any information. If it does, it's an assertion. Say you come up with, "We live in a world of time-saving technology." You can think of lots of examples and even narrow down the "we" to "anyone who cooks today." The setting is obviously the kitchen, but is the revised thesis an assertion? Given the information test, it fails. Your audience already knows what you are supposedly informing them about. But if you revise and come up with "Electronic gizmos have turned the kitchen into a laboratory," you've given the topic a fresher look, one that does contain information.

Sweatin' for Nothin'

Michael Barlow

Unlike many students at the University of New Orleans, Michael Barlow went straight on to college after graduating from high school. As his essay implies, he is not a fitness freak, although he is engaged in a number of college activities. An African American and an education major concentrating in teaching English at the secondary level, he may soon turn up in the classroom on the other side of the desk. No matter what he does, he will try not to emulate Mimi.

WHAT TO LOOK FOR   *Starting and ending an essay are often the most difficult parts of writing. One technique that works well is the one Barlow uses. You'll see that he sets up a framework by first setting out the image of the hamster in the cage and then, in his conclusion, returning to it. The effect is a sense of closure. You can use the same technique by ending your essay with a reference to an idea you bring out in your introduction.*

1   During spring break, I visited my family in Fort Worth. It was a pleasant visit, but my, how things have changed. My mother has purchased a stairmaster and joined a fitness club. My father now jogs at 6:00 every morning, and my sister is contemplating aerobics as one of her first electives when she goes off to college this August. This was not the group of people I last saw in January. These were not the laid-back complacent folks I've known so well. This was not *my* family.

2   One night around 2 a.m., after partying with some friends from high school, I was lying in bed watching Mimi, my pet hamster, crank out revolutions on an exercise wheel. I should have gone to sleep but I was captivated. The creaking of the wheel made me think of the strenuous exercise that seems to have plagued everyone at 301 Lake Country Drive. What was it? What was going on? So I asked myself whether or not Mimi knew that sprinting in a metal cylinder wouldn't get her out of the cage. She probably didn't know—her brain is smaller than a kernel of corn.

3   But what about humans? What about my family? I see millions of Americans, like my family, in Spandex outfits and gel-cushioned shoes trying to get out of their cages. Something is wrong with the

fitness mania that has swept the Western World, and from watching Mimi I know what it is. Entropy.

4   Entropy is the measure of the amount of energy unavailable for useful work in a system—metaphorically speaking, it is a measure of waste. In our throwaway society, we waste energy at a maddening pace. Coal is lit to make a fire, which produces a lot of carbon dioxide, while heating a small amount of water to make steam, which produces electricity, which lights an incandescent bulb in a room in a house where nobody's home. Basic waste.

5   Exercise mania has crippled our culture. It is no coincidence that we are running out of cheap and available energy while at the same time polluting the air, land, and sea with our waste. According to the laws of physics, entropy diminishes in a closed system, meaning that eventually everything will be reduced to an amorphous, undifferentiated blob. The universe is a closed system. There are some parallels to a hamster cage, and Mimi creates entropy at a noisy rate.

6   What did we do for exercise in those past centuries when people did not act like captive hamsters? If a person chopped down wood or ran a long way, it was because he or she needed fuel or wanted to get somewhere. Now we do such things to fit into new pants or to develop our biceps. We have treadmills, rowing machines, stairmasters, stationary bikes, Nordic Tracks, butt busters, and wall climbers, and we labor at them while going nowhere. Absolutely nowhere! We do work that is beyond useless; we do work that takes energy and casts it to the wind like lint. And we don't even enjoy the work. Look at people in a health club. See anybody smiling?

7   There is nothing magical about fitness machines. We can get the exact same result by climbing up stairs in our homes or offices. Take a look at any set of stairs in any building. Anybody in Spandex headed up or down? No. People ride elevators all day, then drive to their fitness centers where they pay to walk up steps.

8   When I was looking at Mimi, I was thinking of Richard Simmons, the King of Entropy, who wants everybody to exercise all the time and has made insane amounts of money saying so. Simmons says that he has raised his metabolism so high that he can eat more without gaining weight. Working out to pig out—an entropy double whammy.

9   I have a solution for such gratuitous narcissism and I think Simmons might find a tearful video in it. Let people on the ma-

chines create useable energy as they burn off their flabby thighs and excess baggage. Hook up engines and cams and drive shafts that will rotate turbines and generate electricity. Let exercisers light the health club itself. Let them air condition it. Let the clubs store excess energy and sell it to nearby shop owners at low rates.

10   Better yet, create health clubs whose sole purpose is the generation of energy. Pipe the energy into housing projects. Have energy nights where singles get together to pedal, chat, and swap phone numbers. Build a giant pony wheel that operates a flour mill, a rock crusher, a draw bridge, a BMW repair shop. Have the poles protrude from the wheel with spots for a couple hundred joggers to push the wheel around. Install magazine racks on the poles. Have calorie collections and wattage wars. Make it "cool" to sweat for the betterment of mankind, not just for yourself.

11   We cannot afford much more entropy. If we forget that, we might as well be rodents in cages, running into the night. Just like Mimi.

THESIS AND ORGANIZATION

1. The essay has a problem–solution structure. In your own words, what does Barlow describe as the problem?
2. Paragraphs 5–7 give examples of kinds of exercise. What distinctions does Barlow draw among them?
3. The solution appears in paragraphs 9–10 and is a humorous one. Summarize it.
4. In your own words, state the serious point made in the last paragraph.
5. What do you find to be the main subject of the essay? Exercise? Fads? Waste? Entropy? American culture? What reasons can you find for your choice?

TECHNIQUE AND STYLE

1. Look up *analogy* in an unabridged dictionary. What analogy does Barlow draw? What does the analogy contribute to the essay?
2. Paragraph 4 defines *entropy*. How necessary is that definition? What does it add to the essay?
3. What does the essay gain with the example of Richard Simmons?
4. Imagine you are one of the people filling up the fitness club. Would you be offended by this essay? Why or why not?

5. The person behind the words always comes through in an essay, sometimes more clearly than others. Explain why you would or would not want Michael Barlow as a classmate or friend.

SUGGESTIONS FOR WRITING

Journal

1. Take a few minutes to write down what you think about the exercise craze or to record your reaction to a television commercial advertising an exercise product.

2. How does exercise make you feel? Write about why you do or do not enjoy exercising.

Essay

Try your own hand at a problem–solution essay, giving detailed examples of both the problem and the solution. Like Barlow, you may want your tone to be humorous, sugarcoating a serious point. As for the problem, you're apt to be surrounded with choices:

getting enough hours into the day
scraping tuition together
keeping up with schoolwork
deciding which pleasure to indulge
sorting out family loyalties

Illustrate the problem by using examples. You may find examples for the solution harder to come by, in which case, like Barlow, you may want to propose something fantastic.

Stop Ordering Me Around

Stacey Wilkins

*Like many students, Stacey Wilkins works in a restaurant waiting on
tables, a job that helps her pay off a student loan but one that also ex-
tracts a price of its own, as her essay points out. The essay appeared in
the January 4, 1993, issue of* Newsweek *in a regular feature, the "My
Turn" column. A person who wants to be treated with respect, Wilkins
also apparently values her privacy, for the only identification that
appears at the end of the essay is the note, "Wilkins lives in
Connecticut." Her forum, however, is a public one, and the readers of*
Newsweek *are her ideal audience in that as educated, middle-class
Americans, they are more likely to patronize the kind of restaurant
Wilkins works at than the local fast-food place.*

WHAT TO LOOK FOR   *The narrative that opens Wilkins' essay
serves as the primary example in the essay, and one that sets the
essay's tone as well. As you read the essay, try to hear it so that you
can identify her tone more exactly. At times, the tone may strike you
as angry, hurt, bitter, sarcastic, and any number of other variations.
How would you characterize it?*

1   I had just sat an extra hour and a half waiting for some country-
club tennis buddies to finish a pizza. They came in 15 minutes after
the restaurant closed—they hadn't wanted to cut short their tennis
match. The owner complied and agreed to turn the oven back on
and make them a pizza. The cook had long since gone home.

2   The customers had no problem demanding service after I explained that the restaurant had closed. They had no problem sitting
there until well after 11 o'clock to recount the highlights of their
tennis game (the restaurant closed at 9:30 p.m.). And, most important, they had no problem making me the brunt of their cruel little
post-tennis match. What fun it was to harass the pathetic little waitress. "Oh, it's just so nice sitting here like this," one man said. After
getting no response, he continued: "Boy, I guess you want us to
leave." I was ready to explode in anger. "I am not going to respond
to your comments," I said, and walked away.

3   He was geared up for a fight. The red flag had been waved. The
man approached me and asked about dessert. A regular customer,

he had never made a practice of ordering dessert before. You know, the '90s low-fat thing. But that night he enjoyed the power. He felt strong, I felt violated.

4   Three dollars and 20 cents later, I went home. Their tip was my payment for this emotional rape. As I drove, tears streamed down my face. Why was I crying? I had been harassed before. Ten years of waitressing should have inured me to this all-too-common situation. But this was a watershed: the culmination of a decade of abuse.

5   I am now at the breaking point. I can't take being the public's punching bag. People seem to think abuse is included in the price of an entree. All sense of decency and manners is checked with their coats at the door. They see themselves in a position far superior to mine. They are the kings. I am the peasant.

6   I would like them to be the peasants. I am a strong advocate of compulsory restaurant service in the United States. What a great comeuppance it would be for the oppressors to have to work a double shift—slinging drinks, cleaning up after kids and getting pissed off that a party of 10 tied up one of their tables for three hours and left a bad tip. Best of all, I would like to see that rude man with tomato sauce on his tennis shorts.

7   Eating in a restaurant is about more than eating food. It is an opportunity to take your frustrations out on the waiter. It is a chance to feel better than the person serving your food. People think there is nothing wrong with rudeness or sexual harassment if it is inflicted on a waiter.

8   Customers have no problem with ignoring the wait staff when they go to take an order. Or they won't answer when the waiter comes to the table laden with hot plates asking who gets what meal. My personal pet peeve is when they make a waiter take a separate trip for each item. "Oh, I'll take another Coke." The waiter asks, "Would anyone else like one?" No response. Inevitably when he comes back to the table someone will say, "I'll have a Coke, too." And so on and so on.

9   I find it odd because no matter what an insolent cad someone might be, they generally make an effort to cover it up in public. The majority of people practice common etiquette. Most individuals won't openly cut in line or talk throughout a movie. People are cognizant of acceptable behavior and adhere to the strictures it demands. That common code of decency does not apply while eating out.

10   Food-service positions are the last bastion of accepted prejudice. People go into a restaurant and openly torment the waiter, leave a small tip and don't think twice about it. Friends allow companions to be rude and don't say a word. The friends of this man did not once tell him to stop taunting me. They remained silent.

11   It doesn't cross their minds that someone has just been rotten to another human being. I have yet to hear someone stick up for the waitress, to insist a person stop being so cruel. This is because people don't think anything wrong has occurred.

12   However, if this man had shouted obscenities at another patron about her ethnicity, say, it would have rightly been deemed unacceptable. Why don't people understand that bad manners are just as unacceptable in a restaurant? Why do they think they have license to mistreat restaurant personnel?

13   I believe it is because food-service workers are relegated to such a low position on the social stratum. Customers have the power. Food-service employees have none. Thus we are easy targets for any angry person's pent-up frustrations. What better sparring partner than one who can't fight back? Most waiters won't respond for fear of losing their jobs. Consequently, we are the designated gripecatchers of society, along with similar service workers.

14   If people stepped down from their spurious pedestals, they might see how wrong they are. We have dreams and aspirations just like everyone else. Our wages finance those dreams. Even an insulting 10 percent tip helps us to move toward a goal, pay the rent, feed the kids.

15   I'm using my earnings to pay off an encumbering graduate-school debt. Our bus girl is financing her education at the University of Pennsylvania. My manager is saving for her first baby. Another waitress is living on her earnings while she pursues an acting career. The dishwasher sends his pay back to his children in Ecuador.

16   Our dreams are no less valid than those of someone who holds a prestigious job at a large corporation. A restaurant's flexible working hours appeal to many people who dislike the regimen of a 9-to-5 day. Our employment doesn't give someone the right to treat us as nonentities. I deserve respect whether I remain a waitress or move on to a different career. And so do the thousands of waiters and waitresses who make your dining experience a pleasant one.

THESIS AND ORGANIZATION

1. How does the opening narrative set the scene? Where else in the essay do you find references to that narrative? Do they unify the essay or distract you? Why?
2. At what point in the essay does the author move from the particular to the general? Which gets the most emphasis?
3. Reexamine the essay as one that poses a problem and a solution. What is the problem? The solution?
4. How successfully does Wilkins position her experience as representative of the experience of others?
5. Where do you find Wilkins' thesis? Explain whether you find that placement effective.

TECHNIQUE AND STYLE

1. How would you characterize the author's tone?
2. Does the opening narrative enlist your sympathies? Why or why not?
3. Some readers may find the essay's aim is more expressive than expository or persuasive, that the author is more concerned with venting her feelings than explaining the problem or persuading her readers to resolve it. Make a case for your interpretation of the author's aim.
4. In paragraph 2, Wilkins repeats variations on "they had no problem." Explain whether you find the repetition effective.
5. At various times in the essay, Wilkins uses words that suggest she is really writing about issues of power and class, as in her use of "peasant" (paragraphs 5 and 6) and "low position on the social stratum" (paragraph 13). What other examples can you find? Would the essay be stronger or weaker if these issues were discussed more openly?

SUGGESTIONS FOR WRITING

Journal

1. We live in a service society, yet as Wilkins points out, sometimes we demand too much of those who provide the services. Record a few examples of rudeness that you have observed.
2. Write an entry recording your reaction to Wilkins' essay. Do you think her complaints are justified?

Essay

The odds are that you have or have had a job similar to Wilkins', if not waiting on tables then some other low-paying job that is also low on the totem pole of status. Like Wilkins, you may have found you were (or are) not treated with respect. On the other hand, your experience may be quite the opposite. Write an essay in which you use examples from your own experience or the experiences of others to explain how you were (or are) treated on your job. You will want to narrow your subject so that you can cover it thoroughly in three to five pages, so you might focus on a specific category of people:

> customers
> coworkers
> supervisor(s)

Another way to approach the topic would be to choose an example from each of those categories, but if you select that route, make sure your examples are representative.

A Black Fan of Country Music Finally Tells All

Lena Williams

The essay that follows is a bit of a departure from Lena Williams' usual beat, but in a way, it fits. Just as it's unusual to find a "black fan of country music," so, too, it's unusual to find a woman who is also a sports writer. A regular contributor to the New York Times *sports section, Williams concentrates on basketball and football, with special attention to the growing sport of women's basketball. The essay that follows appeared in the* New York Times Arts & Leisure *section's coverage of "Pop Music" in a column called "Pop View," Sunday, June 19, 1994.*

WHAT TO LOOK FOR   *At times, you may find yourself writing an essay on a subject that you're somewhat embarrassed about, which is the position Lena Williams found herself in when she wrote the essay that follows. In that case, you'll need to make a decision about your tone, the attitude you take toward your subject and your audience. Williams, as you will see, takes an unapologetic stance, almost daring her readers to challenge her. Yet the overall tone of the essay is not antagonistic because she takes the edge off of her "challenge" with humor and personal narrative, techniques that you can incorporate into your own writing.*

1   I Heard that Reba McEntire's new album, "Read My Mind," shot to No. 5 on the Billboard chart the first weekend of its release.

2   Well, she got my $11.95.

3   I'm a 40-something black woman who spent her youth in Washington, lip-syncing to the Supremes and slow dancing to the Temptations. Now I often come home to my Manhattan apartment and put on Vince Gill, Randy Travis or Reba. Consider me a fan of country music. So there. Deal with it.

4   For most of my adult life, I was a closet country music fan. I'd hide my Waylon Jennings and Willie Nelson albums between the dusty, psychedelic rock. I'd listen to Dolly Parton on my earphones, singing along softly, afraid my neighbors might mistake my imita-

tion twang for a cry for help. I'd enter a music store, looking over my shoulder in search of familiar faces and flip through the rhythm-and-blues section for about five minutes before sneaking off to the country aisle where I'd surreptitiously grab a Travis Tritt tape off the rack and make a beeline for the shortest cashier's line.

5   Just when I'd reached for my American Express card, I'd spot a tall, dark, handsome type in an Armani suit standing behind me with a puzzled look. What's he going to think? "The sister seems down, but what's she doing with that Dwight Yoakum CD?"

6   So now I'm publicly coming out of the closet and proclaiming my affection for country perennials like Ms. McEntire.

7   When I told a friend I was preparing this confessional, he offered a word of caution: "No self-respecting black person would ever admit to that in public."

8   I thought about his comment. As a child growing up in the 1950's, in a predominantly black community, I wasn't allowed to play country-and-western music in my house. Blacks weren't supposed to like country—or classical for that matter—but that's another story. Blacks' contribution to American music was in jazz, blues and funk. Country music was dismissed as poor white folks' blues and associated with regions of the nation that symbolized prejudice and racial bigotry. Even mainstream white America viewed country as lower class and less desirable, often poking fun at its twangy chords and bellyaching sentiments.

9   But I was always a cowgirl at heart. I liked country's wild side; its down-home, aw-shucks musicians with the yodel in their voices and the angst in their lyrics. I saw an honesty in country and its universal tales of love lost and found. Besides, the South didn't have a monopoly on racial hatred, and country artists, like everybody else, were stealing black music, so why should I hold it against country?

10   And while snickering at country, white America also demonstrated a similar cultural backwardness toward black music, be it gospel, ragtime or the blues. So I allowed country to enter my heart and my mind, in spite of its faults. Indeed, when prodded, some blacks who rejected country conceded that there was a spirituality that resounded in the music and that in its heartfelt sentiment, country was a lot like blues. Yet they could never bring themselves to spend hard-earned dollars on Hank Williams Jr.

11   The 1980's saw country (western was dropped, much to my chagrin) become mainstream. Suddenly there was country at the Copa and at Town Hall. WYNY-FM radio in New York now claims the largest audience of any country station, with more than one million listeners. Dolly Parton and Kenny Rogers became movie stars. Garth Brooks became an American phenomenon.

12   Wall Street investment bankers bought cowboy boots and hats and learned to do the two-step. And black and white artists like Patti LaBelle and Lyle Lovett and Natalie Cole and Ms. McEntire now sing duets and clearly admire one another's music.

13   Perhaps the nation's acceptance of country has something to do with an evolutionary change in the music. Country has got edge. It has acquired an attitude. Womens' voices have been given strength. Oh, the hardship and misery is still there. But the stuff about "standing by your man" has changed to a more assertive posture.

14   In "I Won't Stand in Line," a song on Ms. McEntire's new album, she makes it clear to a skirt-chasing lover that "I'd do almost anything just to make you mine, but I won't stand in line." That line alone makes me think of Aretha Franklin's "Respect."

15   One other thing: I don't like sad songs. I've cried enough for a lifetime. Country makes me laugh, always has. Maybe because it never took itself so seriously. Think about it. "Drop-Kick Me, Jesus, Through the Goal Posts of Life." "A Boy Named Sue."

16   Ms. McEntire serves up a humorous touch in "Why Haven't I Heard From You." "That thing they call the telephone/ Now there's one on every corner, in the back of every bar/ You can get one in your briefcase, on a plane or in your car/ So tell me why haven't I heard from you, darlin', honey, what is your excuse?" Call it Everywoman's lament.

17   Well it's off my chest; and it feels good.

18   I will no longer make excuses for my musical tastes. Not when millions are being made by performers exhorting listeners to "put your hands in the air and wave 'em like you just don't care."

19   Compare that with the haunting refrain of Ms. McEntire's "I Think His Name Was John," a song about a woman, a one-night stand and AIDS: "She lays all alone and cries herself to sleep/ 'Cause she let a stranger kill her hopes and her dreams/ And in the end when she was barely hanging on/ All she could say is she thinks his name was John."

THESIS AND ORGANIZATION

1. What paragraph or paragraphs introduce the essay?
2. Paragraphs 4 and 5 detail a short narrative. What is Williams' point?
3. Paragraphs 8–12 sketch the evolution of country-and-western music. Trace the chronology and the changes in attitude toward the genre.
4. What is Williams' point in making the comparison she does in paragraphs 13 and 14?
5. The essay ends with another comparison in paragraphs 18 and 19, one that Williams doesn't spell out. What is it? How does it relate to her thesis?

TECHNIQUE AND STYLE

1. Paragraphs 2 and 17 consist of one sentence each. What effect does Williams achieve with a one-sentence paragraph?
2. Is the essay addressed primarily to a black or white audience or both? What evidence can you find to support your view?
3. Although the essay expresses Williams personal opinion and is subjective, she achieves a balance between the personal and the general. How does she do that?
4. Williams supports her thesis with examples from popular music, both country-western and black. Explain whether you find her examples sufficient evidence for her thesis.
5. Analyze the effectiveness of the essay's title. What other titles can you think of? Which is the more effective and why?

SUGGESTIONS FOR WRITING

Journal

1. Taste in music, as in most everything else, is apt to be idiosyncratic. Think of a band or song or type of music that represents your particular taste and explain why you like it, using examples to support your ideas.
2. Think of a time when you were embarrassed and describe it in such a way that you remove the embarrassment. You might want to use the same techniques that Williams uses—confronting the issue and then modulating your tone. You may want to turn this entry into a full essay.

Essay

If you look back on your tastes, you will probably find that they change over time. Perhaps a type of music that you liked some years ago you would now have a hard time listening to. Or perhaps you were disappointed in a film you recently saw again or a book that you reread, one that had impressed you in the past and belonged to a particular genre such as horror films or adventure stories. You might start by drawing up two columns—then and now—and jotting down examples representing your earlier tastes and your present ones. Like Williams, you may want to write about how your taste has evolved or explain why you like what you like. For a general category, you might think about

music
food
films
books
heroes
sports

Bananas for Rent

Michiko Kakutani

Anyone who reads the book reviews in the New York Times *is familiar with Michiko Kakutani's by-line, for she's the lead reviewer for the
newspaper, covering both fiction and nonfiction. As you might suspect, that sort of extensive analytical reading makes her an astute
critic of the contemporary scene, so it's only fitting that she also contributes to the column "Culture Zone" in the* New York Times
Magazine, *a column in which Ms. Kakutani takes a tough view of
popular culture. Her wide range of interests are reflected in her book*
Poet at the Piano: Portraits of Writers, Filmmakers, and Other Artists
at Work *(1988). In 1998, Ms. Kakutani was awarded the Pulitzer
Prize for Criticism. Her essay "Bananas for Rent" was a "Culture
Zone" piece published on November 9, 1997.*

WHAT TO LOOK FOR *If you are writing about the
contemporary scene and using examples to back up your points, you
may find that some of your readers may not be familiar with the
examples you use. One way out of that bind is to use lots. That is what
Kakutani does in her essay, so be on the look out for multiple
examples as you read. It's easiest to think up multiple examples when
you are making notes for an essay. If you were writing about blue
jeans, for instance, you might be tempted to just put Levi's, but at that
point, it's also easy to think of other brand names as well—Guess,
Gap, Gloria Vanderbilt, and the like.*

1   They are as pervasive as roaches, as persuasive as the weather,
as popular as Princess Diana. They adorn our clothes, our luggage,
our sneakers and our hats. They are ubiquitous on television, unavoidable in magazines and inevitable on the Internet. The average
American, it is estimated, is pelted by some 3,000 advertising messages a day, some 38,000 TV commercials a year.

2   Not so long ago, it was only race cars, tennis stars and sports sta-
diums that were lacquered head-to-toe with ads. Nowadays, school
buses and trucks rent out advertising space by the foot. There are
entire towns that have signed exclusive deals with Coke or Pepsi.
The dead, including Marilyn Monroe (Chanel No. 5), Gene Kelly
(Gap khakis) and Fred Astaire (Dirt Devil vacuum cleaners), have

been hired as pitchmen, and so have New Delhi paraplegics, who now hawk Coca-Cola under bright red-and-white umbrellas. Even bananas have been colonized as billboard space, with stickers promoting the video release of "Space Jam" and the "Got Milk?" campaign turning up on the fruit.

3   As the scholar James Twitchell observes, advertising has become "our cultural literacy—it's what we know." Twitchell, author of a book called "Adcult USA" and a professor at the University of Florida, says his students share no common culture of books or history; what they share is a knowledge of commercials. When he questions them at random about concepts from "The Dictionary of Cultural Literacy," he says he is likely to draw a blank. When, however, he recites a commercial jingle, his students "instantaneously know it, and they're exultant," he says. "They actually think Benetton ads are profound. To them, advertising is high culture."

4   Schoolchildren around the country avidly collect Absolut ads, and college students decorate their walls with poster-size reproductions of ads that are available from a four-year-old company called Beyond the Wall. Forget Monet and Van Gogh. Think Nike, BMW and Calvin Klein. As Brian Gordon, one of the company's founders, sees it, kids regard ads as "a form of self-expression." In today's "short-attention society," he reasons, ads are something people can relate to: they provide "insights into current culture," and they provide them in 30 seconds or less.

5   No doubt this is why entire "Seinfeld" episodes have been built around products like Pez and Junior Mints. The popularity of Nick at Nite's vintage commercials, Rosie O'Donnell's peppy renditions of old jingles, the almost nightly commercial spoofs by Letterman and Leno—all are testaments to the prominent role advertising has assumed in our lives. A whole school of fiction known as Kmart realism has grown up around the use of brand names, while a host of well-known songs (from Nirvana's "Smells Like Teen Spirit" to Oasis' "Shakermaker") satirize old commercials. It used to be that advertisers would appropriate a hit song (like the Beatles' "Revolution") to promote a product; nowadays, the advertising clout of a company like Volkswagen has the power to turn a song (even an old song like "Da Da Da," by the now defunct German band Trio) into a hit.

6   So what does advertising's takeover of American culture mean? It's not just that the world has increasingly come to resemble the

Home Shopping Network. It's that advertising's ethos of spin—which makes selling a means *and* an end—has thoroughly infected everything from politics (think of Clinton's "permanent campaign") to TV shows like "Entertainment Tonight" that try to pass off publicity as information. It's that advertising's attention-grabbing hype has become, in our information-glutted age, the modus operandi of the world at large. "Advertising is the most pervasive form of propaganda in human history," says the scholar Mark Crispin Miller. "It's reflected in every esthetic form today."

7   Miller points out that just as commercials have appropriated techniques that once belonged to avant-garde film—cross-cutting, jump cuts, hand-held camera shots—so have mainstream movies and TV shows begun to ape the look and shape of ads, replacing character and story with razzle-dazzle special effects. For that matter, more and more film makers, including Howard Zieff, Michael Bay, Adrian Lyne and Simon West, got their starts in advertising.

8   Advertising has a more insidious effect as well. Advertisers scouting TV shows and magazines are inclined to select those vehicles likely to provide a congenial (and therefore accessible or upbeat) backdrop for their products, while a public that has grown up in a petri dish of ads has grown impatient with any art that defies the easy-access, quick-study esthetic of commercials—that is, anything that's difficult or ambiguous. "People have become less capable of tolerating any kind of darkness or sadness," Miller says. "I think it ultimately has to do with advertising, with a vision of life as a shopping trip."

9   There are occasional signs of a backlash against advertising—the Vancouver-based Media Foundation uses ad parodies to fight rampant consumerism—but advertising implacably forges ahead like one of those indestructible sci-fi monsters, nonchalantly co-opting the very techniques used against it. Just as it has co-opted rock-and-roll, alienation (a Pontiac commercial features an animated version of Munch's painting "The Scream") and Dadaist jokes (an ad campaign for Kohler featured interpretations of bidets and faucets by contemporary artists), so it has now co-opted irony, parody and satire.

10   The end result of advertising's ability to disguise itself as entertainment and entertainment's willingness to adopt the hard-sell methods of advertising is a blurring of the lines between art and commerce. Even as this makes us increasingly oblivious to advertising's agenda (to sell us stuff), it also makes us increasingly cynical

about everything else—ready to dismiss it, unthinkingly, as junk or fluff or spin, just another pitch lobbed out by that gigantic machine called contemporary culture.

THESIS AND ORGANIZATION

1. Kakutani's opening sentence announces qualities that unify the essay that follows. What paragraph or paragraphs focus on ads as "pervasive"?
2. What paragraph or paragraphs focus on ads as "persuasive"?
3. What paragraph or paragraphs focus on ads as "popular"?
4. Which paragraphs emphasize the effect of ads? What effect do they have?
5. Reread the first and last paragraphs. What is the thesis of the essay? What evidence can you cite to back up your opinion?

TECHNIQUE AND STYLE

1. Kakutani violates a principle of usage in her first paragraph in that the pronoun "they" has no antecedent. What effect does she achieve by not initially specifying to whom the "they" refers?
2. Ads and the culture within which they exist come in for much negative criticism in this essay. How would you characterize Kakutani's tone—negative, reasoned, thoughtful, strident, what?
3. Describe what you perceive to be Kakutani's persona. What evidence can you find to support your view?
4. In a handbook of grammar and usage, look up the uses of the dash. You'll note that Kakutani uses dashes frequently, as in paragraphs 3, and 5–10. What other punctuation could she have used? What reasons can you think of for her choice of the dash?
5. Kakutani uses three similes in her first sentence. Choose one of them and make up three or four of your own. Which do you prefer and why?

Journal

1. Anyone who watches television learns to hate certain ads. Take a minute to write down the ads you dislike the most and then, for each, put down the reasons. You'll end up with the working notes for an essay.
2. Kakutani states that thanks to ads we are becoming "increasingly cynical about everything else—ready to dismiss it, unthinkingly, as junk or fluff or spin, just another pitch lobbed out by that gigantic machine called contemporary culture" (paragraph 10). Write an entry in which you agree or disagree with Kakutani's statement, citing examples to support your views.

Essay

Whether or not you agree with Kakutani, there's no arguing about the prevalence of advertisements. To test out Kakutani's points or simply to analyze advertisements on your own, flip through a popular magazine noting various categories of advertisements—cars, liquor, clothes, perfumes, and the like. Choosing a group of ads for a type of product, examine it as though it were a window into our culture. What do you see? What does it say about our concerns? Fears? Attention span? Tastes? Use your notes to write an essay that illustrates its points through multiple examples. If advertising doesn't seem to be a worthwhile subject, then choose another topic that you can use as a way to examine popular culture. Here are some suggestions:

television shows
films
books
styles
fads
franchises

Electronic Intimacies

Peter Steinhart

Audubon *is the magazine of the National Audubon Society, an organization devoted to protecting birds and their habitats, as well as other wildlife. In addition to publishing* Audubon *six times a year, the organization supports a number of nature reserves and education centers throughout the United States. Peter Steinhart writes frequently for the magazine about the pleasures of nature and the relation of the natural world to our human one. He has also written several books reflecting that interest, the most recent being* The Company of Wolves *(1995), which one reviewer cited as providing "both a scientific and a psychological exploration of the impact wolves have had on humans." In "Electronic Intimacies," Steinhart also examines an "impact," giving his readers numerous examples of the effect television's wildlife shows have had on their viewers. The essay is also a good illustration of how a writer uses various patterns of organization to support a thesis. Here, Steinhart puts example, description, and causal analysis to work.*

WHAT TO LOOK FOR *Steinhart's essay is longer than most of the essays in this book, and longer essays force the writer to group ideas in larger clusters. A short essay may deal with a main point in one or two paragraphs, but a longer one will often take three or more paragraphs to develop an idea. Yet the same principle is at work, the principle of a generalization followed by supporting examples. As you read Steinhart's essay, mark the generalizations so that you are aware of the paragraph blocks that support them.*

1   In Yellowstone National Park a man trotted up to a lone buffalo. The buffalo didn't seem to be doing anything, so the man sought to improve its day by posing it for a picture. The buffalo became annoyed and bluff-charged. Undaunted, the man approached to within a few feet. The buffalo tossed him in the air and gored him.

2   A dozen visitors are injured by buffalo and a few more by bears or elk or moose every year in Yellowstone. Most of them are trying to snuggle up for a photograph. These encounters suggest some-

thing about the way we view wild animals today: We expect them to be available, accessible, and capable of intimacies.

3   Little in our actual experience of wildlife supports that expectation. In real life, our view of most creatures is abrupt and flickering, shadowed and blurred. Much of the content of our encounters comes from imagination or convention. And, since most of the park adventurers who end up in bandages are city slickers, it seems quite likely that they have learned their conventions by viewing wildlife on television.

4   Television has become our chief means of seeing wild creatures. Our living rooms are livelier than any national park. Any day you can switch on *Nature* or the *National Geographic Specials* and watch monkeys cavorting in trees or lions slinking through the grass. Britain's Survival Anglia keeps twenty-two crews in the field around the world. One-third of the programming on The Discovery Channel is wildlife. It's the biggest single subject for nonfiction video.

5   Wildlife film has a relatively short history. In the first decade of this century, Cherry Kearton filmed birds in nests and showed the footage with lectures. Lenses and films were not fast enough to allow telephotos or shots in dim light, so the filmmakers were happy simply to get a shot of, say, a cheetah sauntering along the veldt several hundred yards away. Until the 1950s most wildlife film consisted of simple identification shots—a gazelle grazing in the distance, a zebra running the other way. Most were shown in lecture halls rather than movie theaters. "When color film came out," recalls Karl Maslowski, a filmmaker who for forty years toured on National Audubon's lecture circuit, "if you had a red bird, a yellow bird, and a sunset, people stood up and cheered."

6   In the 1950s Walt Disney changed the field forever. He sought to bring nature to the movie screen and hired cameramen with studio-quality equipment to film close-ups, sustained action, and whole sequences of behavior from several camera angles. Disney brought the animals closer, and his films were immensely popular. But they changed the nature of the animals. Movies dramatize. In a darkened theater, character is everything. In the Disney version, and virtually all the theater films that followed, wildlife was presented as distorted humanity, as bumbling bears, square-dancing tarantulas, adolescent beavers running away from home, or the leering monsters of *Jaws* and *Grizzly.*

7   The big screen has seldom shown animals with what we might consider scientific integrity. Hollywood is a dream factory, and it values emotional intensity over factual accuracy. Modern wildlife filmmakers are quite critical of the Hollywood version. But Disney's popularization combined with increasingly faster films and lenses, lighter equipment, and cheap travel to remote areas allow other filmmakers to go out into the wild for months on end and compile intimate biographies. Bill Burrud began filming wildlife in 1959, and Mutual of Omaha sent out crews in 1962. And they sold their films to television.

8   In the 1960s commercial television hadn't yet sought to displace Hollywood as our dream merchant. It still focused much on fact and event. So television's wildlife descended from the traveling wildlife lecture and the science films produced by the BBC's natural-history unit, whose programs explained how birds navigate or fish live in water. American television borrowed from the movies by weaving humans into the story, for example having Marlin Perkins help a scientist anesthetize a rhino. And there was much emphasis on action, on hunting and being hunted. The British tradition was much enriched when, in the 1960s, Survival Anglia sent crews to live in the field for two or three *years* at a time, to film great cradle-to-grave epics of wildebeest and caribou and elephant. That ushered in a golden age of wildlife film. Today we enjoy hour-long portraits, rich with insight and intimacy. The appetite for such films is enormous.

9   Despite the popularity of wildlife films, they have a way of seeming repetitious. In part, the repetition is real: Much of the stock footage produced by Bill Burrud in the 1960s is still being screened today. Old footage gets dated as better equipment and more skillful photographers raise the level of clarity and intimacy. And new films often recall what we have seen in the old ones. Christopher N. Palmer, executive producer of the *Audubon Television Specials,* cautions, "It takes an enormous amount of time and creativity to make them look fresh."

10   Cameramen are driven to find new species and places to film, and ways to get closer to the animals. Heinz Sielman cut away the side of a tree trunk and installed a window and a blind to film nesting woodpeckers. Dieter Plage disguised a camera as a pelican and swam underwater to film waterfowl. The Oxford Scientific Films

unit built a forty-foot-long indoor trout stream, with pumps to create currents and all the aquatic organisms needed to film a life history of trout.

11   Novelty doesn't come easy. Since the 1960s it has grown harder to make films overseas, because travel is now more expensive and many of the countries are politically unstable or simply hostile. There are fewer places in which animals survive, and so there is competition for the unobstructed view. Des and Jen Bartlett spent four years filming in Namibia's Etosha National Park in part because the wildlife in the more accessible parks of Kenya is always ringed with tour buses.

12   Filming is also more expensive. A complete portrait may take years in the field, and that time costs money. Belinda Wright and Stanley Breeden spent two years and $500,000 filming *Land of the Tiger.* That's more than television will pay for a wildlife film. To cut costs, some filmmakers use trained animals and staged shots.

13   Still, there is a sameness. A local newspaper columnist complains that every time he turns on PBS, he expects to see a show about insects.

14   The problem is not that we're seeing the same creatures over and over again, but that there is an orthodoxy to wildlife films. The organizing idea is almost invariably that a creature struggles to survive the hardships of nature and civilization. Says Bayer, "The typical life story of, say, the mountain lion is a story about survival, and it becomes repetitious."

15   The new orthodoxy is clearly not an interest in science, for the films show a marked preference for mammals and birds, for creatures that are warm-blooded and seemingly approachable, rather than for spiders, jellyfish, or lizards. Nor is the main interest conservation. The films seldom do a good job of explaining who is responsible for a species' decline or what a viewer can do about it. It's not because the filmmaker doesn't care. It's because he wants the film to last long enough to pay back its costs in video rentals and television syndication, so he does not delve into legal or regulatory issues which may be out of date by the time the film is edited and released, let alone rerun in syndication.

16   The focus on survival probably has more to do with television's growing envy of Hollywood than with wildlife's problems. Thinking about survival allows us to personify animals without seeming as anthropomorphic as Disney. And even the most exact-

ing filmmakers have doubts about science and survival as themes. Says James Murray, executive producer of *The Nature of Things:* "You're peering inside and looking at everything in detail, and you're missing the emotional part of it." Photographer and filmmaker Jeff Foott says, "A lot of what's happening in wildlife films is terribly cerebral. I'd love to see films that let people just feel rather than learn."

17   Our real interest is empathy. Humans are designed to mythologize. Give us acres of science and we'll still plant gardens of rhyme. We'll look for spirit anywhere it offers to blossom, and it seems to beckon from the eye shine of the tiger and the flight of the sparrow. We want honesty, but we don't want it to get in the way of vision. That's why, I suspect, the spine of many wildlife films is evolution. It is so abstract that, after a few repetitions, we can conveniently ignore it.

18   If we ignore the message and look for myths, the films may mislead us. For wildlife films suffer from the chief curse of television: They make experience seem accessible and well-organized when in fact it is not. Nature doesn't reveal itself in thirty minutes or an hour. To see wild creatures one needs to train one's senses, to exercise imagination and temper it with effort and experience.

19   To film a red fox and her cubs, Karl Maslowski built a blind forty feet above a den in a black locust tree and then spent four or five days in the blind every spring for twelve years, waiting for a shot of the vixen and her pups. Only twice in those years did he get a shot. Filmmaker Wolfgang Bayer waited three days in a mine shaft, motionless behind a blind, for wild horses to come in to drink, and once waited three weeks for a coyote to come out of its den.

20   The patience and resourcefulness of the wildlife filmmaker are enormous. But they never appear on the screen. In the comfort of our living rooms we escape the cold feet, the mosquito bites, the uncertain glimpses that are part of our real relationship with the wild. And we miss the surges of impulse and imagination that flow out of these gaps in our vision. Still photographs elicit those surges because they usually leave the context of the shot unexplained and let the viewer imagine what has preceded and what follows the shot. But film organizes the experience, sets a context, a place, a meaning. There is at times too little for a viewer to do.

21   By taking the waiting out of watching, wildlife films also make wild creatures appear less modest and retiring than they really are.

Animals become almost promiscuously available on television. We get lingering close-ups. The animals are fully revealed. There are no empty landscapes. That, I suspect, is why visitors to our national parks expect wildlife to be accessible. Says National Park Service naturalist Glen Kaye, "Whatever the hour of the day, the question is, 'Which meadow do I go to to see the deer or the elk or the bear *right now?* There's no sense that the animals may not be available."

22   Films also make the animals seem confiding. Television's close-ups leap across centuries of evolution by taking us within the fight and flight distances that normally separate individuals. That probably explains why we assume a familiarity with movie stars and politicians that we wouldn't attempt with neighbors. We have been electronically intimate, close enough to hear them breathe and see their eyelids flutter. Among real people such things imply familiarity. So we'll barge in on them and demand autographs or recitations, though we are perfect strangers.

23   The same thing is true of wildlife. Filmmakers have taken us into the range of eye shine and body heat and personified the creature by telling us of its struggle. We're apt to feel the same cheap familiarity we feel with Tom Selleck or Oprah Winfrey. Says Mary Meagher, a Yellowstone biologist, "I don't think people have too much sense of flight distance in buffalo or bear, although humans have flight distances themselves. Even when I see that something dangerous is about to happen, if I explain to people that the animal is dangerous, I usually get the finger for my trouble. People can have all the warnings and disregard them."

24   Modern life seems tainted more and more with the expectation of gratification without effort, revelation without knowledge, feeling without understanding. Television is one of the culprits. Too often it absolves us of the responsibility to look for ourselves and sort the real from the perceived. Look at animals in the wild and you get an uncertain image, full of blur and shadow, which requires large measures of imagination and judgment. Look at them on film and you lose the responsibility to organize what you see.

25   Television brings wildlife into our hearts and minds. It makes us aware of humanity's aggrandizement of the Earth. But celluloid is not a substitute for experience. With or without television, we still make much use of animals in our minds. We let them symbolize virtues and vices, carry thoughts and feelings. If wildlife films ever become our only access to wild animals, we may be the less intelligent, perceptive, and imaginative for it.

THESIS AND ORGANIZATION

1. Steinhart begins his essay with a narrative set in a national park. What point does he make later in the essay that most directly relates to that narrative?
2. What paragraphs make up the introduction to the essay? What evidence can you cite to support your opinion?
3. Steinhart includes a short history of wildlife films. What does that explanation contribute to the essay as a whole?
4. How would you summarize Steinhart's point about the effect of the wildlife films we now see on television?
5. Identify the major points in the essay. What paragraphs support those points?
6. What paragraphs provide the conclusion to the essay? How would you restate Steinhart's thesis?

TECHNIQUE AND STYLE

1. Steinhart's prose often provides a perfect example of the kind of paragraph that begins with a topic sentence and then supports it by examples. Select one paragraph that is organized this way and explain the relationship between the particular and the general.
2. It's probably safe to assume that most of Steinhart's readers watch television and occasionally enjoy wildlife programs, programs that Steinhart criticizes. What techniques does he use to avoid offending his readers?
3. Writers often use parallel phrases or clauses to emphasize ideas, as Steinhart does in the first sentence of paragraph 24. Do you find it effective? Why or why not?
4. In paragraphs 22 and 23 the author compares our attitudes toward celebrities and animals. What causal relationship does he draw? How valid does his point seem to be?
5. What sources does the author draw on for his examples? Does the variety seem sufficient?
6. What sense do you get of Steinhart as a person? If you were to describe him based only on what you know of him from this essay, what kind of person would you describe?

SUGGESTIONS FOR WRITING

Journal

1. Take a few moments to record your impression of wildlife shows. Is there one you particularly remember? In general, do you like or dislike them, or does your response fall somewhere in between?

2. Steinhart states that "Modern life seems tainted more and more with the expectation of gratification without effort. . . ." Write an entry testing that statement against your own experience.

Essay

Think about the various categories of shows on television:
cartoons
soap operas
talk shows
dramas
situation comedies
You can probably add any number of others to the list. Like Steinhart, you will be writing an essay in which you analyze the difference between what the type of show presents as reality and reality itself. To make the topic more manageable, you might select one particular show and then use multiple examples from it. If you prefer, choose an advertisement from a magazine instead of a television show.

On Using Division and Classification

The big dark box on the right contains:

5

The next time you shop in a supermarket or clean out a closet, think about how you are doing it and you will understand the workings of **division and classification.** "How often do I wear those shoes?" and "I never did like that sweater" imply that dividing items according to how frequently you wear them would be a good principle for sorting out your closet. Supermarkets, however, do the sorting for you. Goods are divided according to shared characteristics—all dairy products in one section, meat in another, and so on—and then items are placed in those categories. The process looks easy, but if you have ever tried to find soy sauce, you know the pitfalls: Is it with the spices? Sauces? Gourmet foods? Health foods? Ethnic products?

To divide a subject and then classify examples into the categories or classes that resulted from division you must be able to examine a subject from several angles, work out the ways in which it can be divided, and then discern similarities and differences among the examples you want to classify. A huge topic such as animals invites a long list of ways they can be divided: wild animals, work animals, pets; ones that swim, run, crawl; ones you have owned, seen, or read about. These groups imply principles for division—by degree of domesticity, by manner of locomotion, by degree of familiarity. Division and classification often help define each other in that having divided your subjects, you may find that once you start classifying, you have to stop and redefine your principle of division. If your division of animals is based on locomotion, for instance, where do you put the flying squirrel?

Division and classification is often used at the paragraph level. If your essay argues that a particular television commercial for a toilet cleaner

143

insults women, you might want to introduce the essay by enumerating other advertisements in that general category—household products— that you also find insulting to women.

From Julius Caesar's "Gaul is divided into three parts" to a 10-year-old's "animal, vegetable, or mineral," classification and division has had a long and useful history. And, of course, it has a useful present as well. In each of the essays in this chapter, you will see that the system of division and classification supports a thesis, though the essays use their theses for different purposes: to entertain, to explain, to argue.

AUDIENCE AND PURPOSE

Knowing who your readers are and what effect you want to have on them will help you devise your system of classification and sharpen your thesis. Imagine that you are writing an essay for a newsletter put out by a health club or by students in a physical education program and that your subject is the benefits of garlic. You would know that your readers are interested in the positive effects of herbs, but you would also know that their noses may well wrinkle at the mere mention of garlic. Given the negative associations your audience may have, you would do well to begin with the unpleasant connotation, thus starting with what your readers already know, connecting your subject with their experience, and immediately addressing their first and probably negative ideas about garlic. After that, you might move quickly to the many good uses to which garlic can be put, categorizing them according to the herb's different effects. Thus you would inform your readers and at the same time argue for garlic's positive qualities and the idea that it should be more than a pizza topping.

To explain, however, is the more obvious use of division and classification. You may well find that when you start off on a topic that lends itself to this pattern of organization, you need to define some of your terms. Writing about the ways in which a one-year-old can both annoy and delight you, for instance, you may want to define what you mean by your central terms. In so doing, you have a chance to link the definitions to your audience's experiences, so that even if some of your readers have never spent much time around a baby, they can still appreciate your points. For *annoy*, you might define your reaction as similar to hearing a car alarm going off in the middle of the night, and for *delight,* you might remind your readers of how they felt when opening an unexpected but well-chosen present. Both definitions help explain while at the same time drawing on common experiences.

Should you tackle that same topic with a humorous tone, you will not only be informing your audience but entertaining them as well. But humor comes in many forms, evoking everything from belly laughs to giggles to knowing smiles. To produce those responses, you may find yourself using exaggeration (also known as **hyperbole**) or **irony,** or **sarcasm** or a combination of all three, and more. Your title can tip off your readers to your tone: "Baby Destructo" (exaggeration); "Little Baby, Big Problem" (irony); "The Joys of Parenthood" (sarcasm).

SYSTEM OF CLASSIFICATION

To work effectively, a system of classification must be complete and logical. The system that governs how goods are arranged in a supermarket needs to be broad enough to cover everything a supermarket might sell, and it needs to make sense. Can openers should be with kitchen implements, not with vegetables; cans of peas should be with other canned goods, not with milk.

So, too, when you are writing an essay all your examples should be in the correct category. If you were thinking of the subject of campaign spending in the recent presidential election and, in particular, who contributed what to which political party, you would first concentrate on the Republicans and the Democrats, ignoring the campaigns of the minor political groups (the money they raised being minor in comparison). Then you would sort out the kinds of contributions—small donations from private citizens, large ones from individuals, money from PACs, from corporations, and the like—made to each of those two political parties. At that point, you would find you had so much material that you would be better off narrowing your subject, but no matter what you did, you wouldn't mix in intangible gifts such as a volunteer's time or tangible ones such as the "free" donuts handed out to the campaign workers.

More likely, however, as you think about your topic and work on your draft, you will find your classifications are not watertight. Yet you can account for the occasional leak by explaining it or by adjusting your system of division. In the example of campaign contributions, for instance, it would be impossible to put an accurate price tag on the time spent by volunteers or on the goods and services donated to the two political parties, though it's reasonable to assume that the dollar figure would be high. And that's all you need to say. You've explained why you have omitted those kinds of contributions. Adjusting the system of division, the other alternative, so that it included every conceivable kind of donation isn't a reasonable solution as it would make an already large topic even larger, impossibly so.

OTHER PATTERNS OF ORGANIZATION

Earlier in this chapter, you read about what definition can add to classification and division, but description, narration, and example are useful as well. The essay on political contributions, for instance, might open with a brief narrative recounting your having been besieged by a telephone caller who was trying to raise money for a particular candidate. And if that narrative described your having discovered the plea by listening to the caller's recorded message talking to your answering machine, then you could also underscore your point that raising money for campaigns has reached absurd heights (or depths).

Examples are also essential to classification, usually in the form of multiple illustrations. Your practice in using examples in other papers will help you here, for as you know, you can select examples from your own experience or that of others or both. Outside sources such as evidence drawn from books and magazines are also helpful, showing your reader that you have looked beyond your personal experience. When using examples, however, you need think through the most effective way to sequence them, which will often be according to dramatic effect—moving from least to most dramatic—or in chronological order.

THESIS AND ORGANIZATION

Some writers begin their essays by first dividing the subject into their system of classification, then moving on to focus on one of the classes. Say you chose as a topic the electronic gizmos we often take for granted. You might have found yourself making notes that include a huge list. Thinking through that list you might have noticed that you can divide it into machines that can be controlled with a remote device and those that cannot. In one category are items such as microwaves, answering machines, and computers, and in the other you've lumped together CD players, television sets, VCRs. Your lists grow longer, and you begin to wonder what the life of the American consumer will be like in a remote-controlled world. The question interests you, and you want it to interest your audience. If you want the reader to think along with you, you might begin your essay by recreating the process of division that you thought through before focusing on life in the remote lane.

On the other hand, you may find your central question so intriguing that you want to get right to it, in which case you wouldn't need to discuss the division at all; instead, you can leap straight into presenting the category of remote-controlled objects, illustrating it with multiple examples. But before you make up your mind to jump into the subject, consider a third alternative: discussing both remote and nonremote classes, piling examples into each class without telling your reader how you arrived at them.

Perhaps the greatest trap in writing an essay that uses division and classification is that your means don't add up to an end, that what you have is a string of examples that don't lead anywhere. All your examples are well developed, yes, but they don't support an assertion. It's the cardinal sin—an essay without a thesis.

If you find yourself headed in that direction, one solution is to answer your own questions. In the course of thinking about your subject, you may well have come up with a solid, focused, central question, such as "What kind of life will the American consumer have in a remote-controlled world?" Your one-sentence answer to that question can be your thesis.

Often it helps to think of writing as a sort of silent dialogue with yourself. Reading a sentence in your draft and thinking about it, you find that thought leads to another sentence, and so on till you've filled up a number of pages. By the time you have stopped, you may realize that your first draft could more accurately be called a discovery draft, for in the course of writing it, you have found out what you want to say. Sum it up in one sentence that has a debatable point and you have your thesis.

If you are using division or classification to develop only one part of your paper, then where you place it depends on where you think it would be most effective. But if your essay, like most of those in this chapter, is structured primarily by division and classification, then you would do best to use a straightforward pattern of organization, devoting the body of the paper to developing the category or categories involved. Your reader can then follow your reasoning and understand how it supports your thesis. For the sake of clarity—readers can sometimes get lost in a tangle of examples—you may opt for an explicit thesis in an obvious place, such as at the end of your introduction.

USEFUL TERMS

Division and classification Methods of examining a subject. Division involves the process of separating, first dividing the subject into groups so that they can be sorted out—classified—into categories; classification focuses on shared characteristics, sorting items into categories that share a similar feature.

Hyperbole Obvious overstatement, exaggeration.

Irony A statement or action in which the intended meaning or occurrence is the opposite of the surface one.

Sarcasm A caustic or sneering remark or tone that is usually ironic as well.

➣ POINTERS FOR USING DIVISION AND CLASSIFICATION

Exploring the Topic

1. **How can your topic be divided?** What divisions apply? Of those you list, which one is the best suited?
2. **What examples can you think of?** What characteristics do your examples have in common? Which do you have the most to say about?
3. **Are your categories for classification appropriate?** Are the categories parallel? Do they overlap? Do you need to make any adjustments?
4. **Do your examples fit your categories?** Are you sure the examples have enough in common? Are they obvious? Which are not?
5. **What is your principle for classification?** Have you applied it consistently to each category?
6. **Are your categories complete?** Do they cover the topic? Do they contain enough examples?

7. **How can your categories be sequenced?** From simple to complex? Least to most important? Least to most effective?
8. **What is your point?** What assertion are you making? Does your system of classification support it? Are your examples appropriate?
9. **What is your purpose?** Are you primarily making your point to express your feelings, to inform, to persuade, or to entertain?

Drafting the Paper

1. **Know your reader.** Where does your reader stand in relation to your system of classification? Is the reader part of it? If so, how? If the reader is not part of your system, is he or she on your side, say a fellow student looking at teachers? What does your audience know about your topic? About your system of classification? What does the reader not know? Your audience might be biased toward or against your subject and classification system. How can you best foster or combat the bias?
2. **Know your purpose.** If your primary purpose is to express your feelings, make sure that you are not just writing to yourself and that you are not treading on the toes of your audience. Similarly, if you are writing to persuade, make sure you are not convincing only yourself. Check to see that you are using material that may convince someone who disagrees with you or who, at the least, is either sitting on the fence or hasn't given the matter much thought. Writing to inform is probably the easiest here, for though your subject may be familiar, your system of classification is probably new. On the other hand, writing to entertain is difficult and requires a deft use of persona.
3. **Set up your system of classification early in the paper.** You may find that a definition is in order or that some background information is necessary, but make your system clear and bring it out early.
4. **Explain the principle behind the system.** To give your system credibility, you need to provide an explanation for your means of selection. The explanation can be brief—a phrase or two—but it should be there.
5. **Select appropriate examples.** Perhaps you can best illustrate a class by one extended example, or maybe it would be better to pile on examples. If your examples are apt to be unfamiliar to your audience, make sure you give enough detail so that they are explained by their contexts.
6. **Make a point.** Remember that what you have to say about your subject is infinitely more interesting than the subject itself. So, too, your major assertion is more important than your system of classification: it is what your system of classification adds up to. It's easy, in writing this kind of paper, to mistake the means for the end, so make sure that you use classification to support an overall assertion.

Always, Always, Always

Bill Rohde

The essay that follows was written for a class required for students who intended to teach English. Focusing on both writing and the teaching of writing, the course asked students to analyze their own writing habits, including elements in the writing process that gave them problems. No matter what their stage of experience, most writers hit at least one question that sends them to the nearest handbook. The assignment here asked the class to choose one matter of grammar or usage that sent them in search of answers, then to research what the handbooks had to say, and to write an essay explaining both the question and the answers. Since the students were prospective English teachers, they were to use the Modern Language Association's (more familiarly known as the MLA) system of documentation and their audience was the class itself. Bill Rohde questioned the necessity of using a comma before the last item in a series.

WHAT TO LOOK FOR   *It's difficult to write a paper about a dry, well-researched subject in such a way that it has a light tone and an identifiable voice, but that's what Bill Rohde does. As you read the essay, try to imagine the person behind the prose. Also keep in mind that Rohde creates a distinct personality for the narrator of the essay without ever using the first-person I.*

1   A student inquiring about the "correctness" of the serial comma finds conflicting advice in her *Harbrace,* her teacher's *MLA Style Manual,* and the library's *Washington Post Deskbook on Style. Harbrace* tells her she may write either

> *The air was raw, dank, and gray.*

or

> *The air was raw, dank and gray.*

Ever accommodating, the tiny, red handbook considers the comma before the conjunction "optional" unless there is "danger of misreading" (132). *The MLA Style Manual,* with its Bible-black cover, neither acknowledges ambivalence nor allows for options. "Commas are required between items in a series," it clearly states in Section 2.2.4., after which it provides a typically lighthearted sample sentence:

The experience demanded blood, sweat, and tears. (46)

The paperback *Post Deskbook,* so user-friendly it suggests right in the title the handiest place to keep it, advises the student to "omit commas where possible," as before the conjunction in a series (126–27). Apparently written on deadline, the book offers sample sentence fragments:

red, white, green and blue; 1, 2 or 3 (127)

2   What should you, the composition teacher, tell this puzzled student when she approaches with her problem? Tell her she must always use the serial comma—no ifs, ands, or buts about it. Regardless of whether you believe this to be true, you must sound convincing. If the student appears satisfied with your response and thanks you, you may go back to grading papers. If, however, she wrinkles her nose or bites her lip in a display of doubt, then you may safely label her a problem student and select one of the following tailor-made responses.

3   *The struggling student* appreciates any burden a teacher can remove. You should explain to her that out of sympathy for her plight—so much to keep track of when writing—you have just given her one of the few hard-and-fast rules in existence. Tell her to concern herself with apostrophes or sentence fragments, and not with whether the absence of a serial comma might lead to a misreading.

4   *The easily intimidated student* (often ESL) should have accepted your unequivocal answer, but perhaps you do not (yet) strike her as an authority figure. Go for the throat. Say, "Obey the MLA. It is the Bible (or Koran or Bhagavad-Gita) of the discourse community to which you seek entry. Expect blood, sweat, and tears if you do not use the serial comma."

5   *The skeptic* needs an overpowering, multifarious theory to be convinced, so pull out Jane Walpole's *A Writer's Guide* and read the following:

> [A]ll commas indicate an up-pause in the voice contour, and this up-pause occurs after *each* series item up to the final one. Listen to your voice as you read this sentence:

Medical science has overcome tuberculosis, typhoid, small pox, and polio in the last hundred years.

Only *polio,* the final series item, lacks an up-pause; and where there is an up-pause, there should be a comma. The "comma and" combination before the final item also tells your readers that the series is about to close, thus reducing any chance of their misreading your sentence. (95)

While that's still soaking in, drop the names of linguists who have stated that writing is silent speech and reading is listening. Then tell her that omitting the serial comma represents an arrogant, foolish, and futile attempt to sever the natural link between speech and text.

6   Show *the visually oriented student,* possibly an artist, how

Chagall, Picasso, and Dali

are nicely balanced, but

Chagall, Picasso and Dali

are not.

7   Tell *the metaphor-happy student* that commas are like dividers between ketchup, mustard, and mayonnaise; fences between dogs, cats, and chickens; or borders between Israel, Syria, and Lebanon. Without them, messes result. (Dodge the fact that messes may result even if they are present.)

8   If the student is *a journalism major* who cites the *Deskbook* as proof of the serial comma's obsolescence, point out that her entire profession is rapidly approaching obsolescence. Add that editors who attempt to speed up reading by eliminating commas in fact slow down comprehension by removing helpful visual cues.

9   One hopes that reading, seeing, and hearing so many strong arguments in favor of the serial comma has so utterly convinced you of its usefulness that every student from here on in will accept your rock-solid, airtight edict without question.

WORKS CITED

Achtert, Walter S., and Joseph Gibaldi. *The MLA Style Manual.* New York: MLA, 1985.

Hodges, John C., et al. *Harbrace College Handbook.* New York: Harcourt, 1990.

Walpole, Jane. *A Writer's Guide.* Englewood Cliffs: Prentice, 1980.

Webb, Robert A. *The Washington Post Deskbook on Style.* New York: McGraw, 1978.

THESIS AND ORGANIZATION

1. Paragraphs 1 and 2 introduce the essay. What points do they convey to the reader?
2. At what point in the essay does Rohde use division? What does he divide and into what groups?
3. Rohde begins his classification in paragraph 3 and ends it with paragraph 8. What reasons can you infer for the order in which he presents his categories?
4. Where in the essay do you find Rohde's thesis? How effective is that placement?
5. Rohde's thesis is explicit, but what does the essay imply about English teachers? About students? About punctuation and usage?

TECHNIQUE AND STYLE

1. How would you describe Rohde's tone? His persona? What does his research on the topic contribute to his persona?
2. Who is the *you* in the essay? How effective do you find the direct address?
3. Note the use of parentheses in paragraph 4. Check out what your handbook says about parentheses. To what extent does Rohde's use fit the handbook's explanation?
4. A writer's choice of pronoun has become an issue ever since the once generic *he* lost its general nature and gained a specific gender connotation. What is Rohde's solution? Explain why you do or do not find his choice of pronoun effective.
5. The point of documentation is to provide specific and relevant references in an unobtrusive manner. Evaluate how well Rohde uses his research and how well he documents it.

SUGGESTIONS FOR WRITING

Journal Entry

1. Write out your response to Rohde's persona. Would you like to have him as your teacher? Would you like to have him in your class?

2. Commas give many writers fits. Thinking about your own writing, jot down the kinds of problems you have with commas. When you've finished, reread what you have written. Do you find a pattern?

Essay

Given that people's personalities range over a continuum with extremes at either end, the extremes can be good subjects for an essay that uses division and classification. Think about virtually any activity people are involved in and identify the behavior that represents the two extremes, thus dividing the subject. Then choose one of those groups and consider the categories your choice can be classified into. Here are some suggestions:
    drivers
    readers
    writers
    teachers
    professional athletes

The New York Walk: Survival of the Fiercest

Caryn James

Division and classification may seem to play a small part in Caryn James's essay, but it's a crucial one, for misreading the kind of man who hassles women on a city street can have serious consequences. Central to James's essay is the initial division between "a harmless gesture and a threat" (paragraph 13). Faced with either, most women adopt the "'don't mess with me' glare" that James finds natural. But most also wonder about the long-term effects of that glare on the glarer. As the essay explains, James lives in New York City. Her essay was, appropriately, published in the New York Times, *October 17, 1993.*

WHAT TO LOOK FOR *As you write, you'll probably discover that you use a number of patterns of organization. James, for example, begins and ends with narration and description, and the body of her essay incorporates division and classification, example, process, cause and effect, and comparison and contrast. The mixture of modes may make the essay hard to classify, but it also gives it variety.*

1   I know better than to talk back to guys who hassle women on the street. But on one weird August afternoon, I was caught in pedestrian gridlock in Times Square and the humidity turned my common sense to mush. A young man so average-looking he belonged in a Nike commercial planted himself on the sidewalk in front of me, purposely blocking my path, and offered some not-poetic variation on "Hey, baby."

2   What I did next was something no short, slight, sane person should ever do: I stamped my little foot and snapped at him in unprintable terms to get out of my way, right now! And while I was wondering why I had chosen a response that was both ineffectual *and* ridiculous, the street hassler smiled, stepped aside and said in a good-natured, singsong voice, "You're gonna learn to love me."

3   Humor is a desirable quality in a man, but this remark did not make him a person to take home. He was visibly affected by some

155

chemical or other, so I made sure to stay behind him as he woozed his way toward traffic. A basic rule of navigating the New York sidewalks, like driving anyplace, is that it's safer to be behind the drunk driver or drug-addled walker than in front of him.

4   And I didn't want him to see that my deliberately off-putting scowl was turning into a laugh.

5   For an instant I had almost lost the protective covering, the "don't mess with me" glare, that so many of us wear on crowded urban streets. Then I remembered that danger is real—the humor made him seem harmless, but his swaying toward an intersection suggested someone seriously out of control—and that walking in the city is a precise defensive maneuver.

6   This is especially, though not exclusively, true for women. Men are hassled, too, but physical size and social conditioning have made women more likely to be picked on. Walking can become an exhausting series of paralyzing questions. Should you slow down for the guy who seems, quite obviously, about to ask for directions? (I tried it once and was asked to join a theater group.) When is someone being innocently friendly, and when is he sidling up to get a better grip on your wallet or purse? When is a comment an invisible weapon, and when is it just a remark?

7   What's more, 30 years of raised feminist consciousness has taught us all that when men yell out to women on the street, whether to comment on a smile or issue a crude invitation, no compliment is involved. The average street hassler is not a fussy type, and while he may keep an eye out for a 17-year-old with no thighs, he will happily go after whoever crosses his line of vision: your mother, your granny, your self.

8   So most women have mastered the New York Walk for avoiding unpleasant encounters: eyes ahead but with good peripheral vision, bag clutched to your side, a purposeful stride and an unfriendly look. If someone talks to you, think of him as an obscene phone caller. Hang up. Do not acknowledge that he exists. In a big city, this is as necessary as locking your doors, and only a naïf would think otherwise.

9   Most of the time, this survival strategy doesn't bother me. I've always thought that my chilly, don't-talk-to-strangers New England upbringing has given me a Darwinian advantage; I've been naturally selected for this urban life. Ignoring strangers who talk to me

in Times Square—people to whom I have not, after all, been properly introduced—makes me feel right at home.

10   I could have evolved differently. My sister transplanted herself to Virginia, and while walking with her there on a civilized cobblestoned street once, I was shocked to hear her say: "You know, you don't have to grab your bag like that. You're not in New York anymore."

11   At moments like that, it's easy to wonder about the psychic cost of living in a city where such guardedness becomes second nature. Is it even possible, when you step into your house or office, to drop the hostile mask quite so easily or thoroughly as you imagine you can?

12   What residue of snarling distrust must build up over the years, so slowly you'd never notice it accumulating? Those are finally moot questions for someone like me, for whom New York will always be tinged with Holly Golightly glamour. Assuming a defensive posture while walking down the street seems a reasonable trade-off for the advantages of living here. Just as a matter of personal preference. I'd rather be hassled outside the Metropolitan Museum or Tiffany's than on a farm or in the 'burbs. (Don't say it doesn't happen.)

13   Maybe the best one can do is to savor those rare episodes during which it is easy to tell the difference between a harmless gesture and a threat. On another summer day, by a fluke in the law of averages, I happened to be the only person walking by a real-life cliché: a scaffold full of construction workers having lunch at a site on Broadway. As I passed, glare in place and prepared for anything, they started to sing a cheerful version of an oldies song: "There she goes, a-walkin' down the street/Singin' doo-wah-diddy-diddy-dum-diddy-do."

14   Hours later as I left my office, several blocks away, I passed a man who gave a big surprised wave. "Hey, I know you!" he said with a friendly smile of recognition as he passed by. "We sang to you!" I almost said hello.

THESIS AND ORGANIZATION

1. What is the point of James's opening narrative?
2. Paragraph 6 briefly describes various categories of men who approach women on the street. What are they?

3. Paragraph 7 tells the reader that "no compliment is involved." What is?
4. The essay ends with an example of "a harmless gesture" (paragraph 13). What is James's reaction?
5. Think about the division that James makes, her glare and its "psychic cost" (paragraph 11), and in your own words, state the thesis.

TECHNIQUE AND STYLE

1. Though the essay is certainly a literate one, James includes a number of words that best fit the category of slang. What, if anything, do they add to the essay?
2. What evidence can you find to disprove the idea that the essay deals only with the hassling of women?
3. How would you describe James's tone?
4. Where in the essay does James use process? Cause and effect?
5. Explain whether you find James's mixing of modes adds or detracts from the essay.

SUGGESTIONS FOR WRITING

Journal

1. Have you ever been followed, or whistled or yelled at, on the street? Write a paragraph or two about how it made you feel.
2. Describe your behavior when you walk along a crowded street. What do you do or not do? Why?

Essay

We interact with strangers in many different ways according to many different circumstances. The next time you find yourself in one of those situations, note how people act. Think about how various people behave and what categories they can be placed into. Then, when you draft your paper, make your categories come alive through description, narration, and example. Likely spots to observe behavior:

traffic jams
elevators
lines (at a bank, supermarket, movie, cafeteria)
train stations or airports

Intense!

Richard Brookhiser

An editor for the National Review, *Brookhiser is also the author of numerous articles and books, most recently a biography of George* Washington, Founding Father *(1996), and* Rules for Civility *(1997). The latter book is an update of 110 principles based on earlier ones formed by French Jesuits in the fifteenth century that Washington had copied out in the 1740s and used to guide how he lived his life. As you may infer, Richard Brookhiser is an astute observer of people and society and their quirks. The subtitle of Brookhiser's essay— "Reflections on a Paradoxical Personality Type"—points out a particular quirk, so be on the lookout for what's paradoxical about the truly intense. You'll also find that the essay weaves definition into its division. The essay was first published in the* Atlantic *in May, 1993, then reprinted in the* Utne Reader *in the November/December issue of that same year.*

WHAT TO LOOK FOR *If you are writing a reflective essay, a collection of thoughts on a particular subject, you may find it difficult to find a way to bring those thoughts together. Brookhiser does it by weaving his ideas around a conversation with his wife, who provides a kind of audience for his thoughts. You can use a similar device if you set up an opening dialogue. Like Brookhiser, you may want to use division and classification to define a term that captures your imagination.*

1   My wife and I were having lunch. She was talking. "What do my friends mean," she asked, "when they call me intense?"

2   I didn't know what to answer at first, not because I didn't know what she was talking about but because I knew so perfectly that it was hard to put into words.

3   My wife is five feet tall. Of the pocket dictionary of pet names I have bestowed on her over the years, most of which have had a half-life of about a month, one was "bundle," short for "bundle of energy." When I think of her as a car, I think of a sports car, usually a Miata, red—or the cars in the cartoons I watched on TV as a kid, which walked down highways on tire feet and had eyelashes over

their headlights and grins for grillwork. If a pet squirrel accomplished anything by running around in a wheel—if the shaft of the wheel turned on a gas jet, which heated a tea kettle, whose steam floated a small parachute that brushed a light switch as it rose—and if the squirrel understood the process and desired the result, then my wife could be that squirrel.

4   *Intense,* I told my wife, was the word my pothead friends used in college, in the '70s, when they were at that stage of being stoned in which they were fully conscious of the activities of the unstoned but lacked the desire or the capacity to participate in any way. What normal activity is to the stoned, the activity of those who are intense is to those who are normal.

5   I was not making any headway, so I decided to list intense people. "Hillary is intense," I said. "Bill is not." Our forty-second president: hand pumper, hugger, hugger of the tree hugger, smiler, glows with the flow, interested in a hundred policies, committed to about three. Resilient, intelligent, eager to please and be pleased—he is all these things. But he is not intense. The first lady: author of articles in law journals, this year earning less money than her husband probably for the first time in her life, lived in Arkansas not because she was born there but because she chose to. She is intense. My wife began to see.

6   I went through other presidents. Bush: not intense. Reagan: not intense. Carter: intense. Ford: come on. Nixon: so intense that he will probably live, on pure intensity, to give a sound bite at Clinton's funeral. Johnson: not intense (paradoxical—I'll get back to it). Kennedy: not intense. Eisenhower: very intense, though he pretended not to be. George Washington: the most intense president we have ever had. Goebbels, I added, was also intense, though Hitler was not. Lenin was intense. Trotsky was not. Madonna is intense; Marilyn was not.

7   "Give me explanations!" my wife howled. How intense of her, I thought. Here goes.

8   The defining quality of intense is that the motor never stops. The engine always runs, the battery always hums. Within the psychic boiler room of the intense person there is always at least a skeleton crew, and that crew never takes a break.

9   Intense cuts across such categories as good and evil, great and mediocre, success and failure, happiness and the lack of it. Jimmy Carter in office was decent, piddling, unsuccessful, and troubled,

whereas Lenin was wicked, grand, triumphant, and possibly happy (he was known to laugh at the murder of his enemies). But from each man came the whir of wheels endlessly turning.

10   Activity, to be intense, must also be deliberate, directed, self-propelled. Intense requires an exercise of will. This is what distinguishes the achievements of the intense from those of the non-intense.

11   You can be busy without being intense. This thoughtless quality characterizes busy but not intense types—Lyndon Johnson, William F. Buckley Jr., and Francis of Assisi. Even when they seem to be consciously choosing, their choices are driven by uncontrollable personal forces (in Johnson's case, ambition and grievance). Their activity is an exfoliation of their natures. They do not do, they are.

12   Are the intense ever happy? As often as anyone else in this world. The intense are happy when they're coming down the home stretch. Do the intense ever rest? Never.

13   Are you intense? This is the sort of question no one can ever answer for himself. Each of us thinks he is more complicated than anyone else does, possibly more complicated than anyone actually is. If you want to know which you are, ask a friend. If you do, you are probably intense.

THESIS AND ORGANIZATION

1. Paragraphs 1–3 serve as an introduction. What do they lead you to expect about the author's tone?
2. Brookhiser sets out one definition in paragraph 4. What other paragraphs help define the central term?
3. Division enters paragraphs 5 and 6, then is followed by definition. Where does Brookhiser return to his division?
4. Multiple examples make up paragraphs 5, 6, 9, and 11. What are the advantages of using so many examples?
5. Like many reflective essays, this one contains no one sentence that can work as the thesis. Instead, the reader must deduce the thesis from bits and pieces of Brookhiser's ideas about intense people. What is the thesis?

TECHNIQUE AND STYLE

1. Brookhiser uses analogy in paragraph 3. How effective do you find his comparisons?
2. What does Brookhiser achieve by the comparison in paragraph 11?
3. What does the dialogue add to the essay?

4. Brookhiser brings in the topic of happiness in paragraph 12. What reasons can you think of for introducing that idea?
5. Who is the "you" in paragraphs 11 and 13?

SUGGESTIONS FOR WRITING

Journal

1. Use your journal to describe someone you know who, by Brookhiser's definition, is intense.
2. Analyze the degree to which you would call yourself intense or not intense. What examples support your opinion?

Essay

You can write your own "Intense!" essay by drawing up your own list of friends or public figures, using Brookhiser's definitions or your own. Or if you prefer, pick a different category and figure out who belongs where. For examples, you can draw on your own experience and the world of public figures or well-known characters from mythology, books, television, or film. If your examples are not that well known, make sure you provide enough information about them so that your reader can see how they fit your categories. You may want to have a working thesis to keep you on track, and then in your final draft, switch from an explicit to an implied thesis. For possible categories, you can think of who or what is or is not:

"with it"
"in"
overpaid
underrated
bizarre

The Plot Against People

Russell Baker

Russell Baker is best known for his light tone, one that many readers enjoyed during the time he was a regular columnist for the New York Times. *Baker is the author of several collections of essays and autobiographical books—*Growing Up *(1982),* The Good Times *(1989),* There's a Country in My Cellar *(1991)—and the editor of* The Norton Book of Light Verse *(1986) and* Russell Baker's Book of American Humor *(1993). The essay that follows typifies the humorous side of Baker's style, for he has discovered the principles behind the continuing battle between humans and inanimate objects. He discusses these principles as he neatly divides things into three categories and then places objects into his classifications.*

WHAT TO LOOK FOR   *Transitions between paragraphs can be wooden, so obvious that they leap off the page to say "Look at me! I'm a transition." The more effective variety is subtle, and one way to bring that about is to pick up a key word from the previous sentence and repeat it in the first sentence of the paragraph that follows. After you've read Baker's essay, go back over it searching for his transitions between paragraphs.*

1   Inanimate objects are classified into three major categories—those that don't work, those that break down and those that get lost.

2   The goal of all inanimate objects is to resist man and ultimately to defeat him, and the three major classifications are based on the method each object uses to achieve its purpose. As a general rule, any object capable of breaking down at the moment when it is most needed will do so. The automobile is typical of the category.

3   With the cunning typical of its breed, the automobile never breaks down while entering a filling station with a large staff of idle mechanics. It waits until it reaches a downtown intersection in the middle of the rush hour, or until it is fully loaded with family and luggage on the Ohio Turnpike.

4   Thus it creates maximum misery, inconvenience, frustration and irritability among its human cargo, thereby reducing its owner's life span.

5   Washing machines, garbage disposals, lawn mowers, light bulbs, automatic laundry dryers, water pipes, furnaces, electrical fuses, television tubes, hose nozzles, tape recorders, slide projectors—all are in league with the automobile to take their turn at breaking down whenever life threatens to flow smoothly for their human enemies.

6   Many inanimate objects, of course, find it extremely difficult to break down. Pliers, for example, and gloves and keys are almost totally incapable of breaking down. Therefore, they have had to evolve a different technique for resisting man.

7   They get lost. Science has still not solved the mystery of how they do it, and no man has ever caught one of them in the act of getting lost. The most plausible theory is that they have developed a secret method of locomotion which they are able to conceal the instant a human eye falls upon them.

8   It is not uncommon for a pair of pliers to climb all the way from the cellar to the attic in its single-minded determination to raise its owner's blood pressure. Keys have been known to burrow three feet under mattresses. Women's purses, despite their great weight, frequently travel through six or seven rooms to find a hiding space under a couch.

9   Scientists have been struck by the fact that things that break down virtually never get lost, while things that get lost hardly ever break down.

10   A furnace, for example, will invariably break down at the depth of the first winter cold wave, but it will never get lost. A woman's purse, which after all does have some inherent capacity for breaking down, hardly ever does; it almost invariably chooses to get lost.

11   Some persons believe this constitutes evidence that inanimate objects are not entirely hostile to man, and that a negotiated peace is possible. After all, they point out, a furnace could infuriate a man even more thoroughly by getting lost than by breaking down, just as a glove could upset him far more by breaking down than by getting lost.

12   Not everyone agrees, however, that this indicates a conciliatory attitude among inanimate objects. Many say it merely proves that furnaces, gloves and pliers are incredibly stupid.

13   The third class of objects—those that don't work—is the most curious of all. These include such objects as barometers, car clocks,

cigarette lighters, flashlights, and toy train locomotives. It is inaccurate, of course, to say that they never work. They work once, usually for the first few hours after being brought home, and then quit. Thereafter, they never work again.

14   In fact, it is widely assumed that they are built for the purpose of not working. Some people have reached advanced ages without ever seeing some of these objects—barometers, for example—in working order.

15   Science is utterly baffled by the entire category. There are many theories about it. The most interesting holds that the things that don't work have attained the highest state possible for an inanimate object, the state to which things that break down and things that get lost can still only aspire.

16   They have truly defeated man by conditioning him never to expect anything of them, and in return they have given man the only peace he receives from inanimate society. He does not expect his barometer to work, his electric locomotive to run, his cigarette lighter to light or his flashlight to illuminate, and when they don't, it does not raise his blood pressure.

17   He cannot attain that peace with furnaces and keys and cars and women's purses as long as he demands that they work for their keep.

THESIS AND ORGANIZATION

1. In what ways does the introduction, paragraphs 1–2, set up both the system of classification and the major principle at work among inanimate objects?

2. Paragraphs 3–6 explain the first category. What effects does the automobile achieve by breaking down? How do those effects support Baker's contention about "the goal of all inanimate objects"? What other examples does Baker put into his first category? What example does not fit?

3. Paragraphs 7–12 present the second classification. What causes, reasons, or motives are attributed to the examples in this group?

4. Paragraphs 13–16 describe the third group. What are its qualities? Why might Baker have chosen to list it last? What principle of organization can you discern beneath Baker's ordering of the three groups?

5. Consider how each group frustrates and defeats people together with the first sentence of paragraph 2. Combine this information into a sentence that states the author's thesis.

TECHNIQUE AND STYLE

1. In part, the essay's humor arises from Baker's use of anthropomorphism, attributing human qualities to inanimate objects. How effectively does he use the technique?
2. Baker has a keen eye for the absurd, as illustrated by paragraph 10. What other examples can you find? What does this technique contribute to the essay?
3. Baker's stance, tone, and line of reasoning, while patently tongue-in-cheek, are also mock-scientific. Where can you find examples of Baker's explicit or implied "scientific" trappings?
4. The essay's transitions are carefully wrought. What links paragraph 3 to paragraph 2? Paragraph 7 to paragraph 6? Paragraph 10 to paragraph 9? Paragraph 12 to paragraph 11?
5. How an essay achieves unity is a more subtle thing. What links paragraph 8 to paragraph 6? Paragraph 9 to paragraphs 3–6? Paragraph 16 to paragraph 2? Paragraph 17 to paragraphs 10–12 and paragraphs 3–5?

SUGGESTIONS FOR WRITING

Journal

1. Describe a fight you have had with an inanimate object.
2. Of all the inanimate objects that can frustrate you, which one tops the list and why?

Essay

Write your own "plot" essay, imagining something else plotting against people. Like Baker, you can take a "scientific" stance or you may prefer your own humorous tone. Suggestions:

    clothes
    food
    pets
    the weather
    plants
    traffic

The Bench

Mary Ruefle

As you can tell from reading Mary Ruefle's essay, she believes in the imagination and the life of the mind. The essay's language also suggests that she is a poet, which she is. Her most recent collection of poetry is Cold Pluto (1996). Her essay "The Bench" was originally published in The Threepenny Review, a literary quarterly published in Berkeley, California, and then reprinted in the April 1999 issue of Harper's Magazine. You may find the thesis of the essay a bit illusive as it is implied, not openly stated, so be sure you read "The Bench" more than once.

WHAT TO LOOK FOR *Paragraphing often seems a rather mechanical process—new subject, new paragraph. But if you've ever taken a large block of prose and thought about how to break it up into paragraphs, you know that deciding when to start a new paragraph isn't as easy a decision as it may seem to be. Ruefle goes to another extreme, for when she wrote "The Bench," she decided to make the essay one long paragraph. As you read the essay, see if you can figure out why she decided not to break it up into paragraphs.*

My husband and I were arguing about a bench we wanted to buy and put in part of our backyard, a part that is actually a meadow of sorts, a half acre with tall grasses and weeds and the occasional wildflower because we do not mow it but leave it scrubby and unkempt. This bench would hardly ever be used and in the summer when the grasses were high would remain partially hidden from view. We both knew we wanted the bench to be made of teak so that it would last a long time in the harsh weather and so that we would never have to paint it. Teak weathers to a soft silver that might, in November or March, disappear into the gray hills that are the backdrop of our lives. My husband wanted a four-foot bench and I wanted a five-foot bench. This is what we argued about. My husband insisted that a four-foot bench was all we needed, since no more than two people (presumably ourselves) would ever sit on it at the same time. I felt his reasoning was not only beside the point but missed it entirely; I said what mattered most to me was the idea of

10

167

the bench, the look of it there, to be gazed at with only the vaguest
notion that it could hold more people than would ever actually sit
down. The life of the bench in my imagination was more important
20   than any practical function the bench might serve. After all, I argued,
we wanted a bench so that we could look at it, so that we could
imagine sitting on it, so that, unexpectedly, a bird might sit on it, or
fallen leaves, or inches of snow, and the longer the bench, the
greater the expanse of that plank, the more it matched its true function, which was imaginary. My husband mentioned money and I
said that I was happier to have no bench at all, which would cost
nothing, than to have a four-foot bench, which would be expensive.
I said that having no bench at all was closer to the five-foot bench
than the four-foot bench, because having no bench at all served the
30   imagination in similar ways, and so not having a bench became an
option in our argument, became a third bench. We grew very tired
of discussing the three benches, and for a day we rested from our
argument. During this day I had many things to do and many of
them involved my driving past other houses, none of which had
benches—that is, they each had the third bench—and as I drove
past the other houses I could see a bench here and a bench there;
sometimes I saw the bench very close to the house, against the wall
or on a porch, and sometimes I saw the bench under a tree or in the
open grass, cut or uncut, and once I saw the bench at the end of the
40   driveway, blocking the road. Always it was a five-foot bench that I
saw, a long, sleek bench or a broken-down bench, a bench with a
slatted back or a bench with a solid, carved back, and always the
bench was empty. But I knew that for my husband the third bench
was only four feet long and he saw always two people who were
happy to be alive or two people tired from having worked hard
enough to buy the bench they were sitting on. Or they were happy
and tired, happy to have reached the end of some argument, tired
from having had it. For these people, the bench was an emblem of
their days, which were fruitful because their suffering had come to
50   an end. On my bench, which was always empty, no one had sat
down, though the bench was always long enough so that someone,
if he desired to, could lie all the way down. The day passed.
Another day followed it, and my husband and I began, once more,
to discuss the bench. The sound of our voices revealed a renewed
interest and vigor. I thought I sensed in him a coming around to my
view of the bench and I know he sensed in me a coming around to

his view of the bench, because at one point I said that a four-foot
bench reminded me of rough notes toward a real bench while a
five-foot bench was like a fragment of an even longer bench and I
60 admitted it was at times hard to tell the difference. He said he didn't
know anything about the difference between rough notes and fragments but he agreed that between the two benches there was, possibly, just perhaps—he could only imagine—very little difference. It
was, after all, only a foot we were talking about. And I think it was
then, in both of our minds, that a fourth bench came into being, a
bench that was only a foot long, a miniature bench, a bench we
could build ourselves, though of course we did not. This seemed to
be, essentially, the bench we were talking about. Much later, when
the birds came back, or the leaves drifted downward, or the snow
70 fell, slowly and lightly at first, then heavier and faster, it was this
bench that we both saw when we looked out the window at the
bench we eventually placed in the meadow, which continued to
grow as if there were no bench at all.

THESIS AND ORGANIZATION

1. Break the essay into paragraphs. What reasons lie behind your paragraphing? What is gained? Lost?
2. In a sense Ruefle has divided her subject—benches—into real and imaginary ones, and then, in the essay, she classifies the imaginary ones by
   size. What are the characteristics of the four benches?
3. Why is it important that early in the essay Ruefle says, "This bench would
   hardly ever be used and in the summer when the grasses were high
   would remain partially hidden from view"?
4. Obviously, the subject of Ruefle's essay is the bench, but what other subjects does she mention or suggest? What particular words in the essay
   strike you as important?
5. Given the subjects and words you identified in the previous question,
   what is the essay's thesis?

TECHNIQUE AND STYLE

1. What reasons can you find for Ruefle's decision to present the essay as
   one paragraph?
2. If you take a careful look at the essay, you'll find that Ruefle uses a great
   deal of sentence variety. Her sentences, for example, range in length

from 3 to 97 words. Select a sentence that appeals to you and then examine the sentence that precedes it and the one that follows it. What do you find?

3. Ruefle describes her yard, and the argument with her husband reveals something of her personality. How would you describe her persona?

4. Given that an essay's tone can be defined as the attitude the writer takes toward the subject and audience, how would you describe the tone of "The Bench"?

5. Reread the last sentence of the essay. Is the bench real or not? In what ways is the last sentence a fitting ending for the essay?

SUGGESTIONS FOR WRITING

Journal

1. Write a brief entry explaining your response to the essay. What questions do you have about it? Why did you or did you not like it?

2. It has been suggested by people who study such things that fantasizing and imagining specific accomplishments actually influences one's life choices. Imagining what it would be like in college, for example, may have influenced your decision to continue your education. Think about your own experiences, and write a journal entry that analyzes the relative truth of the idea that fantasizing has influenced your decisions.

Essay

Try your own hand at writing a division and classification essay based on your imagination. If, for example, you have always wanted to travel, you would start thinking about all the places you would like to go, listing them and analyzing their characteristics. From those classifications, you can then select the one ideal place, which can be the point of your essay. Your assertion about that place will be your thesis, and your analysis of the alternatives will be your classification. Like Ruefle, you would have divided your topic beforehand, in this case, places you do and do not want to visit. If you chose this assignment, remember that you need to examine a general category and then classify some of the items in it. Possible topics:

your ideal house or apartment
your dream car
your ideal job
your best friend
your ideal class

On Using Comparison and Contrast

6

W hat's the difference?" gets at the heart of **comparison and contrast,** and it is a question that can fit into any context. In college, it often turns up in the form of essay questions; in day-to-day life, it implies the process behind most decisions: "What shall I wear?" "Which movie will I see?" "Should I change jobs?" All these questions involve choices that draw on comparison and contrast. Like description, narration, example, and classification, comparison and contrast forces you to observe, but here you are looking for similarities and differences. In a way, comparison and contrast is the simplest and most analytical form of division and classification in that you are examining only two categories, or perhaps only one example from each of the two categories. "Which sounds better, tapes or records?" compares two categories; "Which sounds better, compact discs or records?" compares two items in the same category.

No matter what you select, however, you need to be sure that the comparison is fair. Deciding where to go out to dinner often depends on how much you are willing to spend, so comparing a fast-food place to an elegant French restaurant doesn't have much of a point unless you want to treat the comparison humorously. If neither is worth the money, however, you have a serious assertion to work from, but you have to work carefully.

Sometimes the similarities will not be readily apparent. If you were writing a paper on Senator Bill Bradley and his campaign for the Democratic nomination for President, you might well wonder how he connected his basketball days with serving in public office. But as you think about what playing on a professional basketball team has in common with his experience serving in the United States Senate, similarities begin to emerge: both positions require teamwork and leadership; both depend on the ability to make quick decisions based on complex situations; both call for stamina and training, including what could be called homework. A cynic might add that both involve fancy footwork and the ability to dodge the opposition, but if you want to keep to a serious tone and carry the comparison further, you'd also realize that both jobs call for many public appearances and the ability to be at ease in front of cameras, to be a public figure, if not a celebrity.

There the similarity ends. One position is relatively short-lived and may pay millions. The other is at least a six-year term and not nearly so well remunerated. And no matter how seriously you take basketball, it is essentially a game, a sport, whereas the other may well affect every citizen in the United States and potentially—as foreign policy is involved—citizens elsewhere as well.

Essays that depend primarily on other modes, such as description, narration, and definition, often use comparison and contrast to heighten a difference or clarify a point, but the pieces in this section rely on comparison and contrast as their main principle of organization, even though their purposes differ.

AUDIENCE AND PURPOSE

Often you may want only to inform your reader: x is better or worse than y; x has a lot in common with y, though not obviously so; x is quite different from y, though superficially similar. If, for instance, your college is primarily residential, you might be interested in how it differs from a nonresidential institution. Assuming that your classmates are your audience, they might be surprised to find that on the average, students at nonresidential campuses are quite different. Compared to those at residential institutions, they are older, work more hours at jobs, miss more classes, carry fewer hours, attend fewer sports events, participate in fewer on-campus activities, and take longer to earn a degree.

You could easily turn what started out as an informative essay into an argumentative one if in the course of writing, you decide that living on a campus that is primarily residential has some drawbacks that may not be apparent at first. A dorm room may not be half as pleasant as an apartment off campus, and eating in the cafeteria can be monotonous.

On the other hand, living on campus makes it easier to form solid friendships, and classes don't have to be over at the bell—the discussion can continue without the pressure of having to race off for a job downtown. As you come up with more and more information, you are able to assess the pros and cons and, therefore, to construct a strong argument in favor of the side you believe is best.

Comparison can also be used to entertain your readers. A seemingly simple job such as washing the dog can be as much of a challenge as performing major surgery. At least at hospitals, you don't have to catch the patient first.

ANALOGY

One useful form of comparison is **analogy,** for it can emphasize a point or illuminate an idea. If you are writing about an abstraction, for example, you can make it more familiar by using an analogy to make it concrete and, therefore, more understandable. An intangible word such as *rumor* becomes more distinct, more memorable, if you write of it as cancer. Or, if you are explaining a process, analogy can often make the unfamiliar familiar; many a tennis instructor has said, "Hold your racquet as though you are shaking hands with a person."

An analogy is an extended **metaphor,** in which a primary term is equated with another quite dissimilar term. The process of writing, for example, is a far cry from making music, but if you think of all the elements of the writing process—coming up with a topic and ideas about it, planning how to organize what you want to say, working on drafts, editing as you go along—then you can see how you can extend the description into a metaphor. You, the writer, are the leader of the orchestra. Organizing your ideas for an essay is rather like getting all the members of the orchestra to play the same tune. Can't find quite the right word? That's similar to having a musician missing from the string section. Wonder if that comma is in the right place? One of the horns skipped a note. Tone not quite what you want it to be? Some of the musicians are flat. Once you have a solid draft, however, it's as though rehearsal is over and the piece is ready for an audience.

So in exposition, analogy clarifies—because by making x analogous to y, you bring all the associations of y to bear on x. If you were to compare the differences in the style of two television newscasters, you might find that one delivers the news in a rush, like a machine gun firing, while the other is more like a single-shot target rifle. The machine gun person fires rapid lines and barely pauses for breath, a sharp contrast to the target rifle person, who hesitates between sentences as though to re-load an idea before aiming it at the viewers.

To use analogy well, however, you have to use it cautiously. Often writers use it sparingly, working one into a sentence or paragraph instead of using it as the basic structure for an entire essay. Five pages of the ship of state can make you and your readers seasick.

METHOD OF COMPARISON

Comparison and contrast essays group information so that the comparison is made by **blocks** or **point by point** or by a combination of the two. if you were to write an essay explaining the differences between an American feast, such as Thanksgiving, and a Chinese one, here is what the two major types of organization would look like in outline form:

Type	Structure	Content
Block	Paragraph 1	Introduction
	Block A, paragraphs 2–4	American culture
	Point 1	Preparation
	Point 2	Courses & types of food
	Point 3	Manners
	Block B, paragraphs 5–7	Chinese culture
	Point 1	Preparation
	Point 2	Courses & types of food
	Point 3	Manners
	Paragraph 8	Conclusion
Point by Point	Paragraph 1	Introduction
	Point 1, paragraph 2	Preparation
		Chinese
		American
	Point 2, paragraph 3	Courses & types of food
		Chinese
		American

And so on. As you can see, sticking rigorously to one type of organization can become boring or predictable, so writers often mix the two.

In this chapter you'll find essays organized by block, point by point, and by a combination of the two. Outlining an essay readily reveals which type of organization the writer depends on. In your own writing, you might first try what comes easiest; then, in a later draft, you might mix the organization a bit and see what you find most effective. Fortunately word processing makes such changes easy, but if you don't have a word processor, try writing each paragraph on a separate piece of paper. Shuffling them around is then a simple task, though you'll have to supply some transitions after you decide on the best sequence for your paragraphs.

OTHER MODES

A close look at any of the essays that follow will show how you can use other modes, such as description, narration, and cause and effect, to help flesh out the comparison and contrast. A brief narrative or anecdote is often a good way to begin an essay as it usually sets a conversational tone and establishes a link between writer and reader. Examples can clarify your points and description can make them memorable, while exploring why the differences or similarities exist or what effect they may have will lead you into pondering cause-and-effect relationships.

THESIS AND ORGANIZATION

The one-sentence thesis placed at the end of an introductory paragraph certainly informs your readers of your subject and stance, but you might find your paper more effective if you treat your thesis more subtly, trying it out in different forms and positions. While some of the essays in this chapter save their major assertion until last, others combine ideas from various points in the essay to form a thesis. And, of course, not all theses are explicit, but if you want to imply it, you have to be sure your implication is clear or the reader may miss the point.

Although some writers begin the writing process with a thesis clearly set out, many find that it is easier to write their way into one. As a result, you may find that the last paragraph in your draft will make a very good introductory one, for by the time you write it, you have refined your thesis. At that point, you'll find writing a new introduction isn't the task it was to begin with; you already know where you ended up and how you got there.

USEFUL TERMS

Analogy An analogy examines a subject by comparing it point by point to something seemingly unlike but more commonplace and less complex. An analogy is also an extended metaphor.

Block comparison A comparison of x to y by grouping all that is to be compared under x and then following with the same information under y.

Comparison and contrast An examination of two or more subjects by exploring their similarities and differences. Similarities and differences are usually developed through literal and logical comparisons within like categories.

Metaphor An implied but direct comparison in which the primary term is made more vivid by associating it with a quite dissimilar term. "Life is a bed of roses" is a familiar metaphor.

Point by point A comparison that examines one or more points by stating the point, then comparing subject x to subject y, and then continuing to the next point.

➤ POINTERS FOR COMPARISON AND CONTRAST

Exploring the Topic

1. **What are the similarities?** What characteristics do your two subjects share? Are the two so similar that you have little to distinguish them? If so, try another subject; if not, pare down your list of similarities to the most important ones.

2. **What are the differences?** In what ways are your two subjects different? Are they so different that they have little in common? If so, make sure you can handle a humorous tone or try another subject; if not, pare down your list of differences to the most important ones.

3. **Should you emphasize similarities or differences?** Which pattern of organization best fits your material? Block? Point by point? A combination of the two?

4. **What examples will work best?** If your reader isn't familiar with your topic, what examples might be familiar? What examples will make clear what may be unfamiliar?

5. **What metaphor does your subject suggest?** Given the metaphor and your subject, what characteristics match? How can the metaphor be extended into an analogy? How can you outline the analogy as an equation? What equals what?

6. **What other modes are appropriate?** What modes can you draw on to help support your comparison and the organization of the essay? Do you need to define? Where can you use description? narration? example? Do any of your comparisons involve cause and effect?

7. **What is your point? your purpose?** Do you want to entertain, inform, persuade? Given your point as a tentative thesis, should you spell it out in the essay or imply it? If you are writing to inform, what information do you want to present? If you are writing to persuade, what do you want your reader to believe or do?

8. **What persona do you want to create?** Is it best for you to be a part of the comparison and contrast or to be an observer? Do you have a strongly held conviction about your subject? Do you want it to show? Does your persona fit your audience, purpose, and material?

Drafting the Paper

1. **Know your reader.** Use your first paragraph to set out your major terms and your general focus and to prepare the reader for the pattern of organization and tone that will follow. Reexamine your list of similarities and differences to see which ones may be unfamiliar to your reader. Jot down an illustration or brief description by each characteristic that the reader may not be familiar with. If your reader is part of the group you are examining, tread carefully, and if your teacher may have a bias about your topic, try to figure out what the bias is so you can counter it. Reread your paper from the perspective of the reader who is biased so that you can check your diction as well as your choice of examples and assertions.

2. **Know your purpose.** If you are writing to persuade, keep in mind the reader's possible bias or neutral view and see how you can use your persona as well as logical and emotional appeals to get the reader on your side. Informative papers run the risk of telling readers something they already know, so use description, detail, example, and diction to present your information in a new light. If your paper's main purpose is to entertain, these techniques become even more crucial. Try adding alliteration, allusions, paradox, and puns to the other techniques you draw on.

3. **If you use an analogy, double-check it.** Make sure your analogy is an extended metaphor, not a statement of fact. See what you want to empha-

size. Also make sure the placement is effective by trying out the analogy in different positions. Perhaps it works best as a framing device or standing alone in a sentence or paragraph.

4. **Use other modes to support your comparison.** Description and example are probably the most obvious modes to use, but consider narration, cause and effect, definition, and analogy as well. Perhaps a short narrative would add interest to your paper, or perhaps cause and effect enters into your comparisons. Definition may be vital to your thesis, and analogy may help clarify or expand a point.

5. **Check your pattern of organization.** If you are using block comparison, make sure you have introduced your two subjects and that your conclusion brings them back together. In the body of the paper, make sure that what you cover for one, you also cover for the other. In point-by-point comparison, check to see that your points are clearly set out. You may want to use both types of organization, though one will probably predominate.

6. **Make a point.** Perhaps you want to use your comparison to make a comment on the way we live, perhaps to clarify two items that people easily confuse, perhaps to argue that one thing is better than the other. Whatever your point, check it to make sure it is an assertion, not a mere fact. Whether your purpose is to inform or to persuade, take a stand and make sure that your thesis clearly implies or states it.

The Two Fundamental Kinds of Pasta

Marcella Hazan

*If you are at all familiar with cooking Italian food, then you already
know Marcella Hazan, for she is the foremost writer of cookbooks focusing on Italian cuisine. A native of Italy with a Ph.D. in biology,
she first began to teach Italian cooking in New York in 1969. She and
her husband now live in Venice, where she taught week-long master
cooking classes until 1998, and she frequently travels to the United
States. Her first book,* The Classic Italian Cookbook *(1973) was a
great success and followed by several others that were also popular.*
Marcella Cucina *is her latest (1997).*

WHAT TO LOOK FOR   *As you read Hazan's essay, you may find
that you are unfamiliar with some of her terms or, indeed, with cooking
pasta at all, to say nothing of knowing the difference between the homemade and store-bought varieties. Often, you will face the same problem
with your own essays, and when that happens, you can use the same
device Hazan uses—an analogy. After you've read the essay as a whole,
reread paragraphs 5 and 6 to understand how Hazan uses an analogy
to make her point about the differences between the two types of pasta.*

1   There are two broad categories within which are grouped all but
a few of the regional pasta specialties: There is homemade pasta
produced by hand, or with hand-operated tools, using soft wheat
flour and eggs; and there is industrially made, boxed pasta produced with semolina—hard wheat flour—and water.

2   Homemade egg pasta includes all the flat noodles—fettuccine,
tagliatelle, *pappardelle, tonnarelli,* lasagne—and the stuffed pastas;
ravioli, tortellini, *tortelloni, agnolotti, pansoti.*

3   When speaking of boxed semolina pasta we refer to such solid
shapes as spaghetti, spaghettini, linguine, fusilli, *farfalle* (bow ties),
and the hollow or cupped shapes such as penne, *maccheroni,* ziti,
rigatoni, *bucatini, conchiglie* (shells), *lumache* (snails).

4   Identifying their attributes, acquiring a sense of which sauces fit
them best, anticipating the different taste and texture sensations
each can deliver—these are the first necessary steps toward becoming a good pasta cook.

5   There is a critical difference in texture between homemade egg pasta and store-bought, boxed semolina pasta, a difference that I hope to make clear by reaching for a comparison outside the field of food. Imagine that there are two fabric houses, one specializing in spinning and weaving the fluffiest, most ethereal cashmere, the other producing linen that possesses a splendidly crisp, firm hand. The same designer may acquire cloth from both, but what he cuts and drapes with the cashmere will be different from what he tailors from the linen.

6   Egg pasta made at home is the cashmere; store-bought, factory-made semolina pasta is the linen. The latter has a hard, impenetrable surface that can carry olive oil-based sauces cleanly without becoming saturated, delivering taste that is lively and fresh. Homemade egg pasta has an almost invisible but open weave; it is porous and absorbent. You would hardly ever want to sauce egg pasta with olive oil, because when it sucks in that oil it develops an unpleasantly slick texture. What it really thirsts for is the luscious butter and cream sauces for which it is the ideal receptacle. Egg pasta embraces sauce; semolina pasta slips it on.

7   Although there exist deplorably ill-conceived machines for extruding spaghetti, *maccheroni* and other semolina pasta shapes in your kitchen, that is a product you don't ever want to make at home. Egg pasta, on the other hand, ought never to be made anywhere else.

THESIS AND ORGANIZATION

1. Where in the essay does Hazan use definition along with division and classification? What reasons can you think of for that placement?
2. Paragraphs 5 and 6 use analogy to explain the difference in the two types of pasta. Spell out the terms of the analogy.
3. Is the primary purpose of the essay to entertain? Argue? Inform? What reasons do you have for your choice?
4. Why is it important to know the difference between the two types of pasta?
5. Reread paragraphs 4, 7, and your answer to question 4. What do you deduce is the thesis?

TECHNIQUE AND STYLE

1. Describe the sort of reader the essay is addressed to. What evidence can you cite to support your opinion?

2. When you write an essay, you may find that you have to use terms the reader may not know. How does Hazan get around this problem? Give examples.
3. Reread paragraph 6, paying particular attention to Hazan's choice of verbs. What examples of unusual verbs can you find?
4. Analyze what you perceive to be Hazan's persona? Is she the kind of person you would like to have as a teacher? Why or why not?
5. What evidence can you find that Hazan's essay appeals to the senses? Which sense does she appeal to the most?

SUGGESTIONS FOR WRITING

Journal

1. Analogy can be a very useful device, one that can clarify yet make vivid a comparison. Consider an abstract term such as education, and then, based on your experiences, write a brief analogy for it. You might start with the idea, "My education can be compared to . . . "
2. This assignment is quite similar to the one above, but this time, think of an analogy for the process you go through when you write.

Essay

You can pattern your own comparison essay after Hazan's, filling in the blank with your idea about the "two fundamental kinds of . . ." Like Hazan, you will want to hedge a bit so that you don't imply that there are *only* two kinds; note that Hazan qualifies her terms with words such as *fundamental* and *broad*, adding that "all but a few of the regional pasta specialties" can fit into her categories. Possible subjects:
drivers
films
friends
teachers
pets
music groups

Lost in a Forrest

Scott Harpt

Scott Harpt transferred to Valley City State University in Valley City, North Dakota, enrolling in the freshman composition class where he wrote this essay. Harpt knew that "telling of achievements or fun times can be interesting. To expand though, it can be helpful to dig deeper and explore that which may be less comfortable." Having just read the novel Forrest Gump *and been moved by it, the book came naturally to mind when the assignment called for a comparison. Harpt comments: "Writing point by point was a great experience for me because it really showed me how to be organized. I found that the more structure I had, the better my thoughts flowed and the less I spent time with my fist under my chin just thinking. Organization and structure is not worth it if it inhibits your creativity, but if you can combine the two, it really works."*

Harpt finds that "If you really want to use your writing as a way to explore your inner feelings, and maybe learn something about yourself, it is vital that you eliminate pride and resolve you may be 'found out' a less than perfect person. That wasn't easy to do," Harpt adds, thinking back on his essay, "but it felt good when it was finished, and I believe readers appreciate the candor and commitment to the work." Those same qualities have followed Harpt through graduation from Valley City State, on to a master's degree at Central Michigan University, and into writing articles for the Journal *of* Evolutionary Psychology, *to say nothing of having a career as a special education teacher and coach (football and baseball) at Shiocton High School in Shiocton, Wisconsin. Given the character of* Forrest Gump, *in both the novel and the film, perhaps Harpt's comparison is ironic, for Gump is naive to the point of simple-mindedness, and his good luck comes more from accident than effort.*

WHAT TO LOOK FOR   *Although you will often want to place your thesis in your first paragraph or toward the end of your introduction, there's no rule that says that's what you have to do. You may find that your thesis carries more weight if you place it at the end of your essay, which is what Scott Harpt does. Note in his first paragraph, however, how he suggests where the essay is going to go.*

> *"Let me say this: Bein' a idiot is no box of chocolates."*
> *Forrest Gump*
>
> *"Let me say this: Being different, in any way, is no box of chocolates."*
> *Scott Harpt*

1   When I started reading the book *Forrest Gump*, I saw Forrest the same way most people did: big and stupid. He was easy to laugh at or make fun of. Half way through the text, I felt like I knew Forrest better, like we were friends. I felt more like defending him than making fun of him. By the end of the story, Forrest Gump was my hero. I cheered for him. I rooted for him. I cried for him. There was something about Forrest Gump that I could relate to personally. I saw myself in this self-proclaimed idiot.

2   As a young boy, Forrest was different than the other kids. He talked slow and had a very low I.Q. In fact, Forrest was permitted to enter the public school only after he first spent some time in a "special" one. He was teased a lot by the "normal kids." They laughed at him. They chased him. They were not his friends. He was alone.

3   As a young boy, I, Scott Harpt, was different than many of the other kids. I was chubby, not very smart, and too outgoing. I was often teased and made fun of by the "big kids," primarily because I was overweight. They laughed at me. They chased me. They were not my friends. Often, I was alone.

4   Eventually, Forrest grew. Although he never did develop much mentally, he excelled physically in several arenas. Forrest became an All-American football star for the University of Alabama. He won the Medal of Honor during the Vietnam War. He even became a world-wide table tennis champion. When Forrest Gump was accomplishing these things, the laughter was discontinued. They weren't making fun anymore. Forrest found himself surrounded with people who wanted to be his friends. He was no longer alone.

5   As time went by for me, my height caught up with my weight. I started exercising and learning about athletics. By the time high school rolled around, I was lean and strong, excelling in five different sports. Along the line somewhere, I became smarter too. I was prevailing in grades as well as sports and had acquired many friendships. On top of the world, I was a football star and a Homecoming King. The kids weren't laughing anymore; they looked up to me. I was their hero. I was no longer alone.

6   Forrest Gump was a hero while enjoying successes, but when his moment in the sun was over, and the spotlight was off of him, he found himself alone again, the idiot to be laughed at.

7   Since my athletic career has come to an end, and inactivity is prevalent, my chubbiness has made a comeback. Away from public attention, I find myself being treated differently. At 21 years old I see myself again, an overweight, lonely, little kid.

8   On the surface Forrest Gump and I are very different, but we share a brotherhood in our struggles: each wanting to be accepted and cared for; each fighting a prejudice that attacks our differences; each wanting "who he is" to be more important than "what he does."

THESIS AND ORGANIZATION

1. Apply the journalistic questions—*who? where? what? why? how?*— to the first paragraph. Which ones does it answer? What does it lead you to expect that follows in the rest of the essay?
2. The essay breaks into groups of paragraphs. What point is made by paragraphs 2 and 3?
3. What is the point of paragraphs 4 and 5?
4. What is the point of paragraphs 6 and 7?
5. The last paragraph sums up Harpt's thesis. State it in your own words.

TECHNIQUE AND STYLE

1. The essay begins with a headnote that quotes both the book and Harpt. How does it set the tone for what follows? How does it prepare you for the essay's organization?
2. Throughout the essay, Harpt carefully constructs his sentences about Gump to be parallel to those about himself. Explain the degree to which you find this technique effective?
3. The last paragraph is composed of one sentence that uses both a full colon and semicolons. Rewrite the sentence either as one sentence or more than one, using different punctuation. Which do you find the more effective and why?
4. How would you describe the tone of the essay? What evidence, if any, do you find that Harpt feels sorry for himself?
5. How would you describe Harpt's persona? Is he someone you would enjoy knowing? Why or why not?

SUGGESTIONS FOR WRITING

Journal

1. If you're familiar with either the book or film of *Forrest Gump,* compare your own experiences with his. Or, if you prefer, discuss whether or not you identified with Gump.

2. Think about the differences or similarities between an earlier version of yourself and the present one. You might think of a time when you started high school and compare it to how you felt when you started college. Focus on the emotions you felt and describe them.

Essay

Harpt compares himself to Forrest Gump, finding a superficial difference and deeper similarities. Think about people, real or fictional, you are familiar with and write your own comparison. Like Harpt, you may want to emphasize similarities, but, if you prefer, you can stress differences. You might want to use Harpt's organizational structure, pairing your paragraphs, but don't try to create parallel sentence structures unless you really want to. Start by making two columns, one for each of your subjects, and then fill in the similarities and differences. After you've worked up your notes into a draft, think about where the thesis will be most effective and place it there. For ideas about a subject, consider comparing yourself to a

parent
celebrity
political figure
friend
sibling

Of Prophets and Protesters

Robert C. Maynard

Huey Newton and Martin Luther King, Jr. are both African Americans, and for most of us the similarity ends there. In "Of Prophets and Protesters," however, Robert C. Maynard shows us that many more similarities tie the two together. Both cared deeply about their people and the poor, both were passionate speakers, both affected their generations, both led movements that affected American history, both died violently, both left legacies. There the similarity ends. One was admired, the other despised; one advocated non-violence, the other violence; one believed in democracy, the other in socialism; one was in the mainstream of the civil rights movement, the other on the radical fringe. Maynard's essay on the two men was published in 1989, appearing in his syndicated column carried by the Times-Picayune *of New Orleans.*

Until his death in 1993, Maynard, one of the most prominent African Americans in American journalism, was the editor and publisher of the Oakland Tribune *and was well known for his efforts to encourage minority journalists. As for Martin Luther King, Jr., biographies abound, and information on Huey Newton is readily available. The most recent account of Newton's life is Bobby Seale's* The Story of the Black Panther Party and Huey P. Newton *(1997).*

WHAT TO LOOK FOR   *When you write about a controversial subject, you have to be careful not to arouse the reader's negative associations. As you read Maynard's essay, notice how he deals with readers who may think of Newton as a racist and radical.*

1   If Huey Newton and Martin Luther King, Jr., ever met, they certainly formed no bond. They are bound nonetheless today by the common threads of how they lived and how each died. In one of history's curious accidents, their deaths help tell the tale of their times.

2   Dr. King and Huey Newton shared a deep concern for their people and for the plight of the poor. They aroused the passions of their generations. They were charismatic figures whose words were remembered and repeated. In different ways, the movements they led helped change America.

3   Dr. King was gunned down in Memphis, probably at the instigation of a hate group. Newton was gunned down in West Oakland,

probably the victim of criminal street activity. The full extent of his own criminal involvement is not altogether clear.

4   What is clear in the first half-light of history is how the two men differed. The work of one is revered in much of the nation, yet the activity of the other was reviled.

5   Newton was representative in the sixties and seventies of sharp and chic radical diversion from the mainstream of the civil rights movement. There were others, such as Stokely Carmichael and H. Rap Brown. Their criticism of Dr. King and the nonviolent movement was that it was too passive, even "Uncle Tom."

6   I covered many of those leaders before and after the split in the movement. I found the differences fascinating. So were some of the similarities. All agreed on one basic tenet: Racism was destroying black lives by the millions.

7   Newton, Carmichael, and Brown, though all critics of Dr. King, differed in their styles and approaches. They shared with each other and with Dr. King a great talent at articulating the nature of the inequities in our society.

8   The radicals differed among themselves and with Dr. King in the solutions they advocated. Newton and the Panthers were socialists and allied themselves with other fringe groups in the white community. Carmichael and Brown preached black nationalism and racial separation.

9   Dr. King preached democracy. He resisted those who would change ours to a socialist system. He also had no patience for those who advanced the idea that black people should have a state of their own. Dr. King believed black Americans contributed mightily to the shaping of America and were entitled to their fair share of the American dream.

10   The struggle of differing views did not die with Dr. King in 1968. Some of those arguments went full force into the decade of the seventies. By then, the Voting Rights Act and other reforms of the nonviolent movement began showing tangible results.

11   The fringe movements died. Their leaders had their 15 minutes of fame. H. Rap Brown took a Muslim life-style and name, and leads a very low-profile life. Stokely Carmichael pops up now and again, but he has a small following.

12   Dr. King, even in death, continues to command the conscience of the nation. This is so because his choice of a remedy was to resort to basic American principles of justice, fairness and equality.

13   To see the urban underclass is to recognize how much remains to be done. It is also worth noting that the violent streets that spawned the radical movements remain violent streets. It was on those streets that Huey Newton's life ended.

14   His death is a reminder that the civil rights movement spawned prophets and protesters. Dr. King pronounced a prophecy that remains a challenge to the conscience of our society. And, although Huey Newton and Dr. King differed on solutions, their deaths are joined as reminders of the nation's unfinished business.

THESIS AND ORGANIZATION

1. What tentative thesis does paragraph 1 suggest?
2. Which paragraphs focus on similarities?
3. Which paragraphs focus on differences? On both similarities and differences?
4. Paragraphs 10–14 deal with the time since Martin Luther King, Jr.'s death. What has changed? What has not changed?
5. Consider your answer to question 1 and the last sentence in paragraph 14. What is the essay's thesis?

TECHNIQUE AND STYLE

1. In what ways does the title fit the essay?
2. Huey Newton was a controversial figure who many readers may think of negatively. What is Maynard's view of Newton? How does he take negative opinions of Newton into account?
3. Maynard frequently uses parallelism to emphasize his points. Choose one example and rewrite the sentence so that the parallelism disappears or is strengthened. What is gained? Lost?
4. To what extent does Maynard rely on first person? What reasons can you find for his use of it?
5. Alliteration, the use of similar initial sounds, is a technique usually associated with poetry, not prose. What examples can you find in Maynard's essay? What do they add?

SUGGESTIONS FOR WRITING

Journal

1. Compare two people you admire and explain why you prefer one over the other.

2. Make a list of the characteristics Maynard associates with Huey Newton, and then explain why Newton should or should not be admired.

Essay

Think about two people who were different yet had an influence on those around them. Once you have chosen your subjects and jotted down some information about them, you are ready to draft an essay about them. The subjects you choose may be people you know or figures drawn from a more public arena. Suggestions based on your personal experience:

    relatives
    teachers
    religious persons

For suggestions based on general experience, think of figures who influenced their fields:

    sports
    music
    film
    medical research
    history
    politics

Two Ways to Belong in America

Bharati Mukherjee

You will find out much about Bharati Mukherjee as you read the essay that follows. What she does not say, however, is that she is the author of five novels, two short story collections, and two nonfiction books. Her sixth novel, Leave It to Me, *was published in 1997. Her essay also does not mention the numerous awards she has received, among them the 1988 National Book Critics' Circle Award (for her collection* The Middleman and Other Stories*) as well as Guggenheim and Canada Council grants and fellowships. Much of Mukherjee's writing focuses on the experiences of immigrants. That is also the focus of the essay that follows, one that appeared in the Op-Ed section of the* New York Times *on September 22, 1996, a time when the U.S. Congress, along with many states, was considering bills that would severely curtail the benefits of legal immigrants.*

WHAT TO LOOK FOR *Like Mukherjee, you may at times find yourself directly affected by a proposed law or political debate and you may want to make yourself heard about it. When that happens, you will probably want to begin by explaining how the proposal affects you personally. Yet to make your point to a wider audience, you will need to broaden it so that you speak not just for yourself, but for a larger group. As you read Mukherjee's essay, look for the ways in which she does just that, moving from the particular to the general, from personal narrative to a more universal stance.*

1   This is a tale of two sisters from Calcutta, Mira and Bharati, who have lived in the United States for some 35 years, but who find themselves on different sides in the current debate over the status of immigrants. I am an American citizen and she is not. I am moved that thousands of long-term residents are finally taking the oath of citizenship. She is not.

2   Mira arrived in Detroit in 1960 to study child psychology and pre-school education. I followed her a year later to study creative writing at the University of Iowa. When we left India, we were almost identical in appearance and attitude. We dressed alike, in saris; we expressed identical views on politics, social issues, love and marriage in the same Calcutta convent-school accent. We

would endure our two years in America, secure our degrees, then return to India to marry the grooms of our father's choosing.

3   Instead, Mira married an Indian student in 1962 who was getting his business administration degree at Wayne State University. They soon acquired the labor certifications necessary for the green card of hassle-free residence and employment.

4   Mira still lives in Detroit, works in the Southfield, Mich., school system, and has become nationally recognized for her contributions in the fields of pre-school education and parent-teacher relationships. After 36 years as a legal immigrant in this country, she clings passionately to her Indian citizenship and hopes to go home to India when she retires.

5   In Iowa City in 1963, I married a fellow student, an American of Canadian parentage. Because of the accident of his North Dakota birth, I bypassed labor-certification requirements and the race-related "quota" system that favored the applicant's country of origin over his or her merit. I was prepared for (and even welcomed) the emotional strain that came with marrying outside my ethnic community. In 33 years of marriage, we have lived in every part of North America. By choosing a husband who was not my father's selection, I was opting for fluidity, self-invention, blue jeans and T-shirts, and renouncing 3,000 years (at least) of caste-observant, "pure culture" marriage in the Mukherjee family. My books have often been read as unapologetic (and in some quarters overenthusiastic) texts for cultural and psychological "mongrelization." It's a word I celebrate.

6   Mira and I have stayed sisterly close by phone. In our regular Sunday morning conversations, we are unguardedly affectionate. I am her only blood relative on this continent. We expect to see each other through the looming crises of aging and ill health without being asked. Long before Vice President Gore's "Citizenship U.S.A." drive, we'd had our polite arguments over the ethics of retaining an overseas citizenship while expecting the permanent protection and economic benefits that come with living and working in America.

7   Like well-raised sisters, we never said what was really on our minds, but we probably pitied one another. She, for the lack of structure in my life, the erasure of Indianness, the absence of an unvarying daily core. I, for the narrowness of her perspective, her uninvolvement with the mythic depths or the superficial pop culture of this society. But, now, with the scapegoating of "aliens" (documented or illegal) on the increase, and the targeting of long-

term legal immigrants like Mira for new scrutiny and new self-consciousness, she and I find ourselves unable to maintain the same polite discretion. We were always unacknowledged adversaries, and we are now, more than ever, sisters.

8   "I feel used," Mira raged on the phone the other night. "I feel manipulated and discarded. This is such an unfair way to treat a person who was invited to stay and work here because of her talent. My employer went to the I.N.S. and petitioned for the labor certification. For over 30 years, I've invested my creativity and professional skills into the improvement of *this* country's pre-school system. I've obeyed all the rules, I've paid my taxes, I love my work, I love my students, I love the friends I've made. How dare America now change its rules in midstream? If America wants to make new rules curtailing benefits of legal immigrants, they should apply only to immigrants who arrive after those rules are already in place."

9   To my ears, it sounded like the description of a long-enduring, comfortable yet loveless marriage, without risk or recklessness. Have we the right to demand, and to expect, that we be loved? (That, to me, is the subtext of the arguments by immigration advocates.) My sister is an expatriate, professionally generous and creative, socially courteous and gracious, and that's as far as her Americanization can go. She is here to maintain an identity, not to transform it.

10   I asked her if she would follow the example of others who have decided to become citizens because of the anti-immigration bills in Congress. And here, she surprised me. "If America wants to play the manipulative game, I'll play it too," she snapped. "I'll become a U.S. citizen for now, then change back to Indian when I'm ready to go home. I feel some kind of irrational attachment to India that I don't to America. Until all this hysteria against legal immigrants, I was totally happy. Having my green card meant I could visit any place in the world I wanted to and then come back to a job that's satisfying and that I do very well."

11   In one family, from two sisters alike as peas in a pod, there could not be a wider divergence of immigrant experience. America spoke to me—I embraced the demotion from expatriate aristocrat to immigrant nobody, surrendering those thousands of years of "pure culture," the saris, the delightfully accented English. She retained them all. Which of us is the freak?

12   Mira's voice, I realize, is the voice not just of the immigrant South Asian community but of an immigrant community of the millions

who have stayed rooted in one job, one city, one house, one ancestral culture, one cuisine, for the entirety of their productive years. She speaks for greater numbers than I possibly can. Only the fluency of her English and the anger, rather than fear, born of confidence from her education, differentiate her from the seamstresses, the domestics, the technicians, the shop owners, the millions of hard-working but effectively silenced documented immigrants as well as their less fortunate "illegal" brothers and sisters.

13   Nearly 20 years ago, when I was living in my husband's ancestral homeland of Canada, I was always well-employed but never allowed to feel part of the local Quebec or larger Canadian society. Then, through a Green Paper that invited a national referendum on the unwanted side effects of "nontraditional" immigration, the Government officially turned against its immigrant communities, particularly those from South Asia.

14   I felt then the same sense of betrayal that Mira feels now. I will never forget the pain of that sudden turning, and the casual racist outbursts the Green Paper elicited. That sense of betrayal had its desired effect and drove me, and thousands like me, from the country.

15   Mira and I differ, however, in the ways in which we hope to interact with the country that we have chosen to live in. She is happier to live in America as expatriate Indian than as an immigrant American. I need to feel like a part of the community I have adopted (as I tried to feel in Canada as well). I need to put roots down, to vote and make the difference that I can. The price that the immigrant willingly pays, and that the exile avoids, is the trauma of self-transformation.

THESIS AND ORGANIZATION

1. It's possible to identify Mukherjee's introduction as her first paragraph or as paragraphs 1–5. Make a case for what you find best serves to introduce the essay.

2. Trace the essay's pattern of organization. Is it block, point by point, or a mixture of the two? If the latter, which paragraphs conform to which pattern?

3. Paragraphs 13 and 14 provide a brief narrative of Mukherjee's experience in Canada. What happened and how did it affect her?

4. Where in the essay does Mukherjee broaden the base of her narrative? Why might she have chosen the examples she uses?

5. The essay deals with a number of topics—the "trauma of self-transformation" (paragraph 15), the injustice of the proposed laws, the concept of citizenship, the plight of the immigrant, the question of what it means to hold a green card. What do you find to be the essay's major focus and what is Mukherjee saying about that subject?

TECHNIQUE AND STYLE

1. How would you describe Mukherjee's tone? Does it change in the course of the essay and if so, where and how?
2. Mukherjee makes extensive use of quotation marks (paragraphs 5–8 and 10–13). To what different uses does she put them? What do they add to the essay?
3. What facts do you come to know about Mukherjee's family? What do they add to the essay's point? To Mukherjee's persona?
4. *Immigrant* has many connotations. What are some of them? Where in the essay does Mukherjee allude to the word's connotations? Why does she do so?
5. Mukherjee poses a question at the end of paragraph 11. What is her implied answer? How does her answer relate to the essay's thesis?

SUGGESTIONS FOR WRITING

Journal

1. Write a page or two that records your associations with the word *immigrant*.
2. If you were to move to another country and work there, would you be more likely to become like Mukherjee or her sister?

Essay

Mukherjee describes two ways of looking at a culture, from the outside looking in and from the inside looking out—perspectives all of us are used to. Write your own essay comparing the two views, drawing on your own experiences and that of others to make your point. For suggestions, think of two ways of examining a topic:

what you thought college was going to be like and what you actually found it to be like

what you expected from a job and what you learned

If you prefer, write an essay in which you analyze what it means to have a certain privilege compared to not having it. Suggestions:

a driver's license

a voter's card

membership in a certain group

a green card

The Raven

Barry Lopez

Although Barry Lopez was born in Port Chester, New York, he spent much of his early life in southern California, and it was there where he first fell in love with landscapes in general and deserts in particular, the Mojave Desert to be precise. After returning to New York and then graduating from Notre Dame with a major in English, he became a professional photographer specializing in nature and landscape scenes. Finding that his lens didn't get close enough to nature, he turned to writing, traveling the world to write about its wonders. His work is published regularly in journals such as Harper's Magazine *and* The Paris Review, *and his list of books is a long and distinguished one.* Of Wolves and Men *(1982) received the John Burroughs Medal for distinguished natural history writing, and* Arctic Dreams: Imagination and Desire in a Northern Landscape *(1986) won the National Book Award for Best Book of Nonfiction. His most recent book is* About This Life: Journeys on the Threshold of Memory *(1998). Lopez's writing has often been compared to that of Henry David Thoreau. According to one interviewer, Lopez "brings an acute sense of obligation to detail and integrity with his every observance, and something that can only be described as a spiritually driven, almost Zen-like regard for non-fiction." The essay that follows appeared in* Desert Notes: Reflections in the Eye of a Raven *(1976).*

WHAT TO LOOK FOR   *You'll find that Lopez's essay rides a fine line between fantasy and reality, although his point is a serious one. In that sense, you can read the piece as a sort of fable, much like those of Aesop, the sixth century Greek who wrote the still familiar tale of the tortoise and the hare, among many others. The idea of depicting animals with human traits is still much with us though the creatures have changed into the likes of the Roadrunner and Mickey Mouse.*

1   I am going to have to start at the other end by telling you this: there are no crows in the desert. What appear to be crows are ravens. You must examine the crow, however, before you can understand the raven. To forget the crow completely, as some have tried to do, would be like trying to understand the one who stayed without talking to the one who left. It is important to make note of who has left the desert.

2   To begin with, the crow does nothing alone. He cannot abide silence and he is prone to stealing things, twigs and bits of straw, from the nests of his neighbors. It is a game with him. He enjoys tricks. If he cannot make up his mind the crow will take two or three wives, but this is not a game. The crow is very accommodating and he admires compulsiveness.

3   Crows will live in street trees in the residential areas of great cities. They will walk at night on the roofs of parked cars and peck at the grit; they will scrape the pinpoints of their talons across the steel and, with their necks outthrust, watch for frightened children listening in their beds.

4   Put all this to the raven: he will open his mouth as if to say something. Then he will look the other way and say nothing. Later, when you have forgotten, he will tell you he admires the crow.

5   The raven is larger than the crow and has a beard of black feathers at his throat. He is careful to kill only what he needs. Crows, on the other hand, will search out the great horned owl, kick and punch him awake, and then, for roosting too close to their nests, they will kill him. They will come out of the sky on a fat, hot afternoon and slam into the head of a dozing rabbit and go away laughing. They will tear out a whole row of planted corn and eat only a few kernels. They will defecate on scarecrows and go home and sleep with 200,000 of their friends in an atmosphere of congratulation. Again, it is only a game; this should not be taken to mean that they are evil.

6   There is however this: when too many crows come together on a roost there is a lot of shoving and noise and a white film begins to descend over the crows' eyes and they go blind. They fall from their perches and lie on the ground and starve to death. When confronted with this information, crows will look past you and warn you vacantly that it is easy to be misled.

7   The crow flies like a pigeon. The raven flies like a hawk. He is seen only at a great distance and then not very clearly. This is true of the crow too, but if you are very clever you can trap the crow. The only way to be sure what you have seen is a raven is to follow him until he dies of old age, and then examine the body.

8   Once there were many crows in the desert. I am told it was like this: you could sit back in the rocks and watch a pack of crows working over the carcass of a coyote. Some would eat, the others would try to squeeze out the vultures. The raven would never be seen. He would be at a distance, alone, perhaps eating a scorpion.

9   There was, at this time, a small alkaline water hole at the desert's edge. Its waters were bitter. No one but crows would drink there, although they drank sparingly, just one or two sips at a time. One day a raven warned someone about the dangers of drinking the bitter water and was overheard by a crow. When word of this passed among the crows they felt insulted. They jeered and raised insulting gestures to the ravens. They bullied each other into drinking the alkaline water until they had drunk the hole dry and gone blind.

10   The crows flew into canyon walls and dove straight into the ground at forty miles an hour and broke their necks. The worst of it was their cartwheeling across the desert floor, stiff wings outstretched, beaks agape, white eyes ballooning, suprising rattlesnakes hidden under sage bushes out of the noonday sun. The snakes awoke, struck and held. The wheeling birds strew them across the desert like sprung traps.

11   When all the crows were finally dead, the desert bacteria and fungi bored into them, burrowed through bone and muscle, through aqueous humor and feathers until they had reduced the stiff limbs of soft black to blue dust.

12   After that, there were no more crows in the desert. The few who watched from a distance took it as a sign and moved away.

13   Finally there is this: one morning four ravens sat at the edge of the desert waiting for the sun to rise. They had been there all night and the dew was like beads of quicksilver on their wings. Their eyes were closed and they were as still as the cracks in the desert floor.

14   The wind came off the snow-capped peaks to the north and ruffled their breath feathers. Their talons arched in the white earth and they smoothed their wings with sleek, dark bills. At first light their bodies swelled and their eyes flashed purple. When the dew dried on their wings they lifted off from the desert floor and flew away in four directions. Crows would never have had the patience for this.

15   If you want to know more about the raven: bury yourself in the desert so that you have a commanding view of the high basalt cliffs where he lives. Let only your eyes protrude. Do not blink—the movement will alert the raven to your continued presence. Wait until a generation of ravens has passed away. Of the new generation there will be at least one bird who will find you. He will see your eyes staring up out of the desert floor. The raven is cautious, but he is thorough. He will sense your peaceful intentions. Let him have the first word. Be careful: he will tell you he knows nothing.

16   If you do not have the time for this, scour the weathered desert shacks for some sign of the raven's body. Look under old mattresses and beneath loose floorboards. Look behind the walls. Sooner or later you will find a severed foot. It will be his and it will be well preserved.

17   Take it out in the sunlight and examine it closely. Notice that there are three fingers that face forward, and a fourth, the longest and like a thumb, that faces to the rear. The instrument will be black but no longer shiny, the back of it sheathed in armor plate and the underside padded like a wolf's foot.

18   At the end of each digit you will find a black, curved talon. You will see that the talons are not as sharp as you might have suspected. They are made to grasp and hold fast, not to puncture. They are more like the jaws of a trap than a fistful of ice picks. The subtle difference serves the raven well in the desert. He can weather a storm on a barren juniper limb; he can pick up and examine the crow's eye without breaking it.

THESIS AND ORGANIZATION

1. Reread paragraph 1. What does it imply about the rest of the essay? How does it set up the focus of paragraphs 2–4?
2. What does Lopez tell you about the crow? Write down the details and the paragraphs they come from.
3. What does Lopez tell you about the raven? Write down the details and the paragraphs they come from.
4. What do paragraphs 15–18 convey about the relationship between humans and ravens?
5. To come up with a thesis for the essay, first think about the crow versus the raven: which one does Lopez prefer and why? Take your answer to that question and add to it your answer to question 4. Then reduce your responses to a one-sentence assertion and that will be the thesis.

TECHNIQUE AND STYLE

1. To what extent does Lopez's essay fit the genre of the fable? Does it have a moral? If so, what is it?
2. How would you describe the tone of the essay?
3. To what extent does Lopez use the first person pronoun *I*? What reasons can you discover for the degree to which he uses it?

4. If you are familiar with the desert, to what extent does Lopez portray it realistically? If you are not familiar with the desert, to what extent does he make you understand what it is like?

5. Reread the essay, marking every time Lopez mentions *patience*, either directly or indirectly. What is he saying about patience? How does that point reinforce the tone of the essay?

SUGGESTIONS FOR WRITING

Journal

1. Take a few minutes to write up your response to Lopez's essay. Do you have questions about it? To what extent did you like or dislike it and why?

2. We often discover human characteristics in animals we know well, pets in particular. Describe an animal you know well attributing human traits to it.

Essay

Write your own version of a fable or semifable. Like Lopez, you may want to mix fantasy and reality, or you may want to shape your tone to the one or the other. To start off with, consider a possible subject such as two similar

> animals
> clothing styles
> foods
> game shows
> text books

Once you have a topic to work with, decide on the kind of tone you want for the essay and then start to play with characteristics that you can attribute to your choices. If it's a fable that you're writing, you can be an observer, like Lopez, or remove yourself from the narrative and have the characters speak for themselves.

On Using
Process

7

I f you have ever been frustrated in your attempts to put together a barbecue grill or hook up a stereo system, you know the value of clear and
complete directions. And if you have tried to explain how to get to a particular house or store, you also know that being able to give clear directions is not as easy as it seems. We deal with this practical, how-to kind of
process analysis every day in recipes, user's manuals, and instruction
booklets. Basic to this process is dividing the topic into the necessary
steps, describing each step in sufficient detail, and then sequencing the
steps so they are easy to follow. You can also help by anticipating trouble
spots. If you were writing a set of directions for a barbecue grill, for example, you might start by describing the parts that must be put together
so that you familiarize the reader with them and force a quick inventory.
And if the plans call for 12 screws but the packaging includes 15, telling
the reader that there are three extra will stave off the inevitable "I must
have done it wrong" that leftover parts usually elicit.

But writing directions is only one kind of process analysis. "How
does it work?" and "How did it happen?" are questions that get at other
sorts of processes—the scientific and the historical. Lab reports exemplify scientific process analysis, as do the kinds of papers published in
Scientific American or the *New England Journal of Medicine*. Like the
practical, how-to process paper, the report of an experiment or explanation of a physical process clearly marks the steps in a sequence. The
same is true of essays that rely on historical process, though sometimes
it's harder to discern the steps. A paper that analyzes how the United
States became involved in the Vietnam War, for instance, identifies the
major stages of involvement and their chronology, the steps that led up
to open warfare. Essays that focus on a historical process often con-
dense time in a way that practical or scientific process analysis does not,
but the chronology itself is still important.

Although process analysis is usually associated with specialized subjects—how to do *x*, how *y* works, or how *z* came about—it also finds its way into less formal prose. If you were to write about how you got interested in a hobby, for instance, you would be using process analysis, as you would if you were writing an explanatory research paper on the history of Coca-Cola. Process analysis is also useful as a means of discovery. If you were to analyze the process you go through to revise a draft of one of your papers, you might find out that you overemphasize a particular stage or leave out a step. It's easy to underrate process analysis as a way of thinking and expressing ideas, because it is often equated with the simpler forms of how-to writing.

AUDIENCE AND PURPOSE

The concept of audience is crucial to process essays, for you must know just how familiar the reader is with the topic so you know what you need to explain and how to explain it. Familiar topics present you with a challenge, for how can you interest your readers in a subject they already know something about? The answer lies in what you have to say about that subject and how you say it. A seemingly dull topic such as making bread can be turned into an interesting paper if you start with the negative associations many readers have about the topic—air bread, that tasteless, white, compactible substance better suited to bread ball fights than human consumption—and then go on to describe how to make the kind of bread that is chewy, substantive, tasty, and worth $4.50 a loaf in a specialty food store.

Your purpose in such an essay is informative, but if you want your essay to be read by people who don't have to read it, then you need to make your approach to your subject interesting as well. A straightforward, follow steps 1–10, how-to essay will get the job done, but unless the need for the information is pressing, no one will read it. But if you relate the bread-baking process, for example, so that your reader enjoys the essay, then even the person who would never willingly enter a kitchen will probably keep reading.

If what you have to say involves a personal subject, you need to present the information in a believable way, and at the same time, adjust it to the level of the audience. The process involved in friends growing apart, for instance, can be explained in terms so personal that only the writer could appreciate it. If that were your topic, you would need to gear your description to the general reader who may have experienced something similar. That way, you would place your personal narrative into a larger, more general context.

On the other hand, if you know not only more but also more specialized information than the reader, you must be careful to make sure your audience is following every step. Sometimes a writer explores a process to inform the reader and other times to persuade, but always the writer has an assertion in mind and is trying to affect the reader. If, for example, you enjoy scuba diving and you're trying to describe the physiological effects the body is subject to when diving, you might first describe the necessary equipment and then take the reader on a dive, emphasizing the different levels of atmospheric pressure—the instant and constant need to equalize the air pressure in your ears, the initial tightness of your mask as you sink to 10 feet, the gradual "shrinking" of your wet suit as the pressure increases with the depth of the dive. Then after a quick tour of the kinds of fish, sea creatures, and coral formations you see during the dive, you would return your reader to the surface, stopping at 15 feet to release the buildup of nitrogen in the blood. The whole process may strike your reader as not worth the risk, so you would want to make sure not only that your thesis counters that opinion, but also that you describe what you see, so the attractions outweigh the hazards and momentary discomfort.

SEQUENCE

Chronology is as crucial to process as it is to narration. In fact, it is inflexible. A list of the ingredients in the bread has to precede baking instructions; a quick safety check of the necessary equipment has to come before the dive. And then you must account for all the important steps. If time is crucial to the process, then you have to account for it also, although in a historical process essay, time is apt to be compressed or deemphasized to underscore a turning point. An essay on the Civil Rights movement, for instance, might well begin with a brief account of the slave trade, even though the body of the paper focuses on the 1950s and 1960s, culminating with the assassination of Martin Luther King in 1968. And if you were to identify King's death as the turning point in the movement, you would emphasize the chronology and character of the events leading up to and following his assassination.

Undergirding the concept of sequence, of course, is the pattern of cause and effect—in the example above, you might want to explore the effect of King's death on the Civil Rights movement. What's most important to process analysis, however, is neither cause nor effect, but the stages or steps, the chronology of events. Without a set sequence or chronology, neither cause nor effect would be clear.

OTHER MODES

In writing a process analysis, you will draw on the same skills you use for description, narration, definition, and example papers, for without supporting details and examples to further and describe the process, a process essay can be tedious indeed. An essay on the Civil Rights movement would probably need to draw on statistics—such as the percentage of the population held in slavery in 1860—as well as examples of protests and boycotts, and quotations from those involved, both for and against equal rights for African Americans. An essay on scuba diving may need to define some terms and bring in examples from mathematics and physiology, as well as from scientific articles on the relative health of coral reefs in the Caribbean. Incorporating references to well-known people—a Mohammed Ali or a Jacques Cousteau—or to current events or adding a narrative example or even an amusing aside can make what might otherwise be little more than a list into an interesting paper.

TRANSITIONS

To make the stages of the process clear, you will need to rely on logically placed transitions that lead the reader from one stage to the next. Most writers try to avoid depending only on obvious links, such as *first, next, next,* and instead use chronology, shifts in tense, and other indicators of time to spell out the sequence. The process itself may have clear markers that you can use as transitions. An essay explaining a historical event, for instance, will have pegs such as specific dates or actions that you can use to indicate the next stage in the sequence.

THESIS AND ORGANIZATION

The body of a process essay almost organizes itself because it is made up of the steps you have identified, and they must occur in a given sequence. Introductions and conclusions are trickier, as is the thesis, for you must not only set out a process but also make an assertion about it. Your thesis should confront the reader with a point, implicit or explicit, about the process involved, and in so doing, head off the lethal response, "So what?"

USEFUL TERMS

Chronology The time sequence involved in events; what occurred when.

Process analysis A type of analysis that examines a topic to discover the series of steps or acts that brought or will bring about a particular result. Whereas cause and effect analysis emphasizes *why*, process emphasizes *how*.

➤ POINTERS FOR USING PROCESS

Exploring the Topic

1. **What kind of process are you presenting?** Is it a practical, "how-to" process? A historical one? A scientific one? Some mixture of types?
2. **What steps are involved?** Which are crucial? Can some be grouped together? Under what headings can they be grouped?
3. **What is the sequence of the steps?** Are you sure that each step logically follows the one before it?
4. **How familiar is your reader with your subject?** Within each step (or group of steps), what information does the reader need to know? What details can you use to make that information come alive? What examples? What connections can you make to what the reader already knows? Do you use any terms that need to be defined?
5. **Is setting or context important?** If so, what details of the setting or context do you want to emphasize?
6. **What is the point you want to make about the process?** Is your point an assertion? Will it interest the reader?

Drafting the Paper

1. **Know your reader.** Using two columns, list what your reader may know about your topic in one and what your reader may not know in the other. If you are writing about a practical process, figure out what pitfalls your reader may be subject to. If you are writing about a historical or scientific process, make sure your diction suits your audience. Be on the lookout

for events or actions that need further explanation to be understood by a general audience. If your reader is apt to have a bias against your topic, know what that bias is. If your topic is familiar, shape your first paragraph to enlist the reader's interest; if the topic is unfamiliar, use familiar images to explain it.

2. **Know your purpose.** If you are writing to inform, make sure you are presenting new information and that you are making an assertion about your topic. Don't dwell on information that the reader already knows if you can possibly avoid it. If you are writing to persuade, remember that you do not know whether your audience agrees with you. Use your persona to lend credibility to what you say, and use detail to arouse your reader's sympathies.

3. **Define your terms.** Think through the process you have chosen for your topic to make sure that your reader is familiar with all the terms associated with it. If any of those terms are technical or unusual ones, be sure you define them clearly.

4. **Present the steps in their correct sequence.** Make sure that you have accounted for all the important steps or stages in the process and that they are set out in order. If two or more steps occur at the same time, make sure you have made that clear. If time is crucial to your process, see that you have emphasized that point. If, on the other hand, the exact time at which an event occurred is less important than the event itself, make sure you have stressed the event and have subordinated the idea of time.

5. **Use details and examples.** Whether you are writing an informative or a persuasive essay, use details and examples that support your purpose. If you are explaining how to make your own ice cream, for example, draw on what the reader knows about various commercial brands and flavors to bolster the case for making your own. After all, your reader may not want to take the time and trouble to complete that process and may have to be enticed into trying it. Choose details and examples that combat your reader's negative associations.

6. **Double-check your transitions.** First mark your stages with obvious transitions or with numbers. After you have turned your notes into a working draft, review and revise the transitions you have used, checking to see that they exist, that they are clear, and that they are not overly repetitious or obvious. Make sure each important stage (or group of stages) is set off by a transition. See if you can indicate shifts by using verb tense or words and phrases that don't call attention to themselves as transitions.

7. **Make a point.** What you say about a subject is far more interesting than the subject itself, so even if you are writing a practical process essay, make sure you have a point. A paper on a topic such as "how to change a tire" becomes unbearable without a thesis. Given an assertion about changing a tire—"Changing my first flat was as horrible as I had expected it to be"—the paper at least has a chance.

Runner

Laura Carlson

Running has been a sport Laura Carlson has enjoyed for the past 10 years, both on her own and for her school. Now a junior at Valley City State University in Valley City, North Dakota, she wrote the essay that follows in a class taught by Noreen Braun, who reprinted the essay on a web page devoted to what she titled as "Some Fine Student Writing from Composition I, Fall Semester, 1997." Thinking about the essay and reading it over, she comments: "I am really taken aback. I remember writing it and thinking that this is my favorite type of writing, descriptive, and that I could really do a good job on it—if I wanted to. It was really hard for me to sit down and write something with a due date. One thing I did was to basically forget that I had to do it for class, but that I had to write the essay for myself."

Stumped for a subject, Carlson thought about what she enjoyed and came up with the topic that is the title of the essay. She notes that the idea for the essay "came naturally to me. I actually went out that day to run." Thinking about that experience, she "tried to remember what it had been like; the feelings that I felt, the cold and the pictures in my mind, and I tried to incorporate them back into my writing. I think it really worked. I really just wrote about what I knew and how I really felt. Visualization was the key to my success with this essay." What worked for Laura may well work for you.

WHAT TO LOOK FOR   *Not everyone knows what it feels like to run for a fairly long distance, and even those who do may not know what it's like to do that on a cold North Dakota morning. To make her experience come alive and to make it immediate, Carlson, therefore, chooses the present tense and descriptive details. The result is an essay that explains the process she goes through when she runs and makes the reader feel what Carlson feels.*

1   When I wake up this morning, I can feel the chill of the air in my joints. I am almost reluctant to give up the warmth of my bed, but I know I need to. Slowly, I step out of my bed and quickly throw on a sweatshirt and pants. Leaving my room, still tired, but slowly awakening, I yawn.

2   I stretch my tired limbs, first my arms, then my legs. Noticing a tightness in my right hip, I take a little extra time to stretch it. I am

still moving slowly as if in a drugged stupor. Maybe I should just go back to bed. Before I change my mind, I hurry outside into the brisk early morning air. I take three or four breaths to acclimate myself to the cold, cold air. I can see my breath on the air in little white puffs. I want to reach out as if I could float away with the rising mist. It is still dark outside. The sun hasn't quite poked his head out to greet the day. The blue black sky is waiting to engulf me as his arms extend as far as I can see.

3   Running on an October morning is so exhilarating! I think it is only about 20 degrees this morning. I am so cold!

4   My steps are slow to start. I feel my legs tighten and restrain me, not wanting to exert the effort to propel me forward, yet I know that it is mind over matter and I am going to win this battle! I tell myself that I need to get ready for the big meet that is coming up at the end of the month. My adrenaline is pumping and my mind is whirling at a mile a minute taking in the frosty scenery that is surrounding me. The trees are covered in a fine layer of crystals forming together to make a wintry scene unlike any other I have seen yet this season. My breathing is accelerating and my pulse is beating in my ears. The biting cold is gnawing at my skin. I refuse to give into the cold of the air and the gripping of my lungs.

5   As I slowly retreat into a solid pace, my body is more aware of my feet steadily pounding on the pavement and of the crunching of the leaves and twigs as they collapse under the weight of my body. The burning in my lungs is lessening as my pace is increasing. The steady flow of traffic helps keep my mind from wandering and keeps me focused. I only have a couple of miles to go. My nose is running just as fast as my feet. I feel the slight burning as if the air were actually freezing the breath entering and exiting my nostrils.

6   I can tell by the landmarks of the city that I am closing in on my destination: home. I pass the fenced-in yard with the barking dog who chooses to torment me each time I pass. I keep running, my pace not faltering. As I come within three blocks of my house, I pick up my pace as if in a race. I am feeling winded as my stride lengthens and my breathing becomes much more shallow. I am almost home. The scenery is changing as the sun has finally approached the horizon. The hues of the sky are changing rapidly with the approaching daylight.

7   My house is in sight. I slow my pace to a fast walk and slowly make my way to my driveway. I take deep breaths to get used to

the different pace. I am done for another day. I feel refreshed and awakened. I am now ready to continue with another day.

THESIS AND ORGANIZATION

1. Which paragraph or paragraphs make up the essay's introduction. What does it tell you?
2. Trace the process of Carlson's preparation for running. What paragraphs describe it?
3. Trace the process of the run itself. What paragraphs describe it?
4. One technique Carlson uses to avoid the stilted *first-next-then* marking of the essay's chronology is to use the progress of the sunlight. Where in the essay does she note that progress?
5. Is Carlson's thesis stated or implied? What evidence can you find to support your idea?

TECHNIQUE AND STYLE

1. Carlson gives the essay unity by frequently referring to the weather. What descriptive details does she use?
2. Throughout the essay, Carlson uses the first person *I*. Does she avoid overusing it or not? How can you back up your opinion?
3. In paragraph 2, Carlson personifies the sun and the sky by referring to them with the pronoun *he*. What would be lost without that personification? What is gained?
4. The first sentence of paragraph 6 uses a full colon. What other punctuation could be used? Which is the most effective and why?
5. Reread the last paragraph. How else might the essay have ended that would fit in with what has come before? Which is the more effective ending and why?

SUGGESTIONS FOR WRITING

Journal

1. Write your own last paragraph for the essay and then, briefly, explain why you think it is better or not as good as Carlson's.
2. Briefly describe the feelings you have when you are involved in a sport, either as a spectator or a participant.

Essay

Like Carlson, you might start by thinking about what you enjoy. Perhaps it's a sport or a hobby, but no matter what the subject you can use Carlson's essay as a model to write your own description of the process involved. You may find it easiest to start with the process, jotting down the steps or stages. Then once you have a rough draft, you can decide on the kind of introduction and conclusion that would be most effective for the essay, and, of course, where best to put the thesis, if you want to state rather than imply it. Suggestions for a topic:

playing a sport
being involved with your hobby
playing a card game
cooking a favorite dish
enjoying a "do nothing" day

How to Swat a Fly

Will Cuppy

Writing in the tradition of American humorists that found humor by poking fun at what is often taken seriously (too seriously, they would say), Will Cuppy's essays appeared in both newspapers and magazines. Born in Indiana, he later moved to Illinois where he earned his BA and MA degrees from the University of Chicago, while at the same time beginning his career in journalism writing for Chicago's newspapers. Most of his career, however, was spent in New York, where he became a book reviewer for the New York Herald Tribune *as well as a frequent contributor to the* New Yorker *and the* Saturday Evening Post.

The Bronx Zoo became one of Cuppy's favorite haunts, and that is where his observations of animal behavior evolved into his mock-scientific essays about humans and other creatures. How to Tell Your Friends from the Apes *(1931) gathered together many of the pieces he wrote for the* New Yorker, *and that same tone is echoed in* The Great Bustard and Other People *(1941) as well as his posthumously published* The Decline and Fall of Practically Everybody *(1950). "How to Swat a Fly," the essay that follows, appeared in* How to Attract the Wombat *(1949), but flies haven't changed much.*

WHAT TO LOOK FOR   *Dullness is a cardinal sin for any piece of prose, and it's the main danger in essays that describe processes. These types of essays are apt to fall too easily into the first-second-third enumerating of steps (*first-next-then *is almost as deadly), and the thesis can easily slide into what is obvious instead of an assertion. Cuppy's essay dodges around being boring by using humor and by commenting on the steps he sets out, techniques you can use in your own writing.*

1   Being as sound in mind and body as I am ever likely to be, I have decided to release my notes on Fly-swatting made from time to time during many years of active service at my Long Island beach cottage, Chez Cuppy. (It's the same old place I used to call Tobacco Road, but I think the new name sort of lends a tone—and, besides, it's a change.) In the belief that Fly-swatting is here to stay for awhile, DDT and other squirts to the contrary notwithstanding, I am passing on the torch in Ten Easy Lessons, as follows:

1. Get set. Be sure you're not going to fall off your chair backwards in the act of swatting. Here as elsewhere, style is everything.

2. Still, don't take too much time with the preliminaries. The Fly won't wait there forever. He has other things to do with his time.

3. Try to ascertain in some unobtrusive way whether the object you're after is actually a Fly or a nail head, such as often occurs in the woodwork of country homes. Don't go poking at the thing to see which it is. When in doubt, swat.

2   Little situations like this are bound to occur in every swatter's routine. For instance, there is a small black spot on the ceiling of my bedroom that has embarrassed me dozens of times, it looks so exactly like a Fly of some large and vicious species. If I have crept up on it once—Oh, well! Stalking an imperfection in the paint and swinging one's heart out at a nail head are not things one likes to remember, but perhaps they have their place in the give and take of daily living. We can't be heroes to ourselves every instant.

3   *4.* In any case, never flirt your swatter back and forth past a Fly before swatting, expecting to get him your next time around. When you finally make up your mind to hit him, he will not be there. The Fly who hesitates is lost. He knows this and acts accordingly.

4   *5.* Take aim quickly but carefully. A complete miss is not good for the morale, either yours or the Fly's.

5   *6.* If possible, fix him with the first swat. Failure to do so may be serious. For one thing, you didn't get him. That alone is bad. Secondly, conditions will never be quite the same again, since you are now dealing with an alert and disillusioned Fly. He is never going to trust you as he did before. He will avoid you in the future.

6   That was one of the many faults of my dear Aunt Etta's swatting. She never hit her Fly the first time and she seldom came anywhere near him on repeated attempts, partly because she employed the worst of all swatting techniques, the folded newspaper, or motion, method. She would lunge at the Fly again and yet again with her antiquated weapon in a free-for-all that left her exhausted and the Fly in the best of health and spirits. A folded newspaper is only about 17 per cent efficient in anybody's hands, and Aunt Etta's form was nothing to boast of. Her batting average must have been something incredible. I'm glad to state that she often thought she had won. Her eyesight wasn't so good, either.

7   I assure you that Aunt Etta was one of the kindest persons I have ever known, though not so soft about Flies as my Uncle Theodore

did so much in his day to encourage the spread of typhoid fever and other diseases. There was certainly no sadistic urge in her swatting activities. She never engaged a Fly in hand-to-hand combat until after she and we children had staged a ceremonious Fly-drive with kitchen aprons and dish towels, then a second and often a third to chase the last one out the open screen door. It was only the Fly or Flies who failed to respect these rites that she tackled, and it always amazed me that there would be any such. If we thought Aunt Etta had one of her headaches, or felt a nap coming on, or couldn't stand such a racket—in which case she would tell us so in no uncertain terms—we disappeared. We vanished utterly, with the usual gift of cookies. But Flies are not brought up that way, apparently. They cannot take a hint.

8   The family would want me to add that Aunt Etta's house was no more Fly-ridden than any other home of the period. In fact, it was less so than most, as it was thoroughly screened. Which reminds me that she never did, to my knowledge, solve the riddle of how they got in. She was always saying there wasn't a crack where they could squeeze through. All right, then, how did the Mouse get in?

7. Don't mind a little incidental breakage around the house. Aunt a was much too careful of her bric-a-brac. She wouldn't strike in yards of her whatnot when a Fly took sanctuary there. For ause I would smash anything in Chez Cuppy to smithereens, possibly my shaving mirror. I'm not having seven years of for any Fly.

'vate patience. It is a beautiful thing in itself, and when er a Fly who will not light, you will need it. Eventually light, and ten to one it will be in some dark, inaccessi-wn behind the stove.

o absolutely refuses to settle is a problem for ad-and not an easy one. Talk about a watched pot! a a Fly too openly, but try to act as though you something else altogether. This involves looking while gazing fixedly in the other direction, but ractice. It is my opinion that a Fly will not set-ng straight at him with a swatter in your fist. ile you are following him around the room, ieve me, he knows what you are up to.

g.
ere
that
low
gain
usted
per is
t Etta's
e been
ght she
ns I have
oby, who

12 I would go so far as to say that a Fly knows the exact moment when you start looking for a swatter, if you should be caught without one. Edge yourself ever so casually in the general direction of a swatter, and notice what happens. Other persons who may be present will simply wonder why you are hitching your chair along in that insane fashion or tiptoeing across the room with one groping hand outstretched and a haunted look in your eyes. They won't have the faintest notion of what goes on, but the Fly will. He has already figured out his first five moves and several of yours.

13 This does not necessarily prove that the Fly is more intelligent than you are. If such things could be measured—and they will be, some day—I have little doubt that you, gentle swatter, would be found to have a higher I.Q. than the average Fly. You may be slow on the uptake, while the Fly is unbelievably fast. His sheer brilliance in planning and executing maneuvers of every sort on the ground and in the air amounts to genius, and you have all you can do to keep from falling over your feet. You cannot make quick decisions, or, if you do, you are generally dead wrong, as everybody at the office knows but yourself. The Fly's decisions are mostly right. They have to be.

14 Yet on the whole, taking it by and large, and allowing for individual exceptions, you are smarter than the Fly. You know more than he does about more things. Above all, you possess the power of abstract reasoning, a faculty which distinguishes mankind from the merely brute creation, such as Flies. You can listen to the radio, look at television, and go to the movies. You can read mystery stories and try to guess who done it. Keep your chin up and always remember that if you are not the Fly's superior in every single respect one might mention, you are at least his equal, mentally. Since you are fighting on practically even terms, then, when you are after a Fly who will not light you must seek for a flaw in his intellectual equipment if you hope to gain the initiative, and I can help you there. The key is his imperfect memory. You can remember as far back as yesterday. The Fly cannot. He forgets. The particular Fly of whom we were speaking will be out of his dark corner in a few brief moments, and you can begin the whole show all over again.

15 *9.* Check up on yourself occasionally. Ask yourself, "Am I a better swatter than I was last year?" The correct answer is No.

16 *10.* Don't be discouraged at a few failures. I don't always get them myself, but I give them pause. It makes 'em think.

THESIS AND ORGANIZATION

1. Examine Cuppy's first paragraph in terms of the journalistic questions *who? where? what? when? why? how?* Which ones does the paragraph answer and how?
2. What is the relationship between paragraph 2 and point 2?
3. What is the relationship between paragraphs 6–8 and point 6?
4. What is the relationship between paragraphs 11–14 and point 8?
5. Consider Cuppy's humor together with his directions, and state the essay's thesis in your own words.

TECHNIQUE AND STYLE

1. Why does Cuppy capitalize the word *fly?* What effects does he achieve by doing it?
2. Describe Cuppy's characterization of the Fly.
3. Examine the first sentence in each of Cuppy's directions. In what way are the sentences parallel or not?
4. Describe Cuppy's tone. How would you characterize his humor?
5. From your reading of the essay, describe the sort of person that Cuppy seems to be? What sort of persona does he present?

SUGGESTIONS FOR WRITING

Journal

1. Briefly outline the steps involved in a familiar chore—cleaning out the bathroom cabinet, washing the car, mowing the lawn, painting a room. Your outline plus a thesis can be the basis of a longer essay.
2. Think of a process you are used to (washing the car, cooking, studying, packing, playing a sport or the like) and find an analogy that fits all or part of the process. For instance, packing for a trip may be like preparing to climb Mr. Everest—you never know what you are going to need so you take almost everything.

Essay

Cuppy's essay deals with a common experience, and you can find your subject in the same general area. Think, for example, of various common actions, how you

wash dishes
study
make a _____ sandwich
wait in line
deal with boring people

Once you have a subject, then consider the steps involved and write them down. Review the list to make sure you have them in an order that makes sense. Like Cuppy, you may want to enumerate the steps, commenting on some of them. Or like Carlson (206), you may want to use a more subtle kind of chronology.

A Woman's Place

Naomi Wolf

Naomi Wolf was working on her Ph.D. at Princeton University when she adapted her dissertation into The Beauty Myth: How Images of Beauty Are Used Against Women, *a best-seller published in 1991. As the title of the book implies, Wolf is concerned with issues that affect women, an interest that runs through all of her work as she tries to redefine and revive feminism. Her most recent book examines the American version of growing up female,* Promiscuities: An Ordinary American Girlhood *(1997). The essay below, however, is more closely related to an earlier work,* Fire with Fire: The New Female Power and How to Use It *(1993), and is adapted from a commencement address she gave at Scripps College, a women's college in California.*

WHAT TO LOOK FOR *Many writers steer away from beginning a sentence with* and *and* because *they are afraid of creating a sentence fragment. But as long as the sentence has a subject and main verb, it can begin with* and *(or, like this one, but* or any other conjunction) *and still be an independent clause, a complete sentence, with the conjunction serving as an informal transition. To see how effective that kind of sentence can be, notice Wolf's last paragraph.*

1   Even the best of revolutions can go awry when we internalize the attitudes we are fighting. The class of 1992 is graduating into a violent backlash against the advances women have made over the last 20 years. This backlash ranges from a senator using "The Exorcist" against Anita Hill, to beer commercials with the "Swedish bikini team." Today I want to give you a backlash survival kit, a four-step manual to keep the dragons from taking up residence inside your own heads.

2   My own commencement, at Yale eight years ago, was the Graduation from Hell. The speaker was Dick Cavett, rumored to have been our president's "brother" in an all-male secret society.

3   Mr. Cavett took the microphone and paled at the sight of hundreds of female about-to-be Yale graduates. "When I was an undergraduate," I recall he said, "there were no women. The women went to Vassar. At Vassar, they had nude photographs taken of the women in gym class to check their posture. One year the photos

were stolen, and turned up for sale in New Haven's redlight district." His punchline? "The photos found no buyers."

4   I'll never forget that moment. There we were, silent in our black gowns, our tassels, our brand new shoes. We dared not break the silence with hisses or boos, out of respect for our families, who'd come so far; and they kept still out of concern for us. Consciously or not, Mr. Cavett was using the beauty myth aspect of the backlash: when women come too close to masculine power, someone will draw critical attention to their bodies. We might be Elis, but we still wouldn't make pornography worth buying.

5   That afternoon, several hundred men were confirmed in the power of a powerful institution. But many of the women felt the shame of the powerless: the choking on silence, the complicity, the helplessness. We were orphaned from our institution.

6   I want to give you the commencement talk that was denied to me.

7   Message No. 1 in your survival kit: redefine "becoming a woman." Today you have "become women." But that sounds odd in ordinary usage. What is usually meant by "You're a real woman now"? You "become a woman" when you menstruate for the first time, or when you lose your virginity, or when you have a child.

8   These biological definitions are very different from how we say boys become men. One "becomes a man" when he undertakes responsibility, or completes a quest. But you, too, in some ways more than your male friends graduating today, have moved into maturity through a solitary quest for the adult self.

9   We lack archetypes for the questing young woman, her trials by fire; for how one "becomes a woman" through the chrysalis of education, the difficult passage from one book, one idea to the next. Let's refuse to have our scholarship and our gender pitted against each other. In our definition, the scholar learns womanhood and the woman learns scholarship; Plato and Djuna Barnes, mediated to their own enrichment through the eyes of the female body with its wisdoms and its gifts.

10   I say that you have already shown courage: Many of you graduate today in spite of the post-traumatic stress syndrome of acquaintance rape, which one-fourth of female students undergo. Many of you were so weakened by anorexia and bulimia that it took every ounce of your will to get your work in. You negotiated private lives through a mine field of new strains of VD and the ascending shadow of AIDS. Triumphant survivors, you have already "become women."

11   Message No. 2 breaks the ultimate taboo for women: *Ask for money in your lives.* Expect it. Own it. Learn to use it. Little girls learn a debilitating fear of money—that it's not feminine to insure we are fairly paid for honest work. Meanwhile, women make 68 cents for every male dollar and half of marriages end in divorce, after which women's income drops precipitously.

12   Never choose a profession for material reasons. But whatever field your heart decides on, for god's sake get the most specialized training in it you can and hold out hard for just compensation, parental leave and child care. Resist your assignment to the class of highly competent, grossly underpaid women who run the show while others get the cash—and the credit.

13   Claim money not out of greed, but so you can tithe to women's political organizations, shelters and educational institutions. Sexist institutions won't yield power if we are just patient long enough. The only language the status quo understands is money, votes and public embarrassment.

14   When you have equity, you have influence—as sponsors, shareholders and alumnae. Use it to open opportunities to women who deserve the chances you've had. Your B.A. does not belong to you alone, just as the earth does not belong to its present tenants alone. Your education was lent to you by women of the past, and you will give some back to living women, and to your daughters seven generations from now.

15   Message No. 3: Never cook for or sleep with anyone who routinely puts you down.

16   Message No. 4: Become goddesses of disobedience. Virginia Woolf wrote that we must slay the Angel in the House, the censor within. Young women tell me of injustices, from campus rape coverups to classroom sexism. But at the thought of confrontation, they freeze into niceness. We are told that the worst thing we can do is cause conflict, even in the service of doing right. Antigone is imprisoned. Joan of Arc burns at the stake. And someone might call us unfeminine!

17   When I wrote a book that caused controversy, I saw how big a dragon was this paralysis by niceness. "The Beauty Myth" argues that newly rigid ideals of beauty are instruments of a backlash against feminism, designed to lower women's self-esteem for a political purpose. Many positive changes followed the debate. But all that would dwindle away when someone yelled at me—as, for in-

stance, cosmetic surgeons did on TV, when I raised questions about silicone implants. Oh, no, I'd quail, people are mad at me!

18 Then I read something by the poet Audre Lorde. She'd been diagnosed with breast cancer. "I was going to die," she wrote, "sooner or later, whether or not I had ever spoken myself. My silences had not protected me. Your silences will not protect you. . . . What are the words you do not yet have? What are the tyrannies you swallow day by day and attempt to make your own, until you will sicken and die of them, still in silence? We have been socialized to respect fear more than our own need for language."

19 I began to ask each time: "What's the worst that could happen to me if I tell this truth?" Unlike women in other countries, our breaking silence is unlikely to have us jailed, "disappeared" or run off the road at night. Our speaking out will irritate some people, get us called bitchy or hypersensitive and disrupt some dinner parties. And then our speaking out will permit other women to speak, until laws are changed and lives are saved and the world is altered forever.

20 Next time, ask: What's the worst that will happen? Then push yourself a little further than you dare. Once you start to speak, people *will* yell at you. They *will* interrupt, put you down and suggest it's personal. And the world won't end.

21 And the speaking will get easier and easier. And you will find you have fallen in love with your own vision, which you may never have realized you had. And you will lose some friends and lovers, and realize you don't miss them. And new ones will find you and cherish you. And you will still flirt and paint your nails, dress up and party, because as I think Emma Goldman said, "If I can't dance, I don't want to be part of your revolution." And at last you'll know with surpassing certainty that only one thing is more frightening than speaking your truth. And that is not speaking.

THESIS AND ORGANIZATION

1. Wolf's essay could easily be retitled "How to Survive the Backlash." What is the backlash?
2. Why does Wolf include the anecdote about Dick Cavett? How is it related to the backlash?
3. What are the four steps for survival?
4. What gender-based stereotypes does Wolf attack?

5. Wolf's essay gives advice and explains how to survive, but it also comments on women's place in society today. Combine those comments with her advice and the result will be the thesis.

TECHNIQUE AND STYLE

1. What saying does Wolf's title refer to? How does her title set up her essay?
2. Throughout the essay, Wolf uses allusion—Anita Hill (paragraph 1), Plato and Djuna Barnes (paragraph 9), Virginia Woolf (paragraph 16), Audre Lorde (paragraph 19), and Emma Goldman (paragraph 21). Use an encyclopedia to look up one of these allusions so that you can explain to the class how it is (or is not) appropriate.
3. To explore the effect of Wolf's repeated use of *and* in her last paragraph, try rewriting it. What is gained? Lost?
4. The original audience for the essay was women, but it was republished for an audience that also includes men. Explain whether men would find the essay offensive. Is it antimale?
5. Wolf is obviously a feminist, but think of feminism as a continuum ranging from conservative to radical. Based on this essay, what kind of feminist is Wolf? What evidence can you find for your opinion?

SUGGESTIONS FOR WRITING

Journal

1. Choose one of Wolf's "messages" and test it out against your own experience. Do you find the advice helpful? Necessary?
2. Relate an experience in which you ran into sexism, either antimale or antifemale. You could use this entry later as the basis for an essay in which you explain how to cope with sexism.

Essay

All of us at one time or another have played a role we didn't believe in or didn't like. Those roles vary greatly. Think about the roles you have had to play and how you broke out of them. Choose one and draft a paper explaining "How to Survive" or "How to Break Out." Some roles to think about:

dutiful daughter
responsible sibling
perfect husband (or wife)
brave man
happy homemaker

You Sure You Want to Do This?

Maneka Gandhi

Ever wonder what goes into a simple tube of lipstick? Maneka Gandhi tells us, though she also warns us that we may find out more than we wanted to know. Gandhi writes a regular column in the Illustrated Weekly *of India, although this essay was published in the Baltimore Sun (1989). A strong voice on the current political scene in India, Maneka Gandhi speaks out in favor of vegetarianism as well as animal rights and protecting the environment. In the essay that follows she uses a technique that you may also find useful—she defines her audience in her first sentence with a very specific you.*

WHAT TO LOOK FOR *Process analysis essays that are built around chronology sometimes fall into predictable transitions such as* first, second, next, then. *Gandhi avoids the obvious, even though chronology is important to her discussion. Be on the lookout for how she gets from one stage to the next.*

1   Are you one of those women who feel that lipstick is one of the essentials of life? That to be seen without it is the equivalent of facial nudity? Then you might like to know what goes into that attractive color tube that you smear on your lips.

2   At the center of the modern lipstick is acid. Nothing else will burn a coloring sufficiently deeply into the lips. The acid starts out orange, then sizzles into the living skin cells and metamorphoses into a deep red. Everything else in the lipstick is there just to get this acid into place.

3   First lipstick has to spread. Softened food shortening, such as hydrogenated vegetable oil, spreads very well, and accordingly is one of the substances found in almost all lipsticks. Soap smears well, too, and so some of that is added as well. Unfortunately, neither soap nor shortening is good at actually taking up the acid that's needed to do the dyeing. Only one smearable substance will do this to any extent: castor oil.

4   Good cheap castor oil, used in varnishes and laxatives, is one of the largest ingredients by bulk in every lipstick. The acid soaks into the castor oil, the castor oil spreads on the lips with the soap and shortening till the acid is carried where it needs to go.

221

5   If lipstick could be sold in castor oil bottles there would be no need for the next major ingredient. But the mix has to be transformed into a rigid, streamlined stick, and for that nothing is better than heavy petroleum-based wax. It's what provides the "stick" in lipstick.

6   Of course, certain precautions have to be taken in combining all these substances. If the user ever got a sniff of what was in there, there might be problems of consumer acceptance. So a perfume is poured in at the manufacturing stage before all the oils have cooled—when it is still a molten lipstick mass.

7   At the same time, food preservatives are poured into the mass, because apart from smelling rather strongly the oil in there would go rancid without some protection. (Have you smelled an old lipstick? That dreadful smell is castor oil gone bad.)

8   All that's lacking now is shine. When the preservatives and the perfume are being poured in, something shiny, colorful, almost iridescent—and, happily enough, not even too expensive—is added. That something is fish scales. It's easily available from the leftovers of commercial fish-packing stations. The scales are soaked in ammonia, then bunged in with everything else.

9   Fish scales, by the way, mean that lipstick is not a vegetarian product. Every time you paint your lips you eat fish scales. So lipsticks without them actually are marked "vegetarian lipstick."

10   Is that it then? Shortening, soap, castor oil, petroleum wax, perfume, food preservatives and fish scales? Not entirely. There is still one thing missing: color.

11   The orange acid that burns into the lips turns red only on contact. So that what you see in the tube looks like lip color and not congealed orange juice, another dye has to be added to the lipstick. This masterpiece of chemistry and art will be a soothing and suggestive and kissable red.

12   But it has very little to do with what actually goes on your face. That, as we said, is—but by now you already know more than you wanted to.

THESIS AND ORGANIZATION

1. What does paragraph 1 make clear about the essay's audience and subject? What expectations does it set up for the reader?
2. Which paragraphs focus on the ingredients that make lipstick work?
3. Which paragraphs focus on making lipstick attractive?

4. Consider the title of the essay and what Gandhi has to say about what goes into a tube of lipstick. What is her thesis?
5. Given the thesis of the essay, do you find Gandhi's purpose more informative than argumentative or the reverse? Explain.

TECHNIQUE AND STYLE

1. Considering what you have learned about Gandhi's thesis and purpose, how would you characterize the tone of the essay?
2. What provides the transitions between paragraphs 3 and 4? Between paragraphs 10 and 11? How effective do you find this device?
3. Examine the verbs Gandhi uses in paragraphs 2 and 3. What do they contribute to the essay's tone?
4. Paragraph 9 is more of an aside, a "by the way" comment, than a furthering of the essay's forward motion. What reasons can you think of that make the paragraph appropriate?
5. The last paragraph contains two references that may seem vague at first. What does "it" refer to in paragraph 12's first sentence? What does "That" refer to in the second sentence? Would a summary add to or detract from the conclusion? Explain.

SUGGESTIONS FOR WRITING

Journal

1. Did Gandhi's essay change the way you think or feel about lipstick? Write a brief entry explaining how the essay affected you.
2. Get hold of your favorite junk food and jot down what is listed as its ingredients. Write a short entry explaining your response to that list.

Essay

Think about other items we take for granted, and then find out if their ingredients contain a few surprises. You might start with a product, first noting the ingredients listed on the package and then consulting an unabridged dictionary. Given that information and your response to it, you are in a position to write an essay similar to Gandhi's. Your thesis would be your response (surprise, disgust, dismay), and the body of the paper would explain the role of the ingredients. Suggestions:

hot dogs
marshmallows
frozen pies or cakes
shampoo
perfume or aftershave

Inspiration? Head Down the Back Road, and Stop for the Yard Sales

Annie Proulx

As you will be able to tell from reading Annie Proulx's essay, her interests and travels are many and varied, some would even say strange. A graduate of Colby College in Maine, Proulx has lived in Vermont and is now in Wyoming, places that fostered her interest in gardening, fly fishing, and making cider (all of which she has written about), and led to her astute observations about people and landscapes. You can read about her keen sense of character and landscapes in her novels: Postcards *(1993), which won the PEN/Faulkner Award;* The Shipping News *(1994), which won both a Pulitzer Prize and National Book Award; and* Accordion Crimes *(1996). Proulx's short stories frequently appear in magazines such as the* New Yorker, *the* Atlantic Monthly, Harper's, *and* GQ, *some of which are reprinted in her books* Heart Songs and Other Stories *(1994) and the recent* Close Range *(1999). The essay that follows is part of a series—Writers on Writing—published by the* New York Times *where it appeared on May 10, 1999.*

WHAT TO LOOK FOR   *Proulx's essay is as far removed from the lock-step, how-to essay as a chocolate mousse is from a Tootsie Roll, yet she is writing about a process—how she finds her sources of inspiration for her writing. As you read her essay, try to identify both the sources for her ideas and how she uses those sources and you will reveal the process that is embedded in the essay.*

1   The Irish singer Christy Moore clips out "Don't Forget Your Shovel," a song I like not only for its tripping rhythm and sly social commentary but for its advice to the diggers of the world, a group to which I belong.

2   A whole set of metaphoric shovels is part of my tool collection, and for me the research that underlies the writing is the best part of the scribbling game. Years ago, alder scratched, tired, hungry, and on a late return from a fishing trip, I was driving through Maine when a hubbub on the sidewalk caught my eye: milling customers at a yard sale. I stop for yard sales.

3   Pay dirt. I found the wonderful second edition unabridged Webster's New International Dictionary with its rich definitions and hundreds of fine small illustrations. On a collapsing card table nearby sat Harper's Dictionary of Classical Literature and Antiquities, The Oxford Companion to English Literature and other weighty reference works, discards from a local library and the best catch of the trip.

4   I am an inveterate buyer of useful books on all possible subjects. Collectors pass up ex-libris books, but I need reading copies. And because I often fold down page corners and scribble in margins, it is best to keep me away from first editions.

5   On the jumbly shelves in my house I can find directions for re-placing a broken pipe stem, a history of corncribs, a booklet of Spam recipes, a 1925 copy of "Animal Heroes of the Great War" (mostly dogs but some camels); dictionaries of slang, dialect and re-gional English; a pile of Little Blue Books (none are blue) from the 1920's featuring titles like "How to Be a Gate-Crasher" and "Character Reading From the Face." One of these, "Curiosities of Language," treats us to the tortured orthography our grandparents thought hilarious:

> There was a young man, a Colonel,
> Who walked in the breezes volonel;
> He strolled in the aisles,
> Of the wooded maisles,
> And, returning, read in his jolonel.

6   This digging involves more than books. I need to know which mushrooms smell like maraschino cherries and which like dead rats, to note that a magpie in flight briefly resembles a wooden spoon, to recognize vertically trapped suppressed lee-wave clouds; so much of this research is concerned with four-dimensional observation and notation. These jottings go into cheap paper-covered notebooks that I keep in a desultory fashion, more often onto the backs of en-velopes and the margins of newspapers, from there onto the floor of the truck or onto the stair landing atop a stack of faxes and bills.

7   The need to know has taken me from coal mines to fire towers, to hillsides studded with agate, to a beached whale skeleton, to the sunny side of an iceberg, to museums of canoes and of windmills, to death masks with eyelashes stuck in the plaster, to shipyards and log yards, old military forts, wildfires and graffiti'd rocks, to rough water and rusty shipwrecks, to petroglyphs and prospectors' dig-

gings, to collapsed cotton gins, down into the caldera of an extinct volcano and, once or thrice in the middle distance, in view of a snouty twister.

8   I listen attentively in bars and cafes, while standing in line at the checkout counter, noting particular pronunciations and the rhythms of regional speech, vivid turns of speech and the duller talk of everyday life. In Melbourne I paid money into the hand of a sidewalk poetry reciter to hear "The Spell of the Yukon," in London listened to a cabby's story of his psychopath brother in Paris, on a trans-Pacific flight heard from a New Zealand engineer the peculiarities of building a pipeline across New Guinea.

9   The grand digging grounds are still the secondhand bookshops. Every trip ends with boxes of books shipped back, dusty old manuals on the hide business or directions for the dances of Texas with footprints and dotted lines reeling across the pages. But bookstores are changing. Recently I rattled the latch of a favorite in Denver before I saw the sign announcing that it was forever closed, but the inventory could be "accessed" on the Internet. Another dealer, a specialist in local histories, operated from his living room for years and put out an interesting catalogue from time to time. Both the catalogue and a visit to his bookshelves are things of the past, rendered obsolete by chilly cyber-lists.

10   I rarely use the Internet for research, as I find the process cumbersome and detestable. The information gained is often untrustworthy and couched in execrable prose. It is unpleasant to sit in front of a twitching screen suffering assault by virus, power outage, sluggish searches, system crashes, the lack of direct human discourse, all in an atmosphere of scam and hustle.

11   Nor do I do much library research these days, though once I haunted the stacks. Libraries have changed. They are no longer quiet but rather noisy places where people gather to exchange murder mysteries. In bad weather homeless folk exuding pungent odors doze at the reading tables. One stands in line to use computers, not a few down for the count, most with smeared and filthy screens, running on creaky software.

12   I mourn the loss of the old card catalogues, not because I'm a Luddite, but because the oaken trays of yesteryear offered the researcher an element of random utility and felicitous surprise through encounters with adjacent cards: information by chance that is different in kind from the computer's ramified but rigid order.

13   This country swims in fascinating pamphlets. In a New Mexico greasy spoon I pick up a flyer that takes St. Paul sharply to task on the subjects of hair style, clothing and women. ("Shorts, miniskirts, halters, bikinis, etc., are all O.K. You don't have to listen to Paul. . . . God wants women to look nice and be in style with the times. As far as men, Jesus had long hair. Paul must have been a religious fanatic.") A hundred miles later I read a narrow sheet with advice on how to behave in the presence of a mountain lion. ("Do not make direct eye contact. . . . Try to appear as big as possible.")

14   Food and regional dishes are important research subjects. Some you can order in restaurants, but others exist only in out-of-print cookbooks and must be prepared at home, like a duck roasted inside a watermelon, a dish called Angel in a Cradle, or another called the Atlanta Special, which sounds like a train, although the ingredient list begins, "1 beaver (8 to 10 pounds.)"

15   I like to drive the West, making a slow drift over caliche and gravel roads, volume cranked up and listening to music (this, too, is research), usually regional subtexts of alternative genres. But two that I never tire of hearing are Glenn Ohrlin singing "Barnacle Bill, the Sailor," in his two-tone voice, and the good ol' boy Texas country-and-western yodeler Don Walser with the Kronos String Quartet, sliding a heartaching "Rose Marie" straight at me.

16   The truck wanders around intersecting roads as tangled as fishing line. At times topographic maps, compass bearings or keeping the sun at my shoulder are better direction guides than signs, usually nonexistent or bullet-blasted into unreadability. The rules of road drift are simple: Always take a branching side route, stop often, get out and listen, walk around, see what you see. And what you see are signs, not direction signs but the others, the personal messages. We live in a world of signs.

17   I am amazed when people mourn the loss of the Burma Shave jingles. Better stuff is all around us, in public restrooms, in phone booths, on rocks, stapled to telephone poles, stuck on lawns. I remember a large billboard that stood for many years on a back-country road in Colorado. The community used it as a kind of enormous greeting card, welcoming home a son on leave from the Navy, congratulating a child on her fifth birthday, inviting neighbors to a party.

18   The signs of urban panhandlers seem to indicate that many of them took creative-writing courses. These messages are always

printed in neat capital letters: "WILL KILL FOR FOOD," "BIG DUMB UGLY BUM NEEDS YOUR HELP," "MY MOTHER LOVED ME BUT NOW SHE'S GONE."

19   The digging is never done because the shovel scrapes at life itself. It is not possible to get it all, or even very much of it, but I gather what I can of the rough, tumbling crowd, the lone walkers and the voluble talkers, the high lonesome signers, the messages people write and leave for me to read.

THESIS AND ORGANIZATION

1. Paragraphs 1–3 introduce the essay and its central metaphor. What does it lead you to expect from what follows?
2. What do you learn about Proulx's taste in books in paragraphs 3–5? About how she uses them?
3. When Proulx says that her "digging involves more than books" (paragraph 6), what is she referring to, what does she do? What is it that she does in paragraphs 7 and 8?
4. Paragraphs 9–12 describe changes, lost sources of information. What are they? What has been lost?
5. Proulx notes other sources that she uses in paragraphs 13–18. What are they?
6. Given your answers to the previous questions, make a list of the sources Proulx uses combined with the actions she takes to gather them. What general statement can you make about them? To what extent is that statement an adequate thesis for the essay?

TECHNIQUE AND STYLE

1. Proulx introduces the metaphor of digging in paragraph 1, then mentions it several times later in the essay (paragraphs 2, 3, 6, 9, and 19). In what ways is the metaphor appropriate for the process she describes? What does it add to the essay?
2. What is gained or lost by including the limerick in paragraph 5? What does it illustrate about Proulx's cast of mind?
3. Chose one of the paragraphs that brims with examples. What do they contribute to Proulx's point in the paragraph? To her thesis?
4. Reread the essay, noting the times Proulx mentions something relating to books or to writing. What reasons can you find for the frequency of the references?
5. Explain what line, if any, Proulx draws between research and inspiration. What evidence can you find for your opinion?

6. The last paragraph concludes the essay by summarizing without repeating. Reread the second sentence. What paragraph or paragraphs does "rough, tumbling crowd" refer to? "The lone walkers"? "The voluble talkers"? "The high lonesome signers"? "The messages people write and leave for me to read"?

SUGGESTIONS FOR WRITING

Journal

1. In paragraph 10, Proulx has some harsh comments for the Internet. Use your journal to test out her assertions against your own experience.
2. Proulx coins the expression "road drift" for pleasurable and informative wandering around on side roads (paragraph 16). Recreate a time when you "followed the rules of road drift."

Essay

What are your sources of inspiration for your writing or for some aspect of your life? Jot them down along with the actions you take to obtain them, and you'll have the skeleton of an essay that you can model along the lines of Proulx's. If you prefer, you might choose to write about how you write, thinking of the central term as broadly as possible and not just from the point at which you start to produce words on paper or the screen. If that idea doesn't appeal, think about the last time you had to do research and retrace the process you went through.

On Using
Cause and
Effect

8

Process analysis focuses on *how;* causal analysis emphasizes *why.* Though writers examine both **cause and effect,** most will stress one or the other. Causal analysis looks below the surface of the steps in a process and examines why they occur; it analyzes their causes and effects, why *X* happens and what results from *X*. As a way of thinking, causal analysis is a natural one.

Let's say you've followed the directions that came with your new stereo system and have finally reached the moment of truth when it's ready. You load your favorite tape, push the switch marked "power"; it clicks, nothing happens. The receiver is on, as are the CD player and tape deck, but no sound comes out of the speakers. Probably you first check for the most immediate possible cause of the problem—the hookups. Are all the jacks plugged into the correct sources? Are they secure? Are the speaker wires attached correctly? If everything checks out, you start to search for less immediate causes, only to discover that the wrong switch was depressed on the receiver so that it's tuned to a nonexistent turntable. You push "Tape," and music fills the room. The problem is solved.

Essays that analyze cause and effect usually focus on one or the other. If you are writing about your hobby, which, let's say, happens to be tropical fish, you could emphasize the causes. You might have wanted a pet but were allergic to fur; you might have been fascinated with the aquarium in your doctor's office, and your aunt gave you two goldfish and a bowl. These reasons are causes that you would then have to sort out in terms of their importance. But if you wished to focus on effect, you might be writing on how your interest in tropical fish led to your majoring in marine biology.

You can see how causal analysis can be confusing in that a cause leads to an effect, which can then become another cause. This kind of causal chain undergirds Benjamin Franklin's point that "a little neglect may breed great mischief . . . for want of a nail the shoe was lost; for want of a shoe the horse was lost; and for want of a horse the rider was lost."

You can avoid the traps set by causal analysis if you apply some of the skills you use in division and classification and in process analysis:

1. Divide your subject into two categories—causes and effects.
2. Think about the steps or stages that are involved and identify them as possible causes or effects.
3. List an example or two for each possible cause or effect.
4. Sort out each list by dividing the items into primary or secondary causes and effects, that is, those that are relatively important and those that are relatively unimportant.

When you reach this final point, you may discover that an item you have listed is only related to your subject by time, in which case you should cross it out.

If you were writing a paper on cheating in college, for instance, your notes might resemble these:

	Possibilities	**Examples**	**Importance**
Causes	Academic pressure	Student who needs an A	Primary
	Peer pressure	Everybody does it	Primary
	System	Teachers tolerate it	Secondary
		No real penalty	
	Moral climate	Cheating on income taxes	Secondary
		False insurance claims	
		Infidelity	
		Breakup of family unit	
Effects	Academic	Grades meaningless	Primary
	Peers	Degree meaningless	Primary
	System	Erodes system	Secondary
	Moral climate	Weakens moral climate	Secondary

The train of thought behind these notes chugs along nicely. Looking at them, you can see how thinking about the moral climate might lead to speculation about the cheating that goes undetected on tax and insurance forms, and for that matter, the cheating that occurs in a different context, that of marriage. The idea of infidelity then sets off a causal chain: infidelity causes divorce, which causes the breakup of families. Pause there. If recent statistics show that a majority of students have cheated, and if recent statistics also reveal a large number of single-parent households, is it safe to conclude that one caused the other? No. The relationship is one of time, not cause. Mistaking a **temporal relationship** for a causal one is a **logical fallacy** technically called **post hoc reasoning.**

It is also easy to mistake a **primary cause** or effect for a **secondary** one. If the notes above are for an essay that uses a narrative framework, and if the essay begins by relating an example of a student who was worried about having high enough grades to get into law school, the principle behind how the items are listed according to importance makes sense. To bring up his average, the student cheats on a math exam, justifying the action by thinking, "Everybody does it." The essay might then go on to speculate about the less apparent reasons behind the action—the system and the moral climate. For the student who cheated, the grade and peer pressure are the more immediate or primary causes; the system and climate are the more remote or secondary causes.

AUDIENCE AND PURPOSE

What you know or can fairly safely assume about the intended audience determines both what to say and how to say it. If you went straight from high school into a full-time job, for example, and wanted to write an essay about deciding five years later to enroll in college, you know your reader is familiar with both high school and college but knows nothing about you—your job and what led to your decision. The reality of your work—perhaps you found it wasn't sufficiently demanding and that your lack of a higher education stood in the way of promotion—and your expectations of what college will do to enrich your life are the reasons, the causes, behind your change in direction.

Perhaps your subject is less personal but still one that your reader knows something about, say the high school dropout rate. Like your reader, you know that it's high in your city because you remember a story in the local newspaper pointing that out. What you didn't know your reader probably doesn't know either: How high is high? Why do students drop out? What happens to them after that? You'll have to do some research to find out some answers (the news story is a good place to start), but you'll find plenty to say. And as you amass information on your topic, you'll start to sense a purpose. Perhaps you simply want to inform your reader about the magnitude of the problem, or perhaps you will want to argue that more needs to be done about it.

An awareness of the reader and that person's possible preconceptions can also guide your approach to the topic. If, for example, your topic is the single-parent family, and you want to dispel some ideas about it that you think are misconceptions, you might safely assume that your audience regards single-parent families as at best incomplete and at worst irresponsible. It's obvious that you won't win your argument by suggesting that anyone with such ideas is a fool and possibly a bigot as well; it's also obvious that making your point while not offending some readers requires a subtle approach. One way to avoid offense is to put yourself in the shoes of the reader who has the negative associations. Then just as you learned more about the topic and became enlightened, so, with any luck, may your reader.

VALID CAUSAL RELATIONSHIPS

As noted earlier, it is easy to mistake a temporal relationship for a causal relationship and to assign significance to something relatively unimportant. That's another way of saying that evidence and logical reasoning are essential to cause-and-effect essays. If, for instance, you find yourself drawn to one example, you need to think about how to avoid resting your entire argument on that one example. Writing about collegiate sports, for instance, you might have been struck by the story of a high school basketball star who wanted to play proball but didn't have the educational background necessary to be admitted to an NCAA Division I basketball school. After playing at several junior colleges, he finally transferred to an NCAA I institution, where with tutoring and a lot of individual attention, he was able to keep his grades high enough to maintain his academic eligibility only to have all the academic support vanish a year short of graduation, for he had used up his time limit and was no longer eligible to play. The effect—no degree, little education, and few chances for review by pro scouts—was devastating. You want to write about it. You want to argue that college sports take advantage of high school athletes, but you have only one example. What to do?

You can use your one example as a narrative framework, one that is sure to interest your reader. But to make that example more than an attention-getting device that enlists the reader's emotions, you have a number of alternatives. If your research shows that a fair number of athletes have a similar story, then you have multiple examples to support your point. If only a few share the experience, you'll need to modify your thesis to argue that even a few is too many. And if you can't find any other examples, then you have to narrow your argument to fit what you have, arguing that this particular individual was victimized. While you can ask how many more like him there may be, you cannot state that they exist.

THESIS AND ORGANIZATION

Although a cause can lead to an effect that then becomes a cause leading to another effect and so on, most essays are organized around either one or the other: why high school students drop out, why a person returns to college, what happens if a college takes advantage of a basketball player, what effect does being a working mother in a one-parent household have on the children. That's not to say that if your essay focuses on cause, you have to avoid effect and vice versa. Whichever one you don't emphasize can make a good conclusion. Your introduction, however, is a good place for your thesis; the reader can then follow the logical relationships between ideas as you develop your main point.

USEFUL TERMS

Cause and effect An examination of a topic to discover, explain, or argue why a particular action, event, situation, or condition occurred.

Logical fallacy An error in reasoning. Assigning a causal relationship to a temporal one and reaching a general conclusion based on one example are both logical fallacies.

Post hoc reasoning A logical fallacy in which a temporal relationship is mistaken for a causal one. The fact that one event preceded another only establishes a temporal not a causal relationship.

Primary cause The most important cause or causes.

Secondary cause The less important cause or causes.

Temporal relationship Two or more events related by time rather than anything else.

➤ POINTERS FOR USING CAUSE AND EFFECT

Exploring the Topic

1. **Have you stated the topic as a question that asks why X happened?** What are the possible causes? The probable causes? Rank the causes in order of priority.
2. **Have you stated the topic as a question that asks what results from X?** What are the possible effects? The probable effects? Rank the effects in order of priority.
3. **Is a temporal relationship involved?** Review your lists of causes and effects, and rule out any that have only a temporal relationship to your subject.
4. **Which do you want to emphasize, cause or effect?** Check to make sure your focus is clear.
5. **What is your point?** Are you trying to show that something is so or to explore your topic? Are you making an argument?
6. **What evidence can you use to support your point?** Do you need to cite authorities or quote statistics? If you depend on personal experience, are you sure your experience is valid, that is, representative of general experience?
7. **What does your reader think?** Does your audience have any preconceived ideas about your topic that you need to account for? What are they? How can you deal with them?
8. **Do you need to define any terms?** What words are crucial to your point? Are any of them abstract and, therefore, need to be defined? Have you used any technical terms that need definition?
9. **What role do you want to play in the essay?** Are you an observer or a participant? Is your major intention to inform, to persuade, or to entertain? What point of view best serves your purpose?

Drafting the Paper

1. **Know your reader.** Figure out what attitudes your reader may have about your topic. If the causal relationship you are discussing is unusual, you might want to shape your initial attitude so that it is as skeptical as your reader's. On the other hand, you may want to start with a short narrative that immediately puts the reader on your side. Consider how much your reader is apt to know about your topic. If you are the expert, make

sure you explain everything that needs to be explained without being condescending.

2. **Know your purpose.** Adjust your tone and persona to suit your purpose. If you are writing a persuasive paper, make sure your persona is credible and that you focus your ideas so that they may change the mind of a reader who initially does not agree with you—or, short of that, so your ideas make the reader rethink his or her position. If you are writing an informative paper, choose a persona and tone that will interest the reader. Tone and persona are even more crucial to essays written to entertain, in which the tone can range from ironic to lighthearted.

3. **Emphasize a cause or effect.** Essays that focus on cause will more than likely cover a variety of probable reasons that explain the result. Though there may be only one effect or result, you may want to predict other possible effects in your conclusion. For instance, an essay that explores the causes of violence may examine a number of reasons or causes for it but may then conclude by speculating on the possible effects of a rising crime rate. On the other hand, essays that focus on effect will more than likely cover a number of possible effects that are produced by a single cause, though again you may want to speculate on other causes. If you are writing about the effects of smoking, at some point in the essay you may want to include other harmful substances in the air such as dust, hydrocarbons, and carbon monoxide.

4. **Check for validity.** Don't hesitate to include quotations, allusions, statistics, and studies that support your point. Choose your examples carefully to buttress the relationship you are trying to establish, and be sure you don't mistake a temporal relationship for a causal one.

5. **Make a point.** The cause-and-effect relationship you examine should lead to or stem from an assertion: video games not only entertain, they also stimulate the mind and improve coordination; video games are not only habit-forming, they are also addictive.

Still a Mystery

Edna Buchanan

Although many people associate Edna Buchanan with mystery novels, those who read the Miami Herald *also know her as a Pulitzer Prize–winning crime reporter. That background has served her well. After writing one nonfiction book about her journalistic career in crime, Buchanan turned to the more structured world of fiction, creating Britt Montero, a* Miami Herald *police reporter who has now appeared in a series of adventures. The latest,* You Only Die Twice, *appeared in hardback edition in 2001. The essay that follows was one of several published in an advertising supplement to the April 21, 1996, the* New York Times Magazine *that announced the 1996 Edgar Allan Poe Awards. The supplement was compiled and edited for the Mystery Writers of America. As you read Buchanan's essay, ask yourself how much of it is explanation and how much is persuasion.*

WHAT TO LOOK FOR   *Buchanan's essay is a good example of how various patterns of organization can be used together. You'll find that although her main pattern is cause and effect, she also draws on definition, narration, description, process, and comparison and contrast. As you read the essay, try to spot where and how she uses these other modes.*

1   She looked like a broken doll, pale and naked, crumpled in a mangrove tangle at the water's edge. The little girl had been stolen from her bedroom during a dark and steamy Miami night.

2   Her murder, a quarter of a century ago, still haunts those who remember. The lead homicide detective never forgot. I sat at his bedside as he lay dying. During his final breaths, he spoke again of the case, still unsolved, still a mystery.

3   Too many disturbing mysteries weigh upon real life, the last pages forever elusive, frustratingly out of reach. In the case of that little girl I finally fashioned my own solution. I wrote about a similar child, a similar case. A central character in that novel was a dying detective, still obsessed by her fate. But this time there was

closure, her murder was solved. Justice at last. Good therapy for me, for all of us. What joys there are in writing and reading mysteries. More truth can be told in fiction than in real life. The writer can address society's problems, mirror the community, inform as well as entertain, expose wrongs and injustices and create characters who vent his or her own outrage. Fictional officials can be endowed with dedication, intelligence and common sense, so unlike most in real government.

4   Everybody is interested in mysteries, in crime. We are all touched by it. We are all fascinated by evil. We all yearn for resolution. Our system rarely provides it. Even if a crime is solved, even if there is an arrest and if—after hearing after hearing and deposition after deposition—there should be a conviction, it still never really ends. There are appeals and more appeals, basic gain time, incentive gain time, good time, pre-trial release, work release, conditional release and early release, to say nothing of furloughs, parole and probation—and escape. There is no last page.

5   Real life can be grim, unlike mystery fiction, where writers can wrap up those loose ends, solve the mysteries and best of all, write the last chapter, where the good guys win and the bad guys get what they deserve—so unlike real life.

6   The genre is an escape, a sanctuary, in an increasingly chaotic world overtaken by unresponsive government agencies, rush hour traffic, voice mail and other unspeakable torments. Mystery novels offer intellectual challenge, structure and the triumph of logic and order in a world where such comforts are increasingly rare.

7   Readers assume the role of detective, sharpening deductive skills and honing their talents for problem and puzzle solving. Mystery aficionados love logic and having the strands spun out of an original premise weave together satisfyingly at the end.

8   They experience wonderful literature, memorable characters, roller-coaster adventure, breathtaking suspense, and pumped up heart rates, all without exposing themselves to bullets, tear gas, rocks, bottles, or actual exercise.

9   The writer has even more fun.

10   We provide the only world in which our readers are certain to find swift and sure justice—or any real justice. We all need endings and it is a joy, as a novelist, for me to be able to give them to readers, and to myself.

11   Two fewer ghosts, one a little girl and the other an aging detective, haunt my dreams these dark and steamy nights. Who says there is no justice?

THESIS AND ORGANIZATION

1. Buchanan uses a framing device to open and close her essay. Explain whether you find it effective.
2. Which paragraphs focus on the writer of mysteries? What reasons does Buchanan give for writing mystery stories?
3. Which paragraphs focus on the reader of mysteries? What reasons does Buchanan give for reading mystery stories?
4. Paragraph 4 discusses the "system." What is Buchanan's point? How does it relate to the other ideas in the essay?
5. Consider what Buchanan has to say about why people write and read mysteries and how the world of fiction relates to the world of reality. In one sentence, state her thesis.

TECHNIQUE AND STYLE

1. Rewrite Buchanan's first sentence deleting the adjectives. What is gained? Lost?
2. The essay was one of several in an advertising supplement promoting the 1996 Edgar Allen Poe Awards in particular and mysteries in general. Analyze the degree to which Buchanan is "selling" mysteries.
3. Many people regard reading mystery stories as at best a waste of time, at worst a morbid interest. How does Buchanan counter that opinion?
4. What point is Buchanan making by comparing mystery fiction to real life crime? How valid do you find her opinion?
5. Quite intentionally, Buchanan chooses to have paragraph 9 consist of a single sentence. What reasons can you come up with for Buchanan's choice?

SUGGESTIONS FOR WRITING

Journal

1. Explain why you read what you read. If you only read what is assigned for your classes, explain why you do not read for pleasure.
2. Buchanan states "We are all fascinated by evil. We all yearn for resolution." Explore the degree to which you think she is correct.

Essay

Almost everyone uses leisure time to relax by pursuing some form of pleasure. Think about what you do for day-to-day fun and make a list of what you come up with. Choose one subject and consider why you do it as well as its effects on you. Then draft an essay in which you explain what you do and why. You may want to emphasize cause rather than effect or vice versa.

Tiffany Stephenson—An Apology

Bjorn Skogquist

Bjorn Skogquist came to Concordia College in Moorhead, Minnesota, with a firm interest in drama (having been in productions at Anoka High School that were recognized for excellence by the Kennedy Center for the Performing Arts) but a distinct aversion to writing. His freshman year, however, when his instructor, James Postema, encouraged him to "include anything I wanted, anything that I felt to be important," Skogquist "began to find it rather easy, and in a way, almost entertaining." He comments, "About halfway through, after I had written about various mishaps and comical incidents in my life, I decided to write about the things that a person would rather forget." The result is the essay that follows, although the name of the subject has been changed to Tiffany Stephenson. Skogquist relates "one of those things that I would rather forget, but instead of forgetting it, I apologized. It was something that I began and couldn't put down until I had finished."

WHAT TO LOOK FOR   *If you find yourself thinking about an incident that occurred to you and mulling over its effect, you may well be on the way to an essay that takes a personal narrative and reexamines it through the lens of cause and effect. That is what Bjorn Skogquist does with what happened to him in the fourth grade. As you read the essay, look for the ways he handles different time periods— what had been happening before he entered his new school, his first day there, the incident that occurred, and the present.*

1   When I was in the fourth grade, I moved from a small Lutheran school of 100 to a larger publicly funded elementary school. Lincoln Elementary. Wow. Lincoln was a big school, full of a thousand different attitudes about everything from eating lunch to how to treat a new kid. It was a tough time for me, my first year, and more than anything, I wanted to belong.

2   Many things were difficult; the move my family had just made, trying to make new friends, settling into a new home, accepting a new stepfather. I remember crying a lot. I remember my parents fighting. They were having a difficult time with their marriage, and

whether it was my stepfather's drinking, or my mother's stubbornness, it took an emotional toll on both me and my siblings. Despite all this, the thing that I remember most about the fourth grade is Tiffany Stephenson.

3   The first day of fourth grade at Lincoln Elementary School was an emptiness, and it felt enormous. I wasn't the only one who felt this way, but I was too absorbed in my own problems to notice anyone else's. I was upset that my father, my blood father, was in the hospital for abusing alcohol. Among other things, he was a schizophrenic. I was too young to understand these diseases, but I understood all too well that my daddy was very sick, and that I couldn't see him any more.

4   My first day at Lincoln was a very real moment in my life. The weather was both cloudy and intolerably sunny at the same time. Maybe it wasn't that the sun was so bright, maybe it was just that our eyes were still adjusted to morning shadows. It was one of those sequences that somehow stand out in my memory as unforgettable. I remember feeling gray inside. I think that all of us felt a little gray, and I would guess that most of us remember that first day as you might remember your grandmother's funeral, whether you liked it or not.

5   I walked in and sat near the back of the class, along with a few others. If you were different or weird or new, from another planet, you sat in the back because those were the only desks left. I sat at the far left of the room, in the back near the windows. For a while I just stared out into the playground, waiting for recess to come. Our teacher, Mrs. Bebow, came into the room and started talking to us. I don't remember exactly what she said that day, because I wasn't listening. I was numb to the world, concentrating solely on that playground. She seemed distant, far away, and I think that my whole day might have stayed numb if it weren't for a boy named Aaron Anderson.

6   Aaron, who sat to my right, leaned over and whispered, "My name's Aaron. And that's Tiffany Stephenson. Stay away from her. She's fat and ugly and she stinks." At that, a few others laughed, and I felt the numbness leaving me. Mrs. Bebow remarked that if we had something so terribly amusing to say, everyone had a right to know just what it was. Of course, we all quieted down. Then I asked which one was Tiffany, and Aaron pointed. There she was,

coloring contentedly, sitting alone in the corner, in the very back, just like me. She was not fat or ugly, and as far as I knew, she didn't stink either. I even remember thinking that she was cute, but I quickly dismissed the thought because I already had a new friendship, even though it was in the common disgust of Tiffany Stephenson.

7   While all this was happening, our teacher Mrs. Bebow managed to take roll, after which she proceeded to lecture the boys on good behavior and then the girls on being young ladies. Every time she turned her back, airplanes and garbage flew across the room at Tiffany, along with a giggle. I don't think Tiffany Stephenson thought too much of us, that day or ever.

8   A few days later, one of the girls passed Tiffany a note. It ended up making her cry, and it got the girl a half an hour of detention. I was too busy trying to fit in to notice though, or didn't notice, or was afraid to notice, or simply didn't care.

9   That fall, both the boys and girls would go up to Tiffany on the playground and taunt her. They made absurd accusations, accusations about eating boogers at lunch, or about neglecting to wear underwear that day. Interestingly, this was the only activity that we participated in where a teacher didn't command, "OK, boys and girls need to partner up!" What we did to Tiffany Stephenson was mean, but in using her we all became common allies. I wonder if the teachers knew what we were up to when we made our next move, or if they thought that we were actually getting along. I think they knew at first, but we got craftier as time passed. And Tiffany had quit telling the teacher what happened. She knew that when we were ratted on, her taunts got worse. And they did get worse. We were mean, but we kept on because there was no one to stand out and say, "Enough."

10   When I think about that year, and about Tiffany, I remember that she was almost always alone. Toward the second half of the year, a retarded girl named Sharon Olsen befriended her. Sharon and Tiffany were a lot alike. They spent most of their time together coloring and drawing pictures, and those pictures always found their way to the prize board at the end of the week. The teacher knew that they needed a little encouragement, but mostly that "encouragement" ended up making us hate them more. We picked on Sharon a lot too, but not as much as we targeted Tiffany.

11   Through the long winter, our taunts became hateful jeers, and our threats of pushing and shoving became real acts. We carried our threats out against Tiffany, but with no real reason to hate her. A couple of times when we walked down to lunch, we even pushed her around the corner to an area under the stairs. We knew that if no other classes followed us, we could get away with our plan, which was to tease her until tears flowed. We always asked her if she was scared. She never gave us the right answer. In a quiet voice she would reply, "No. Now leave me alone." Sometimes we left her alone, and sometimes we just laughed. Tiffany must have felt so very scared and alone, but she had more than us, she had courage. We didn't care. The more we could scare her, the better, the closer, the stronger knit we somehow felt.

12   One afternoon, heading for lunch, a few of us stayed behind and blocked the doorway. Tiffany was there, alone again, and cornered by three boys. Looking back, I realized why we began pushing her around. We felt unbelievably close, so close to each other through our hatred. It was a feeling that I have experienced only a few times since. And not only was the experience ours to cherish, it was a delight for Mrs. Bebow's entire fourth grade class. We were a purpose that afternoon, and we knew it. Looking back to that moment, I feel more remorse for my coldness than I have felt for any other passing wrong. But then, there, I felt alive, unafraid, and strangely whole.

13   That afternoon changed me forever.

14   By the time we sent Tiffany Stephenson to the green linoleum, she was no longer a person. Her full name, given to her at birth as a loving gesture, was now a fat, smelly, ugly title. There, on the green linoleum of Mrs. Bebow's fourth grade classroom, amidst the decorations and smell of crayfish aquariums, Tiffany Stephenson received many kicks, punches and unkind words. We didn't kick or punch her very hard, and the things we said weren't especially foul, but they were inhuman. This event was the culmination of the inhumane hate and vengeance that had been growing inside of us all year long. And yet, if any one of us stopped for a second to look, to really take a good look at who it was lying there on the ground, curled up in a ball crying, we would have realized that she was one of us.

15   At the beginning of the year, all of us had felt like we were in the back of the room. We were all unknowns. But somehow during that year we had put ourselves above her by force, and I admit that for a long time I couldn't see my wrong. But I had wronged. I had

caused someone pain for my own personal ambitions. I was now popular, and it was at Tiffany Stephenson's expense. I was a coward, stepping on her courage for one moment in the warm sunlight, above my own pale clouds.

16   Only recently do I realize my error. I wish I could have been the one to say, on that first fall afternoon, "Tiffany's not ugly, fat or stinky. She's just like you and me, and we're all here together." Really, I wish anyone would have said it. I know now that people need each other, and I wish I could tell the fourth grade that we could all be friends, that we could help each other with our problems. I wish that I could go back. But all I can do is apologize. So Tiffany, for all my shortcomings, and for sacrificing you for the sake of belonging, please forgive me.

THESIS AND ORGANIZATION

1. What paragraph or paragraphs introduce the narrative?
2. Trace the causal relationships in paragraphs 1–5. What does the author feel and why?
3. Trace the causal relationship in paragraphs 6–14. What does the author feel and why?
4. Paragraphs 15 and 16 sum up the incident that occurred "that afternoon." What did the author realize then? Now?
5. Consider all the cause-and-effect relationships in the narrative and state the thesis of the essay.

TECHNIQUE AND STYLE

1. Tiffany Stephenson's name first appears in paragraph 2 but not again until paragraph 6. Explain what is gained by the delay.
2. How does the author try to connect his experience with that of the reader? Why might he have chosen to do that?
3. In paragraph 15 Skogquist says "I was a coward, stepping on her courage for one moment in the warm sunlight, above my own pale clouds." What does he mean by "the warm sunlight, above my own pale clouds"?
4. Paragraph 13 consists of one sentence. Explain its function and effect.
5. Skogquist gives his audience a lot of information about his family. Explain why he may have chosen to do that and what it contributes to the essay.

Suggestions for Writing

Journal

1. Do you identify with the author or with Tiffany Stephenson?

2. If you were Tiffany Stephenson, would you forgive Skogquist? Why or why not?

Essay

Write your own personal narrative about an experience in which you explore the effect it had on you. Like Skogquist, you will probably want to have a dual perspective: the effects then and now. For a subject, consider your first

day at a new school
attempt at a sport
acquaintance with death
friendship
visit to the dentist or doctor or hospital

Wrestling with Myself

George Felton

When not teaching writing and copywriting at the Columbus College of Art and Design, George Felton is a freelance writer whose topics cover the hot spots of popular culture—Richard Simmons, the "Healthism" craze, not understanding how things work, and the like. Here, he investigates his (and our) fascination with pro wrestling. The essay was originally published in Sun *Magazine, the supplement to the* Baltimore Sun, *on November 11, 1990. Felton has also published his work in the* New York Times, Newsweek, *and* Advertising Age *and has been a contributor to the Bread Loaf Writers' Conference.*

WHAT TO LOOK FOR   *Felton's audience is composed of readers who share his enthusiasm for pro wrestling, those who regard it as silly or worse, and those who know little if anything about it. At times, you may find yourself faced with a similar variety of readers, which is when you can employ some of the techniques Felton uses. As you read his essay, look for the ways he addresses the attitudes of these various readers.*

1   It's Saturday morning, 11 a.m., right after the cartoons: time for "The NWA Main Event." As I watch the ringside announcer set up today's card, a huge wrestler—topless and sweating, wearing leather chaps and a cowboy hat, carrying a lariat with a cowbell on it— bursts into the frame, grabs the announcer by his lapels, and, chunks of tobacco spraying out of his mouth, begins to emote: "Well lookee here, this is just what eats in my craw. . . . I don't care if you're the president or the chief of police, it don't matter, I'm gonna do what I wanna do," and what he mostly wants to do is wrassle somebody good for once—enough nobodies in the ring, enough wimps running the schedule. As quickly as he spills into camera, he veers out, having delivered exactly the 20-second sound bite required. Our announcer blithely sends us to a commercial, and another Saturday's wrestling hour has begun. I feel better already.

2   I soon find out this cowboy's name is Stan Hanson, he's from Border, Texas, and lately he's been getting disqualified in all his matches for trying to kill his opponents and then "hogtying" them

247

with his lariat. We get to watch a recent match in which he kicks some poor guy's stomach furiously with his pointed-toe cowboy boots and drop-slams his elbow into his neck and, after getting him down, hits him over the head with the cowbell, and first whips, then strangles him with his lariat. It's great stuff, with the bell ringing madly and the referee waving his arms, but Stan's already yanked the guy outside the ring onto the apron and he's still on top, trying to kill him.

3   Why do I love this? Why am I crazy about Stan Hanson, who's old and fat and a man the announcer warns us "ought to be in a straitjacket and chains"? Because he personifies the great redemption of pro wrestling, the way it delivers me from civilization and its discontents. Not only is Stan Hanson mad as hell and not taking it anymore, but he's doing it all for me—getting himself disqualified so that I won't run the risk myself, but inviting me to grab one end of the rope and pull. He is my own id—the hairy beast itself—given a Texas identity and a push from behind, propelled out there into the "squared circle" where I can get a good look at it: sweat-soaked, mean, kicking at the slats, looking for an exposed neck. My heart leaps up, my cup runneth over.

4   Obviously I can't tell my friends about too much of this. If I even mention pro wrestling, they just stare at me and change the subject. They think I'm kidding. I am not supposed to like pro wrestling—its demographics are too downscale, its Dumb Show too transparent. They complain that it's fake and silly, which to me are two of its great charms. If it were real, like boxing, it'd be too painful to watch, too sad. I like knowing it's choreographed: the staged mayhem lets me know someone has studied me and will toss out just the meat the dark, reptilian centers of my brain require to stay fed and stay put. Sadomasochism? Homoeroticism? I am treated to the spectacle of Ric "The Nature Boy" Flair, astride the corner ropes and his opponent. His fist may be in the air, triumphant, but his groin is in the other guy's face, and he keeps it there. For once the ringside announcers are speechless as we all stare, transfixed, at this clearest of symbolic postures. Consciously I am squirming, but my reptilian center feels the sun on its back.

5   Racism? Ethnocentrism? Am I unsettled about Japanese hegemony? No problem. There is, in the World Wrestling Federation, a tag team of scowling, unnervingly business-oriented Japanese toughs—the Orient Express, managed by Mr. Fuji—who invite me to

hate them, and of course I do. Their failure is my success, and I don't even have to leave the living room. Two oversized, red-trunked Boris types used to parade around the ring under a red flag and insist, to our booing, on singing the Russian national anthem before wrestling. Since the Cold War has become passé, however, I've noticed matches pitting Russians *against each other,* and that, as my newspaper tells me, is not passé. I hear groans of delight from below, as this reprise of Cain and Abel croons its libidinal tune.

6   I mean where else can I take my id out for a walk, how else to let it smell the sweaty air, root its nose through the wet leaves? Cartoons? No amount of Wile E. Coyote spring-loaded bounces, no pancakings of Roger Rabbit, none of the whimsical annihilations of Cartoonville can approximate the satisfactions of a real boot in a real belly, a man's head twisted up in the ropes, the merry surfeit of flying drop kicks, suplexes, sleeper holds, and heart punches, all landed somewhere near real bodies. Pro sports? I get more, not less, neurotic rooting for my teams—my neck muscles ache, my stomach burns with coffee, after enduring another four-hour Cleveland Browns loss on TV. The Indians? Don't even get me started. The violence of movies like *The Last Action Hero* and *Cliffhanger?* Needlessly complicated by storyline.

7   No, give it to me straight. Wrestling may be a hybrid genre—the epic poem meets Marvel Comics via the soap opera—but its themes, with their medieval tone, could hardly be simpler: warrior kings doing battle after battle to see who is worthy, women pushed almost to the very edges of the landscape, *Beowulf*'s heroic ideal expressed in the language of an after-school brawl: "I wanna do what I wanna do. You gonna try to stop me?"

8   I also appreciate the pop-culture novelty of pro wrestling, its endearing way of creating, a little smudged and thick-fingered, but with a great earnest smile ("Here, look at this!") new *bêtes noires* for our consumption. One of the newest is something called Big Van Vader, a guy in a total upper torso headgear that looks like Star Wars Meets a Mayan Temple. He carries a stake topped with a skull and can shoot steam out of ventricles on his shoulders, but it looks like all he can do to keep from toppling over. He's horrifying and silly all at once, an atavistic nightdream wearing a "Kick Me" sign.

9   Such low rent Show Biz, this admixture of the asylum and the circus, is central to wrestling's double-tracked pleasure. Its emotional *reductio ad absurdum* taps my anger like a release valve, but

its silliness allows me to feel superior to it as I watch. I can be dumb and intelligent, angry and amused, on all fours yet ironically detached, all at the same moment.

10   It's a very satsifying mix, especially since my life between Saturdays is such an exercise in self-control, modesty, and late twentieth-century angst. To my students I am the helpful Mr. Felton. To my chairman I am the responsible Mr. Felton. To virtually everybody and everything else I'm the confused and conflicted Mr. F. My violence amounts to giving people the finger, usually in traffic. When I swear I mutter. To insults I quickly add the disclaimer, "just kidding," a move I learned from watching David Letterman temper his nastiness. I never yell at people, threaten them, twist my heel into their ears, batter their heads into ring posts, or catch them flush with folding chairs. I don't wear robes and crowns and have bosomy women carry them around for me, either. In short, I never reduce my life to the satisfying oversimplification I think it deserves.

11   I'm a wimp. Just the sort of guy Cactus Jack or old Stan himself would love to sink his elbows into, a sentiment with which I couldn't agree more. And that brings us to the deepest appeal of pro wrestling: It invites me to imagine the annihilation of my own civilized self. When Ric Flair jabs his finger into the camera and menaces his next opponent with, "I guarantee you one thing—Junkyard Dog or no Junkyard Dog, you're going to the hospital," when another of the Four Horsemen growls, "I'm gonna take you apart on national television," the real thrill is that they're coming for me. And when Stan offers me one end of the rope, we both know just whose neck we're pulling on. Ah, redemption.

THESIS AND ORGANIZATION

1. What paragraph or paragraphs make up Felton's introduction? What are the reasons for your choice?
2. Paragraphs 4 and 5 rely heavily on examples. What ideas do Felton's examples illustrate?
3. Comparisons take up much of paragraphs 6 and 10. What are the comparisons? What are Felton's points in using them?
4. Where in the essay does Felton discuss the effect pro wrestling has on him? What reasons can you find for his placement of the effects?
5. Felton saves his most important reason till his last paragraph. Putting that reason together with the others in the essay, state Felton's thesis in your own words.

TECHNIQUE AND STYLE

1. Felton uses dashes in paragraphs 1, 3, and 7. After examining those examples, what conclusions can you draw about the proper function of dashes?
2. What impression do you have of Felton's persona? Explain whether it fits his self-description in paragraphs 10 and 11.
3. Both the first and last paragraph use dialogue. What does it add?
4. Paragraph 3 is riddled with allusions: to Freud's *Civilization and Its Discontents*, to the film *Network*, to a poem by Wordsworth, to the *Bible*. What do these allusions contribute to Felton's persona? To the essay as a whole?
5. Although the essay is written in first person, Felton uses *we* in paragraphs 2 and 11. Who does *we* refer to? What is gained or lost by switching pronouns?

SUGGESTIONS FOR WRITING

Journal

1. Which category of readers do you belong to—wrestling fan, wrestling debunker, wrestling innocent, or some other? Evaluate the effectiveness of the essay from your perspective.
2. Felton maintains that pro wrestling appeals to the id, to "the hairy beast itself." What other sports can you think of that appeal to the id? Select one and detail its appeal.

Essay

Whether or not you are a fan, there's no arguing with the popularity of watching sports events. Select a sport that you enjoy or one of which you cannot understand the appeal, and use it as the subject for an essay in which you explain or speculate on its popularity. Suggestions:

football or baseball
tennis or golf
racing (cars, horses, dogs)
roller derby, amazon contests, demolition derby
motocross

Black Men and Public Space

Brent Staples

Any woman who walks along city streets at night knows the fear Brent Staples speaks of, but in this essay we learn how that fear can affect the innocent. We see and feel what it is like to be a tall, strong, young black man who enjoys walking at night but innocently terrifies any lone woman. His solution to his night walking problems gives a delightful twist to nonviolent resistance.

The irony of Staples's situation was not lost on Jesse Jackson. Speaking in Chicago in 1993, he pointed out an equally distressing irony: "There is nothing more painful to me at this stage in my life than to walk down the street and hear footsteps and start thinking about robbery. Then [I] look around and see someone white and feel relieved."

Brent Staples holds a Ph.D. in psychology from the University of Chicago and writes on politics and culture for the New York Times *editorial board. His memoir,* Parallel Time: Growing Up in Black and White, *(1994) is published by Pantheon Books. The essay reprinted here was first published in* Harper's Magazine *in 1986. He's still whistling.*

WHAT TO LOOK FOR *Before you read the essay, look up the dash in a handbook of usage so you'll be on the lookout for Staples's use of it. He uses it in two different ways, but always appropriately.*

1   My first victim was a woman—white, well-dressed, probably in her early twenties. I came upon her late one evening on a deserted street in Hyde Park, a relatively affluent neighborhood in an otherwise mean, impoverished section of Chicago. As I swung onto the avenue behind her, there seemed to be a discreet, uninflammatory distance between us. Not so. She cast back a worried glance. To her, the youngish black man—a broad 6 feet 2 inches with a beard and billowing hair, both hands shoved into the pockets of a bulky military jacket—seemed menacingly close. After a few more quick glimpses, she picked up her pace and was soon running in earnest. Within seconds she disappeared into a cross street.

2   That was more than a decade ago. I was 22 years old, a graduate student newly arrived at the University of Chicago. It was in the echo of that terrified woman's footfalls that I first began to know the unwieldy inheritance I'd come into—the ability to alter public

space in ugly ways. It was clear that she thought herself the quarry of a mugger, a rapist, or worse. Suffering a bout of insomnia, however, I was stalking sleep, not defenseless wayfarers. As a softy who is scarcely able to take a knife to a raw chicken—let alone hold one to a person's throat—I was surprised, embarrassed, and dismayed all at once. Her flight made me feel like an accomplice in tyranny. It also made it clear that I was indistinguishable from the muggers who occasionally seeped into the area from the surrounding ghetto. That first encounter, and those that followed, signified that a vast, unnerving gulf lay between nighttime pedestrians—particularly women—and me. And I soon gathered that being perceived as dangerous is a hazard in itself. I only needed to turn a corner into a dicey situation, or crowd some frightened, armed person in a foyer somewhere, or make an errant move after being pulled over by a policeman. Where fear and weapons meet—and they often do in urban America—there is always the possibility of death.

3   In that first year, my first away from my hometown, I was to become thoroughly familiar with the language of fear. At dark, shadowy intersections, I could cross in front of a car stopped at a traffic light and elicit the *thunk, thunk, thunk, thunk* of the driver—black, white, male, or female—hammering down the door locks. On less traveled streets after dark, I grew accustomed to but never comfortable with people crossing to the other side of the street rather than pass me. Then there were the standard unpleasantries with policemen, doormen, bouncers, cabdrivers, and others whose business it is to screen out troublesome individuals *before* there is any nastiness.

4   I moved to New York nearly two years ago and I have remained an avid night walker. In central Manhattan, the near-constant crowd cover minimizes tense one-on-one street encounters. Elsewhere—in SoHo, for example, where sidewalks are narrow and tightly spaced buildings shut out the sky—things can get very taut indeed.

5   After dark, on the warrenlike streets of Brooklyn where I live, I often see women who fear the worst from me. They seem to have set their faces on neutral, and with their purse straps strung across their chests bandolier-style, they forge ahead as though bracing themselves against being tackled. I understand, of course, that the danger they perceive is not a hallucination. Women are particularly vulnerable to street violence, and young black males are drastically

overrepresented among the perpetrators of that violence. Yet these truths are no solace against the kind of alienation that comes of being ever the suspect, a fearsome entity with whom pedestrians avoid making eye contact.

6   It is not altogether clear to me how I reached the ripe old age of 22 without being conscious of the lethality nighttime pedestrians attributed to me. Perhaps it was because in Chester, Pennsylvania, the small, angry industrial town where I came of age in the 1960s, I was scarcely noticeable against a backdrop of gang warfare, street knifings, and murders. I grew up one of the good boys, had perhaps a half-dozen fistfights. In retrospect, my shyness of combat has clear sources.

7   As a boy, I saw countless tough guys locked away; I have since buried several, too. They were babies, really—a teenage cousin, a brother of 22, a childhood friend in his mid-twenties—all gone down in episodes of bravado played out in the streets. I came to doubt the virtues of intimidation early on. I chose, perhaps unconsciously, to remain a shadow—timid, but a survivor.

8   The fearsomeness mistakenly attributed to me in public places often has a perilous flavor. The most frightening of these confusions occurred in the late 1970s and early 1980s, when I worked as a journalist in Chicago. One day, rushing into the office of a magazine I was writing for with a deadline story in hand, I was mistaken for a burglar. The office manager called security and, with an ad hoc posse, pursued me through the labyrinthine halls, nearly to my editor's door. I had no way of proving who I was. I could only move briskly toward the company of someone who knew me.

9   Another time I was on assignment for a local paper and killing time before an interview. I entered a jewelry store on the city's affluent Near North Side. The proprietor excused herself and returned with an enormous red Doberman pinscher straining at the end of a leash. She stood, the dog extended toward me, silent to my questions, her eyes bulging nearly out of her head. I took a cursory look around, nodded, and bade her good night.

10   Relatively speaking, however, I never fared as badly as another black male journalist. He went to nearby Waukegan, Illinois, a couple of summers ago to work on a story about a murderer who was born there. Mistaking the reporter for the killer, police officers hauled him from his car at gunpoint and but for his press creden-

tials would probably have tried to book him. Such episodes are not uncommon. Black men trade tales like this all the time.

11   Over the years, I learned to smother the rage I felt at so often being taken for a criminal. Not to do so would surely have led to madness. I now take precautions to make myself less threatening. I move about with care, particularly late in the evening. I give a wide berth to nervous people on subway platforms during the wee hours, particularly when I have exchanged business clothes for jeans. If I happen to be entering a building behind some people who appear skittish, I may walk by, letting them clear the lobby before I return, so as not to seem to be following them. I have been calm and extremely congenial on those rare occasions when I've been pulled over by the police.

12   And on late-evening constitutionals I employ what has proved to be an excellent tension-reducing measure: I whistle melodies from Beethoven and Vivaldi and the more popular classical composers. Even steely New Yorkers hunching toward nighttime destinations seem to relax, and occasionally they even join in the tune. Virtually everybody seems to sense that a mugger wouldn't be warbling bright, sunny selections from Vivaldi's *Four Seasons*. It is my equivalent of the cowbell that hikers wear when they know they are in bear country.

THESIS AND ORGANIZATION

1. Reread paragraph 1. What expectations does it evoke in the reader? For paragraph 2, state in your own words what Staples means by "unwieldy inheritance." What effects does that inheritance have?

2. The body of the essay breaks into three paragraph blocks. In paragraphs 3–5, what effects does the author's walking at night have on others? On himself?

3. In paragraphs 6 and 7, Staples refers to his childhood. Why had he been unaware of his effect on others? What effect did the streets he grew up on have on him?

4. Staples uses examples in paragraphs 8–10. What do all three have in common? What generalization does Staples draw from them?

5. Summarize the causes and effects Staples brings out in paragraphs 11 and 12, and in one sentence, make a general statement about them. What does that statement imply about being a black male? About urban life? About

American culture? Consider your answers to those questions, and in one sentence state the thesis of the essay.

TECHNIQUE AND STYLE

1. A large part of the essay's impact lies in the ironic contrast between appearance and reality. What details does Staples bring out about himself that contrast with the stereotype of the mugger?
2. In paragraph 1, Staples illustrates the two uses of the dash. What function do they perform? Rewrite either of the two sentences so that you avoid the dash. Which sentence is better and why?
3. Trace Staples's use of time. Why does he start where he does? Try placing the time period mentioned in paragraphs 6 and 7 elsewhere in the essay. What advantages does their present placement have? What is the effect of ending the essay in the present?
4. Examine Staples's choice of verbs in the second sentence of paragraph 5. Rewrite the sentence using as many forms of the verb *to be* as possible. What differences do you note?
5. Staples concludes the essay with an analogy. In what ways is it ironic? How does the irony tie into the essay's thesis?

SUGGESTIONS FOR WRITING

Journal

1. All of us have been in a situation in which we felt threatened. Select an incident that occurred to you and describe its effect on you.
2. Think about a time when, intentionally or unintentionally, you threatened or intimidated someone. Describe either the causes or effects.

Essay

You can develop either of the journal ideas above into a full-fledged essay. Or, if you prefer, think about a situation in which you have been stereotyped and that stereotype determined your effect on others. Among the physical characteristics that can spawn a stereotype are

age
race
gender
physique
clothing

Why Don't We Like the Human Body?

Barbara Ehrenreich

Essayist, novelist, journalist, activist, Barbara Ehrenreich has written extensively on almost every imaginable subject, though politics and the media are her prime targets. A regular contributor to Time *and* The Nation *as well as numerous other magazines, her work also appears in the electronic magazine Z, and her voice is often heard on* Today, Nightline, *and* All Things Considered, *among other radio and television shows. When asked about her large number of publications and venues, she replied, "If I don't write, we don't eat."*

For Ehrenreich, the writing process is anything but calm: "Each article, column, or even short review is a temporary obsession, characterized by frantic research and moments of wild mania, tempered with crushing self-doubt. Adding up to a heady, thrill-filled life." You can also tell something about her sense of humor from the titles of her collections of essays: The Worst Years of Our Lives: Irreverent Notes From a Decade of Greed *(1990) and* The Snarling Citizen *(1995). Her latest book, however, has a different tone:* Blood Rites: Origins and History of the Passions of War *(1997). In 1980, Ehrenreich shared the National Magazine Award for Excellence in Reporting, excellence also reflected in her numerous fellowships and honorary degrees. The essay that follows was published in* Time *in July, 1991.*

WHAT TO LOOK FOR   *You've probably heard that the first paragraph of an essay should "grab the reader's attention," something easily said but hard to do. Ehrenreich, however, succeeds by using lots of details that, thanks to the examples, are lurid ones. If you're stuck for a first paragraph, try writing your draft without one and then go back to write the introduction. Then when you write it, like Ehrenreich, you can use examples and describe them in detail.*

1   There's something wrong when a $7 movie in the mall can leave you with post-traumatic stress syndrome. In the old days killers merely stalked and slashed and strangled. Today they flay their victims and stash the rotting, skinless corpses. Or they eat them filleted, with a glass of wine, or live and with the skin still on when

there's no time to cook. It's not even the body count that matters anymore. What counts is the number of ways to trash the body: decapitation, dismemberment, impalings and (ranging into the realm of the printed word) eye gougings, power drillings and the application of hungry rodents to some poor victim's innards.

2   All right, terrible things do happen. Real life is filled with serial killers, mass murderers and sickos of all degrees. Much of the 20th century, it could be argued, has been devoted to ingenious production and disposal of human corpses. But the scary thing is not that eye gougings and vivisections and meals of human flesh may, occasionally, happen. The scary thing, the thing that ought to make the heart pound and the skin go cold and tingly, is that somehow we find this fun to watch.

3   There are some theories, of course. In what might be called the testosterone theory, a congenital error in the wiring of the male brain leads to a confusion between violence and sex. Men get off on hideous mayhem, and women, supposedly, cover their eyes. Then there's the raging puritan theory, which is based on the statistical fact that those who get slashed or eaten on the screen are usually guilty of a little fooling around themselves. It's only a tingle of rectitude we feel, according to this, when the bad girl finally gets hers. There's even an invidious comparison theory: we enjoy seeing other people get sautéed or chain-sawed because at least it's not happening to us.

4   The truth could be so much simpler that it's staring us in the face. There's always been a market for scary stories and vicarious acts of violence. But true horror can be bloodless, as in Henry James' matchless tale, *The Turn of the Screw*. Even reckless violence, as in the old-time western, need not debauch the human form. No, if offerings like *American Psycho* and *The Silence of the Lambs* have anything to tell us about ourselves, it must be that at this particular historical moment, we have come to hate the body.

5   Think about it. Only a couple of decades ago, we could conceive of better uses for the body than as a source of meat or leather. Sex, for example. Sex was considered a valid source of thrills even if both parties were alive and remained so throughout the act. Therapists urged us to "get in touch with our bodies"; feminists celebrated "our bodies, ourselves." Minimally, the body was a cuddly personal habitat that could be shared with special loved ones. Maximally, it was a powerhouse offering multiple orgasms

and glowing mind-body epiphanies. Skin was something to massage or gently stroke.

6   Then, for good reasons or bad, we lost sex. It turned out to spread deadly viruses. It offended the born-again puritans. It led to messy entanglements that interfered with networking and power lunching. Since there was no way to undress for success, we switched in the mid-'80s to food. When we weren't eating, we were watching food-porn starring Julia Child or working off calories on the Stairmaster. The body wasn't perfect, but it could, with effort and willpower, be turned into a lean, mean eating machine.

7   And then we lost food. First they took the red meat, the white bread and the Chocolate Decadence desserts. Then they came for the pink meat, the cheese, the butter, the tropical oils and, of course, the whipped cream. Finally, they wanted all protein abolished, all fat and uncomplex carbohydrates, leaving us with broccoli and Metamucil. Everything else, as we know, is transformed by our treacherous bodies into insidious, slow-acting toxins.

8   So no wonder we enjoy seeing the human body being shredded, quartered, flayed, filleted and dissolved in vats of acid. It let us down. No wonder we love heroes and megavillians like RoboCop and the Terminator, in whom all soft, unreliable tissue has been replaced by metal alloys. Or that we like reading (even, in articles deeply critical of the violence they manage to summarize) about diabolical new uses for human flesh. It's been, let's face it, a big disappointment. May as well feed it to the rats or to any cannibalistically inclined killer still reckless enough to indulge in red meat.

10   No, it's time for a truce with the soft and wayward flesh. Maybe violent imagery feeds the obsessions of real-life sickos. Or maybe, as some argue, it drains their sickness off into harmless fantasy. But surely it cheapens our sense of ourselves to think that others, even fictional others, could see us as little more than meat. And it's hard to believe all this carnage doesn't dull our response to the global wastage of human flesh in famine, flood and war.

11   We could start by admitting that our '70's-era expectations were absurdly high. The body is not a reliable source of ecstasy or transcendental insight. For most of our lives, it's a shambling, jury-rigged affair, filled with innate tensions, contradictions, broken springs. Hollywood could help by promoting better uses for the body, like real sex, by which I mean sex between people who are often wrinkled and overweight and sometimes even fond of each

other. The health meanies could relax and acknowledge that one of the most marvelous functions of the body is, in fact, to absorb small doses of whipped cream and other illicit substances.

12   Then maybe we can start making friends with our bodies again. They need nurture and care, but they should also be good for a romp now and then, by which I mean something involving dancing or petting as opposed to dicing and flaying. But even "friends" is another weirdly alienated image. The truth, which we have almost forgotten, is that Bodies "R" Us.

THESIS AND ORGANIZATION

1. Paragraphs 1 and 2 introduce the essay. What do they lead you to expect in what follows?
2. Paragraphs 3 and 4 explore the reasons we enjoy watching mayhem on the screen and in the pages of a book. What are they?
3. Paragraphs 5–8 trace the causes of what Ehrenreich perceives as our hatred of the body. What are they?
4. In paragraph 9, Ehrenreich spells out why we need to change our attitudes, and in paragraph 10, she argues for specific changes. What are they?
5. Consider the structure of Ehrenreich's essay that your answers to questions 1–4 have revealed, and in your own words, state the thesis.

TECHNIQUE AND STYLE

1. Reread paragraph 1, paying particular attention to the verbs. What do you notice about them?
2. Ehrenreich incorporates specific allusions to films, books, products, a food celebrity, and a toy store. What do these allusions add to the essay?
3. How would you describe Ehrenreich's tone? How serious is she about her main point? What examples can you find to back up your opinion?
4. How would you describe Ehrenreich's persona? How informed does she appear to be? How credible?
5. You've probably been warned about using the pronoun *they* without its referring to something specific, yet that's just what Ehrenreich does in paragraph 7. What reasons can you think of for her choice?

SUGGESTIONS FOR WRITING

Journal

1. Ehrenreich believes that the violence we find in popular culture is caused by our hating our bodies. Write a short response of your own to that claim.

2. Ehrenreich coins the term "food-porn" (paragraph 6) to summarize our cultures preoccupation with food. To what extent do you think we are obsessed with what we eat?

Essay

While most of us would agree that violence is part of our culture, what that means is open to debate. Some of that violence is intended, such as what is involved in crimes and depicted in books, films, and other examples from the popular culture. Some, however, is accidental, as in automobile accidents. Think about violence and the role it plays in our society. Perhaps you wish to speculate on what causes it or on its effects. If you have witnessed it in person, you could write about its effect on you, though you may find that topic too personal in which case, you can always turn to the media and the electronic world around you to find a topic. Suggestions:

film
books
television
video games
the Internet

On Using
Argument

9

Up to this point, this book has focused on patterns of organization that can be used singly and in combination for various aims—to express how you feel, to explain, and, to a lesser extent, to argue. Those modes or patterns are the means to an end, ways to achieve your goal of self-expression, exposition, or argument. This chapter directly addresses the goal of argument, but because book after book has been written on the art of argument, think of what you have here as a basic introduction. In this chapter you will discover how to construct a short argumentative essay and how the various modes are used to support that aim. It's only appropriate, therefore, that the discussion start with a definition.

In everyday speech, **argument** is so closely associated with *quarrel* or *fight* that it has a negative connotation, but that connotation does not apply to the word as it is used in the writing of essays. If you were to analyze an essay by examining its argument, you would be looking at the writer's major assertion and the weight of the evidence on which it rests. That evidence should be compelling, for the ideal aim of all argumentative writing is to move the reader to adopt the writer's view. In writing argumentative papers, you might want to go further than that and call for a particular action, but most of the time you'll probably work at convincing your reader at least to keep reading and at best share your position on the issue. Many of the subjects of argumentative essays are ones your readers already have an opinion about, so if all you accomplish is having someone who disagrees with you keep on reading, you have constructed a successful argument.

Because an argumentative essay bases its thesis primarily on reason, the word *logic* may pop into your mind and raise images of mathematical models and seemingly tricky statements stringing together sentences beginning with *if*s and leading to one starting with *therefore*. Don't worry. The kind of argumentative essays you will be asked to write are simply an extension of the kinds of essays you've written all along: your thesis is the heart of your argument, and examples, definitions, descriptions and the like provide your supporting evidence.

It's useful to distinguish between self-expression and argument. Open your local newspaper to the editorial pages, and you'll probably find examples of both. If you found a letter to the editor that rants about the "sins" of the Democratic Party and describes the "sinners" as "dishonest, lying, cheats," it's unlikely that the letter will be read all the way through by a Democrat. The writer was letting off steam rather than trying to argue a point, and the steam was based on emotion, not reason. But if there's an editorial on the same page on the same general subject, you'll find it uses reason to support its point as it argues in favor of specific reforms in the laws governing campaign contributions. Such an editorial may well state that although the media's focus highlights abuses within the Democratic party, the Republicans are not altogether innocent. Both Democrats and Republicans are apt to read the editorial all the way through, and many from both parties may come to agree with the editor's thesis.

Slipping from argument into self-expression, relying on emotion instead of reason, is easy to do, particularly if you're writing on a subject about which you feel strongly. One way to avoid that trap is to start work on your topic by brainstorming on the subject as a whole, not your position on it. Phrase the subject as a question, and then list the pros and cons.

If you are writing on gambling, for instance, you would ask, "Should gambling be legalized?" Then you would define your terms: Who would be legalizing it—the federal government, the state, the county, the city? What kind of gambling is involved—betting on horse races, on sports? Playing games such as bingo, video poker, slot machines, roulette? Buying tickets for a lottery? Answering those kinds of questions will help you to draw up your pros and cons more easily because your focus will be more specific. Once you've listed the arguments that can be used, you can then sort through them, noting the evidence you can cite and where to find it. Having done all that, you then are in a position to choose which side you wish to take, and you know the arguments that can be used against you.

The next step is to think about the ways in which you can appeal to your readers. Citing facts and precedents will appeal to their reason; exploring moral issues will appeal to their emotions; and presenting a persona that is thoughtful and, therefore, credible will appeal to their sense of fairness.

Reason is the primary appeal in most argumentative writing, and to use it successfully, you may need to do some research on your subject (each of these appeals—reason, emotion, and persona—is discussed in greater detail following this overview). Once your argument begins to take shape, however, you will find that dealing with one or two of the opposing views will not only strengthen your own case but will also earn you some points for fairness.

Argumentative writing ranges from the personal to the abstract and draws on the various patterns that can be used to structure an essay. For instance, waiting tables in a restaurant may have convinced you that tips should be automatically included in the bill. To make the case that the present system is unfair to those in a service trade, you might draw primarily on your own experience and that of others, though you need to make sure that your experience is representative. If you don't, your reader may discount your argument, thinking that one example isn't sufficient evidence. A quick check among others who are similarly employed or a look at government reports on employment statistics should show that your example is typical and, therefore, to be trusted.

The technical term for an entire argument based on only one example is **hasty generalization,** one of many logical fallacies that can occur in argumentative writing. **Logical fallacies** are holes or lapses in reasoning and, therefore, to be avoided. If you were to argue that the reader should consider only the present system of tipping or the one you propose, you will be guilty of **either-or reasoning,** which is false because it permits no middle ground such as requiring a minimum tip of five percent. Quote Michael Jordan on the subject and you will be citing **false authority;** he knows basketball but not the restaurant industry. And obviously, if you call a 10-percent tipper a cheap idiot, you will be accused quite rightly of name-calling, the **ad hominem** (to the person) fallacy.

Say you noticed one evening that as closing time loomed, your tips got smaller. Is that because people who dine late tip minimally or because your customers felt rushed or because someone miscalculated the tip or some unknown reason? If you conclude that people who dine late are poor tippers, you may well be mistaking a temporal relationship for a causal one. Two events may occur at times close to each other (small tip, late hour) without implying a valid cause and effect relationship. To confuse the two is called **post hoc reasoning.**

Often the best topic for an argumentative essay is the one you come up with on your own, but at times you may be assigned a topic. If that happens, you may find your chances for success increase if you shape the topic so that you have a direct connection to it. Because you already know something about the subject, you have done some thinking about it instead of starting from scratch or using secondhand opinions. Even

abstract topics such as euthanasia can be made concrete and will probably be the better for it. Though you may have never been confronted directly by the issue of mercy killing, you probably have had a member of
your family who was terminally ill. Would euthanasia have been an
appropriate alternative? Should it have been? In addition to using your
own experience, consider using your local newspaper as a resource.
Newspaper accounts and editorials can also help give form and focus to
an abstract issue, and in addition to the book and periodical sources you
may consult, they will help you delineate your topic more clearly.

AUDIENCE AND PURPOSE

Audience plays a greater role in argument than in any other type of writing, and therein lies a problem: you must adapt both form and content
to fit your audience, while at the same time maintaining your integrity. If
you shape your argumentative position according to its probable acceptance by your readers rather than your own belief, the result is propaganda or sensationalism, not argument. Knowingly playing false with an
audience by omitting evidence or shaping facts to fit an assertion or by
resorting to logical fallacies are all dishonest tricks.

Imagine, for example, that you are on the staff of your campus newspaper and have been given the assignment of investigating the rumors
that the Dean of the College of Business is going to resign. You know
that the dean has been fighting with the president of your university, arguing that the College of Business is "grossly underfunded," a phrase
you found in an earlier story on university finances. But you also read
an interview with the dean and know that she has close ties to the local
business community and may be offered a job heading a local company.
Add to that your suspicion that not many colleges of business have
deans who are women, a suspicion borne out by statistics you can
quote, and you begin to scent a story. If you choose to write one that
plays up the conflict with the president and implies sexism while ignoring the possibility of the dean's being hired away from the university,
you are not being true to your evidence and are, therefore, misleading
your readers.

Within honest bounds, however, you have much to draw on, and a
sense of what your audience may or may not know and of what the audience believes about a topic can guide you. Even if your topic is familiar, what you have to say about it will be new information. Censorship is
a tired subject, but if you were to write on the banning of a particular

book from a particular public school library, you would probably give the topic a new twist or two. A concrete example, often in the form of a short introductory narrative, makes an abstract issue more accessible and is apt to keep your reader reading.

If your subject is one many readers know little about, then you can begin by explaining the issue and its context. If your classmates are your readers, for example, they will know little about your personal life. And if you have an aunt whose health insurance was cancelled after her cancer returned, the action may compel you to research an insurance company's right to drop those it insures. Put your indignation together with what you discovered through your research and what your classmates don't know, and you have all the makings of a successful argumentative paper protesting what you see as an injustice.

Whether you start with what your audience does or does not know or with a narrative that illustrates the general situation and makes it concrete, your aim is to convince your readers to adopt your convictions, perhaps even to act on them. Not all readers will be convinced, of course, but if they at least respond, "Hmm, I hadn't thought of that" or "Well, I may have to rethink my position," you will have presented an effective argument.

ARGUMENTATIVE APPEALS

When you write an argumentative essay, you will find that you are appealing to the reader's emotions and reason by creating a credible persona, the ethical appeal. **Reason,** however, is the most important. To present a logical pattern of thought, you will probably find yourself drawing on one or more modes, particularly definition, comparison, and cause and effect. If, for instance, you have a part-time job at a fast-food franchise, you may have noticed that most of the other employees are also part-time. The situation may strike you as exploitive, and you want to write about it.

You might start sketching out a first draft with the example of your job, then define what part-time means, using cause and effect to argue that franchise companies that depend primarily on part-time labor exploit their workers to create greater profits for the company. As you work, you will find that you are laying out a line of reasoning, the assertions—probably the topic sentences for paragraphs or paragraph clusters—that support your thesis. You will also have to do some research so that you place your example in a larger context, showing that it is clearly typical. Then, armed with some facts and figures, you can test each of your supporting sentences by first asking "Am I making an assertion?" If the answer is yes, then you can test your line of reasoning and hence your appeal to reason by asking "Is it supported by evidence?" and "Is the evidence sufficient?"

Logical thinking must undergird all argumentative essays, even those that use an **emotional** appeal, an appeal that often rests on example, description, and narration. In the example of the essay about health insurers, you would be using an emotional appeal if you began your essay with a brief narrative of your aunt's battle with cancer and the crisis caused by her loss of health insurance. And although the bulk of the essay would be taken up with the essay's appeal to reason, you might choose to close with an emotional appeal, perhaps reminding your readers of the number of people who cannot afford any kind of medical insurance and calling for a general reform of health care.

But the emotional appeal has its dangers, particularly when you are close to the subject. You would not want your description of your aunt's problems to slide into the melodramatic, nor would you want to create so powerful an impression that anything that comes after, which is the heart of your argument, is anticlimactic. Emotional appeals are often best left to snagging the reader's attention or calling for action, relatively small roles, than serving a primary function in the essay. Emotion will have an impact, but reason will carry the argument.

The appeal of **persona,** known in classical rhetoric as *ethos* (which translates somewhat ambiguously as "the ethical appeal"), is more subtle than the others; the writer is not appealing directly to the reader's emotions or intellect but instead is using his or her persona to lend credence to the essay's major assertion. The point gets tricky. A fair and honest writer is one who is fair and honest with the reader. Such a writer takes on a persona, not like donning a mask to hide behind but like selecting a picture to show those elements in the personality that represent the writer at his or her best.

For a good example of how persona functions, think of the last time you took an essay test. What you were writing was a mini-argument maintaining that your answer to the question is a correct one. Your persona, which you probably didn't even think about, was intended to create a sense of authority, the idea that you knew what you were writing about. You are so used to writing within an academic context, that the elements of your persona come naturally. The tone you use for essay tests is more formal than informal, which means that your choice of words, your diction, is more elevated than conversational. And if a technical vocabulary is appropriate—the vocabulary of physics, sociology, the arts, and the like—you use it. Successful essay answers also use evidence and are tightly organized so that the line of thought is clear and compelling, all of which comes under the appeal of reason, but don't underestimate the appeal of persona. If two test answers contain the exact same information, the one that is written in the more sophisticated style that implies a more thoughtful response is apt to receive the higher grade.

LOGICAL FALLACIES

Logical fallacies abuse the various appeals. The introduction to this chapter has already pointed out the more obvious ones—hasty generalization, false authority, name-calling, post hoc and either-or reasoning—but there are many others as well. Advertising and political campaigns are often crammed with them.

If you receive a flyer asking you to vote for a candidate for the school board because he is a Vietnam veteran who has a successful law practice, the logic doesn't follow, a literal translation of the Latin term **non sequitur:** the claim leaves you wondering what being a veteran and an attorney have to do with the duties of a member of the school board. And if the flyer goes on to maintain that because the candidate has three children he can understand the problems of students in the public schools when you know that his three children go to private schools, then you've spotted a **false analogy,** a double one—public and private schools are quite different, and three children from the family of a professional are not representative of the public school student population.

Such a flyer is also guilty of **begging the question,** another fallacy. The main question for a school board election is "Can this person make a positive contribution?" Being a Vietnam veteran and the father of three children doesn't answer that question. A **shift in definition** is another form of begging the question. If this hypothetical candidate also claims to be a "good citizen" and then goes on to define that term by example, citing service to his country and fatherhood as proof, then as a voter, you're left with a very narrow definition. Good citizenship involves much more.

Often when you read or hear about the holes in an argument, you may also hear the term **straw man.** With this technique (yet another form of begging the question), your attention is drawn away from the main point, and instead the argument focuses on a minor point with the hope that by demolishing it, the main one will also suffer. Imagine that there's a move to increase local taxes, and you want to argue against it in a letter to the local paper. As you consider the points you can make, you come up with a short list: that the taxes are already high, that existing funds are not being spent wisely, and that all that the taxes support—schools, roads, government and the like—while not outstanding are adequate. You start to gather information to use as evidence for each of these points (probably discovering several more) and run across a news story about a large amount of local taxpayers' money having been spent on rebuilding a bridge on a back road that averaged all of three cars a day. If you were to stop there and construct a thesis arguing taxes should not be raised because of waste in government, then making your case by basing it on the example of the building of the bridge, you would be constructing a straw man argument, one that avoids the major issues.

THESIS AND ORGANIZATION

The thesis of an argumentative essay should be readily identifiable: it is the conviction that you want an audience to adopt. Sometimes the thesis may be stated in the title, but more often you will state your position early on, then back it up with evidence in the body of your essay. If you organize your ideas by moving from the general (the thesis) to the particular (the evidence), you are using **deductive reasoning.** Most of the argumentative essays you run across will be using this kind of logical organization. As for the order in which you choose to present the evidence on which your thesis rests, you'll probably arrange it from the least important to the most important so that the essay has some dramatic tension. Putting the most important first doesn't leave you anywhere to go, rather like knowing from the start that the butler did it.

Although some times you may want to put your thesis as your first sentence, usually you will want to lead up to it, *introduce* it in the literal sense. Starting right off with the thesis will probably strike the reader as too abrupt, too sudden, a bit like being hit over the head. Often an argumentative essay will begin with a narrative or some explanation, ways of setting the scene so that when the thesis appears, it seems natural. As for the ending, you may want to return to the same narrative or information you started with or call for action or point out what may happen unless your view is adopted. Remember, by the time your reader finishes reading what you have to say, if all you have done is make the person reconsider ideas and rethink the argument, you will have succeeded. It's rare, though not impossible, for one essay to change a person's mind.

Now and then, you'll find yourself reading an argument that is organized by moving from the particular to the general, from evidence to thesis. What you have then is called **inductive reasoning,** and it's usually more difficult to write because it demands tight focus and control. Think of the essay's organization as a jigsaw puzzle. Your reader has to recognize each piece as a piece, and you have to build the evidence so that each piece falls into a predetermined place. The completed picture is the thesis.

If you want to construct an essay using inductive reasoning, you may find it easier to do if in your first draft you state your thesis at the beginning, baldly, just so you stay on track. Then, when you've shaped the rest of the paper, you simply move the thesis from the beginning to the last paragraph, perhaps even the last sentence.

You'll find that the essays in this section represent both kinds of organization, so you'll have a chance to see how others have developed their ideas to argue a particular point.

Useful Terms

Ad hominem argument Name-calling, smearing the person instead of attacking the argument. A type of logical fallacy. Smearing the group the person belongs to instead of attacking the argument is called an *ad populum* logical fallacy.

Appeal to emotion Playing or appealing to the reader's emotions.

Appeal to persona The appeal of the writer's moral character that creates the impression that the writer can be trusted and, therefore, believed.

Appeal to reason Presenting evidence that is logical, well thought out, so as to be believed.

Argument The writer's major assertion and the evidence on which it is based.

Begging the question Arguing off the point, changing direction. A type of logical fallacy.

Deductive reasoning Reasoning that moves from the general to the particular, from the thesis to the evidence.

Either-or reasoning Staking out two extremes as the only alternatives and, therefore, excluding anything in between. A type of logical fallacy.

False analogy An analogy that does not stand up to logic. A type of logical fallacy.

False authority Citing an expert on one subject as an expert on another. A type of logical fallacy.

Hasty generalization Reasoning based on insufficient evidence, usually too few examples. A type of logical fallacy.

Inductive reasoning Reasoning that moves from the particular to the general, from the evidence to the thesis.

Logical fallacy An error in reasoning, a logical flaw that invalidates the argument.

Non sequitur Literally, it does not follow. No apparent link between points. A type of logical fallacy.

Persona The character of the writer that comes through from the prose.

Post hoc reasoning Assuming a causal relationship where a temporal one exists. A type of logical fallacy.

Shifting definition Changing the definition of a key term, a form of begging the question. A type of logical fallacy.

Straw man Attacking and destroying an irrelevant point instead of the main subject.

➤ POINTERS FOR USING ARGUMENT

Exploring the Topic

1. **What position do you want to take toward your subject?** Are you arguing to get your audience to adopt your thesis or to go further and take action? What is your thesis? What action is possible?

2. **How is your audience apt to respond to your assertion if you state it baldly?** How much background do you need to provide? Do you need to use definition? What arguments can the reader bring against your assertion?

3. **What examples can you think of to illustrate your topic?** Are all of them from your own experience? What other sources can you draw upon?

4. How can you appeal to your readers' emotions? How can you use example, description, and narration to carry your emotional appeal?

5. How can you appeal to your readers' reason? How can you use example, cause and effect, process, comparison and contrast, analogy, or division and classification to strengthen your logic?

6. What tone is most appropriate to the kind of appeal you want to emphasize? Does your persona fit that tone? How can you use persona to support your argument?

Drafting the Paper

1. Know your reader. Estimate how familiar your reader is with your topic and how, if at all, the reader may react to it emotionally. Keeping those ideas in mind, review how the various patterns of development may help you contend with your audience's knowledge and attitudes, and decide whether your primary appeal should be to emotion or reason.

Description, narration, and example lend themselves particularly well to emotional appeal; process, cause and effect, comparison and contrast, analogy, example, and division and classification are useful for rational appeal. Use definition to set the boundaries of your argument and its terms as well as to clear up anything the reader may not know.

2. Know your purpose. Depending on the predominant appeal you find most appropriate, your essay will tend toward persuasion or argument; you are trying to get your reader not only to understand your major assertion but also to adopt it and perhaps even to act on it. Short of that, a successful writer of argument must settle for the reader's "Well, I hadn't thought of it that way" or "Maybe I should reconsider."

The greatest danger in argumentative writing is to write to people like yourself, ones who already agree with you. You need not think of your audience as actively hostile, but to stay on the argumentative track, it helps to reread constantly as you write, playing the devil's advocate.

3. Acknowledge the opposition. Even though your reader may be the ideal—someone who holds no definite opposing view and indeed is favorably inclined toward yours but hasn't really thought the topic through—you should bring out one or two of the strongest arguments against your position and demolish them. If you don't, the reader may, and there goes your essay. The ideal reader is also the thinking reader who says, "Yes, but. . . . "

4. Avoid logical pitfalls. Logical fallacies can crop up in unexpected places; one useful way to test them is to check your patterns of development. If you have used examples, does your generalization or assertion follow? Sometimes the examples are too few to support the assertion, leading to a hasty generalization; sometimes the examples don't fit, leading to begging the question or arguing off the point or misusing authority; and sometimes the assertion is stated as an absolute, in which case the reader may think of an example that is the exception, destroying your point.

If you have used analogy, double-check to see that the analogy can stand up to scrutiny by examining the pertinent aspects of the things compared. If you have used cause and effect, you need to be particularly careful. Check to see that the events you claim to have a causal relationship do not have a temporal one instead; otherwise, you fall into the post hoc fallacy. Also examine causal relationships to make sure that you have not merely assumed the cause in your statement of effect. If you claim that "poor teaching is a major cause of the high dropout rate during the freshman year in college," you must prove that the teaching is poor; if you don't, you are arguing in a circle or begging the question.

Non sequiturs can also obscure cause-and-effect relationships when an element in the relationship is missing or nonexistent. Definition also sets some traps. Make sure your definition is not only fully stated but also commonly shared and consistent throughout.

5. Be aware of your persona. The ethical appeal, the rational appeal, and the emotional appeal are fundamental concepts of argument, and it is the persona, together with tone, that provides the ethical appeal. To put it simply, you need to be credible.

If you are writing on an issue you feel strongly about and, for example, are depending primarily on an appeal to reason, you don't want to let your dispassionate, logical persona slip and resort to name-calling (formally known as arguing ad hominem or ad populem). That's obvious.

Not so obvious, however, is some slip in diction or tone that reveals the hot head behind the cool pen. Your reader may feel manipulated or use the slip to discount your entire argument, all because you lost sight of the ethical appeal. Tone should vary, yes, but never to the point of discord.

6. Place your point where it does the most good. Put each of your paragraphs on a separate piece of paper so that you can rearrange their order as you would a hand of cards. Try out your major assertion in different slots. If you have it at the beginning, try it at the end and vice versa. Or extend the introduction so that the thesis comes closer to the middle of the paper. See which placement carries greater impact.

You may want to organize your material starting with examples that lead up to the position you wish to attack and to the conviction you are arguing for; in that case your thesis may occur somewhere in the middle third or at the end of the paper. On the other hand, you may want to use deduction—starting with the opposition, stating your position, and then spending 90 percent of the remaining essay supporting your case. Remember that you want to win your reader over, so put your thesis where it will do the greatest good.

Last Rites for Indian Dead

Suzan Shown Harjo

Writing as a Cheyenne, Suzan Shown Harjo points to a problem that affects Native Americans and, she argues, that raises an ethical issue for the rest of us. Her essay, which appeared on the editorial page of the Los Angeles Times *in September of 1989, is a good example of deductive reasoning.*

WHAT TO LOOK FOR *Conclusions are often difficult to write, but one way of ending an argumentative essay is to call for a specified action. That is what Harjo does for her essay, and it's a technique you can adapt for your own arguments.*

1   What if museums, universities, and government agencies could put your dead relatives on display or keep them in boxes to be cut up and otherwise studied? What if you believed that the spirits of the dead could not rest until their human remains were placed in a sacred area?

2   The ordinary American would say there ought to be a law—and there is, for ordinary Americans. The problem for American Indians is that there are too many laws of the kind that make us the archaeological property of the United States and too few of the kind that protect us from such insults.

3   Some of my own Cheyenne relatives' skulls are in the Smithsonian Institution today, along with those of at least 4500 other Indian people who were violated in the 1800s by the U.S. Army for an "Indian Cranial Study." It wasn't enough that these unarmed Cheyenne people were mowed down by the cavalry at the infamous Sand Creek massacre; many were decapitated and their heads shipped to Washington as freight. (The Army Medical Museum's collection is now in the Smithsonian.) Some had been exhumed only hours after being buried. Imagine their grieving families' reaction on finding their loved ones disinterred and headless.

4   Some targets of the Army's study were killed in noncombat situations and beheaded immediately. The officer's account of the decapitation of the Apache chief Mangas Coloradas in 1863 shows the

pseudoscientific nature of the exercise. "I weighed the brain and measured the skull," the good doctor wrote, "and found that while the skull was smaller, the brain was larger than that of Daniel Webster."

5   These journal accounts exist in excruciating detail, yet missing are any records of overall comparisons, conclusions or final reports of the Army study. Since it is unlike the Army not to leave a paper trail, one must wonder about the motive for its collection.

6   The total Indian body count in the Smithsonian collection is more than 19,000, and it is not the largest in the country. It is not inconceivable that the 1.5 million of us living today are outnumbered by our dead stored in museums, educational institutions, federal agencies, state historical societies and private collections. The Indian people are further dehumanized by being exhibited alongside the mastodons and dinosaurs and other extinct creatures.

7   Where we have buried our dead in peace, more often than not the sites have been desecrated. For more than 200 years, relic hunting has been a popular pursuit. Lately, the market in Indian artifacts has brought this abhorrent activity to a fever pitch in some areas. And when scavengers come upon Indian burial sites, everything found becomes fair game, including sacred burial offerings, teeth and skeletal remains.

8   One unusually well-publicized example of Indian grave desecration occurred two years ago in a western Kentucky field known as Slack Farm, the site of an Indian village five centuries ago. Ten men—one with a business card stating "Have Shovel, Will Travel"—paid the landowner $10,000 to lease digging rights between planting seasons. They dug extensively on the 40-acre farm, rummaging through an estimated 650 graves, collecting burial goods, tools and ceremonial items. Skeletons were strewn about like litter.

9   What motivates people to do something like this? Financial gain is the first answer. Indian relic-collecting has become a multi-million-dollar industry. The price tag on a bead necklace can easily top $1000; rare pieces fetch tens of thousands.

10   And it is not just collectors of the macabre who pay for skeletal remains. Scientists say that these deceased Indians are needed for research that someday could benefit the health and welfare of living Indians. But just how many dead Indians must they examine? Nineteen thousand?

11   There is doubt as to whether permanent curation of our dead really benefits Indians. Dr. Emery A. Johnson, former assistant surgeon general, recently observed, "I am not aware of any current medical diagnostic or treatment procedure that has been derived from research on such skeletal remains. Nor am I aware of any during the 34 years that I have been involved in American Indian . . . health care."

12   Indian remains are still being collected for racial biological studies. While the intentions may be honorable, the ethics of using human remains this way without the full consent of relatives must be questioned.

13   Some relief for Indian people has come on the state level. Almost half of the states, including California, have passed laws protecting Indian burial sites and restricting the sale of Indian bones, burial offerings and other sacred items. Representative Charles E. Bennett (D-Fla.) and Sen. John McCain (R-Ariz.) have introduced bills that are a good start in invoking the federal government's protection. However, no legislation has attacked the problem head-on by imposing stiff penalties at the marketplace, or by changing laws that make dead Indians the nation's property.

14   Some universities—notably Stanford, Nebraska, Minnesota and Seattle—have returned, or agreed to return, Indian human remains; it is fitting that institutions of higher education should lead the way.

15   Congress is now deciding what to do with the government's extensive collection of Indian human remains and associated funerary objects. The secretary of the Smithsonian, Robert McC. Adams, has been valiantly attempting to apply modern ethics to yesterday's excesses. This week, he announced that the Smithsonian would conduct an inventory and return all Indian skeletal remains that could be identified with specific tribes or living kin.

16   But there remains a reluctance generally among collectors of Indian remains to take action of a scope that would have a quantitative impact and a healing quality. If they will not act on their own— and it is highly unlikely that they will—then Congress must act.

17   The country must recognize that the bodies of dead American Indian people are not artifacts to be bought and sold as collectors' items. It is not appropriate to store tens of thousands of our ancestors for possible future research. They are our family. They deserve to be returned to their sacred burial grounds and given a chance to rest.

18   The plunder of our people's graves has gone on too long. Let us rebury our dead and remove this shameful past from America's future.

THESIS AND ORGANIZATION

1. Paragraphs 1 and 2 introduce the essay by presenting a "what if" situation. Why might Harjo have chosen this kind of opening?

2. Summarize the examples Harjo presents in paragraphs 3–8.

3. Paragraphs 9–12 explain why people dig up Indian burial sites. What reasons does Harjo give?

4. Harjo explains what is being done and what needs to be done about the situation in paragraphs 13–18. What solution does she call for?

5. Considering the situation Harjo describes, the steps that are being taken to address that situation, and what remains to be done, what is the thesis of the essay?

TECHNIQUE AND STYLE

1. Describe the audience the essay is aimed at as precisely as you can. What evidence do you base your description on?

2. How would you characterize the diction Harjo uses in connection with her examples? Choose one or two examples and substitute more or less loaded words. What is gained? Lost?

3. Based on the way the essay is written, what kind of person does Harjo appear to be? How would you describe her?

4. To what extent does the essay rest its appeal on Harjo's persona? On emotion? On logic? Which appeal predominates?

5. The essay concludes with a call for action. Evaluate its effectiveness.

SUGGESTIONS FOR WRITING

Journal

1. Imagine that you are on the board of a museum that owns Indian skeletons. Explain your response to Harjo's essay.

2. Explain whether you would like to meet Harjo.

Essay

Think of an action that was considered acceptable in the past but today is either questionable or unacceptable. Fifty years ago, for instance, no one thought much about the hazards of smoking, nor of cholesterol levels, nor of needing to inspect meat. Segregation was acceptable, as were other forms of racism. Choose a subject and think about the ethics involved and how present knowledge has changed how we live. Other suggestions:

the sale of cigarettes
the advertising of alcoholic beverages
the popularity of natural foods
the sale of diet products

Gay Marriages: Make Them Legal

Thomas B. Stoddard

What is traditional is not always what is right, or so Thomas B. Stoddard argues in the essay that follows. He calls for a redefinition of marriage that accommodates the legal status of matrimony to the present times. Stoddard is an attorney and executive director of the Lambda Legal Defense and Education Fund, a gay rights organization. Stoddard's essay was published as an opinion piece in the New York Times *in 1989. Since that time, the narrative Stoddard opens with has developed a different ending: Kowalski's parents stopped paying the bills for the nursing home, and she was then released into the care of Karen Thompson.*

WHAT TO LOOK FOR   *Definition is a key element in argument. Note how careful Stoddard is to define* marriage *in paragraphs 4 and 5. When you write your own argumentative paper, you'll probably find it helpful first to identify the most important term and then make sure early on in your paper that you define it carefully.*

1   "In sickness and in health, 'til death do us part." With those familiar words, millions of people each year are married, a public affirmation of a private bond that both society and the newlyweds hope will endure. Yet for nearly four years, Karen Thompson was denied the company of the one person to whom she had pledged lifelong devotion. Her partner is a woman, Sharon Kowalski, and their home state of Minnesota, like every other jurisdiction in the United States, refuses to permit two individuals of the same sex to marry.

2   Karen Thompson and Sharon Kowalski are spouses in every respect except the legal. They exchanged vows and rings; they lived together until November 13, 1983—when Ms. Kowalski was severely injured when her car was struck by a drunk driver. She lost the capacity to walk or to speak more than several words at a time, and needed constant care.

3   Ms. Thompson sought a court ruling granting her guardianship over her partner, but Ms. Kowalski's parents opposed the petition and obtained sole guardianship. They moved Ms. Kowalski to a

nursing home 300 miles away from Ms. Thompson and forbade all visits between the two women. Last month, as part of a reevaluation of Ms. Kowalski's mental competency, Ms. Thompson was permitted to visit her partner again. But the prolonged injustice and anguish inflicted on both women hold a moral for everyone.

4   Marriage, the Supreme Court declared in 1967, is "one of the basic civil rights of man" (and, presumably, of woman as well). The freedom to marry, said the Court, is "essential to the orderly pursuit of happiness."

5   Marriage is not just a symbolic state. It can be the key to survival, emotional and financial. Marriage triggers a universe of rights, privileges and presumptions. A married person can share in a spouse's estate even when there is no will. She is typically entitled to the group insurance and pension programs offered by the spouse's employer, and she enjoys tax advantages. She cannot be compelled to testify against her spouse in legal proceedings.

6   The decision whether or not to marry belongs properly to individuals—not the government. Yet at present, all 50 states deny that choice to millions of gay and lesbian Americans. While marriage has historically required a male partner and a female partner, history alone cannot sanctify injustice. If tradition were the only measure, most states would still limit matrimony to partners of the same race.

7   As recently as 1967, before the Supreme Court declared miscegenation statutes unconstitutional, 16 states still prohibited marriages between a white person and a black person. When all the excuses were stripped away, it was clear that the only purpose of those laws was, in the words of the Supreme Court, "to maintain white supremacy."

8   Those who argue against reforming the marriage statutes because they believe that same-sex marriage would be "antifamily" overlook the obvious: marriage creates families and promotes social stability. In an increasingly loveless world, those who wish to commit themselves to a relationship founded upon devotion should be encouraged, not scorned. Government has no legitimate interest in how that love is expressed.

9   And it can no longer be argued—if it ever could—that marriage is fundamentally a procreative unit. Otherwise, states would forbid marriage between those who, by reason of age or infertility, cannot have children, as well as those who elect not to.

10   As the case of Sharon Kowalski and Karen Thompson demonstrates, sanctimonious illusions lead directly to the suffering of others. Denied the right to marry, these two women are left subject to the whims and prejudices of others, and of the law.

11   Depriving millions of gay American adults the marriages of their choice, and the rights that flow from marriage, denies equal protection of the law. They, their families and friends, together with fairminded people everywhere, should demand an end to this monstrous injustice.

THESIS AND ORGANIZATION

1. Paragraphs 1–3 present an example that holds a "moral for everyone." What is it?
2. Paragraphs 4 and 5 define marriage. What point does Stoddard make about marriage?
3. Paragraphs 6–9 are aimed at countering arguments that can be used against Stoddard's view. Summarize them.
4. What is the effect of paragraph 10? What other paragraphs does it connect with?
5. The essay concludes with a statement of thesis and a call to action. Who should demand what, and how?

TECHNIQUE AND STYLE

1. What paragraph or paragraphs appeal to the reader's emotions?
2. What paragraph or paragraphs appeal to the reader's reason?
3. Where in the essay can you identify an ethical appeal, an appeal based on the author's persona?
4. Stoddard cites the arguments that can be used against his. Does he cite obvious ones? Is his treatment of them fair? How so?
5. Stoddard's subject is a sensitive one and his views may not be shared by many readers. Where in the essay can you find evidence that he is aware of his readers and their potential sensitivity to the issue he writes about?

SUGGESTIONS FOR WRITING

Journal

1. Stoddard's subject is an explosive one. What do you think about this issue?
2. Select one of the points Stoddard makes and either support or refute it.

Essay

Think of an issue that ought to be covered by a law or one that is governed by law and should not be. The best place to start is probably with your own experience and what irks you, but after that you'll need to do some research so that you can present your position in a more objective and reasoned way. The use of outside sources will lend more weight to your ideas. Suggestions for laws that do exist but that some think should not:

    the given speed limit
    the legal drinking age
    particular zoning or IRS regulations
    banning of prayers in public schools

Suggestions for laws that some think should exist but don't (varies by state):

    car insurance
    automobile safety seats for infants
    helmets for motorcycle riders
    neutering of pets

But Is It Art?

Daniel Slate

A student at the University of New Orleans, Daniel Slate wrote "But Is It Art?" in Kim McDonald's freshman composition course following a discussion of the controversy caused by the rap group 2 Live Crew, their album "Nasty as They Wanna Be," and Henry Louis Gates Jr.'s article defending the group and their recording. At the center of the controversy was a ruling by a federal judge in Florida that found the album obscene, a ruling that caused a number of record stores and several major retail chains to stop selling it, not only in Florida but also in a number of other states, and led to the arrest of two members of the band.

As a writer for the University newspaper, The Driftwood, *Slate sometimes faces the threat of censorship of his own work. Often a compromise is reached, but he acknowledges that sometimes he chooses not to have a piece published rather than allowing it to be altered. "Depending on what year it is when you read this," Slate comments, "[I] may have actually attained sophomore status."*

WHAT TO LOOK FOR   *Sometimes when you are writing about a subject that you feel strongly about, it's hard to stay on the main point and not let your feelings overshadow your appeal to reason. One way around that problem is to distance yourself from the topic by putting it within a larger context. That's exactly what Slate does when he set up the bulleted examples that open and close his essay, a device that you may also find useful.*

- Riots break out in the streets of Paris after a musical performance.
- This singer can only be shown from the waist up on television, for fear that his hips contribute to juvenile delinquency.
- Mass hysteria, fainting and "swooning" are becoming the norm at concerts everywhere this new crooner appears.
- The lyrics on this album are so offensive that the artists have been summoned to court.

1   You may recognize a few, if not all, of the preceding events from music history. If not, let me elaborate: the riots took place in 1910 after Igor Stravinsky's "Firebird Suite" premiered at the Paris opera

house; the singer filmed from the waist up on the Ed Sullivan show in 1956 was Elvis Presley; the crooner who made the girls swoon in the 1940s was Frank Sinatra (although Rudy Vallee did too); and the so-called offensive lyrics were penned by a group called "2 Live Crew" in the late 1980s.

2   Art has always been a source of controversy, and music, perhaps the most accessible form of art, has arguably been the most controversial. It is accessible because it travels through the air. It can't really be contained; it doesn't exist on a canvas or in a museum, or even in the vinyl, plastic or digital tape it was recorded on. It resides there, only waiting to be set free into the open air where it lives and breathes. Music comes out at the listener. Music envelops the listener in a way that no other art form can. The reason music is such a popular form of art is due to the fact that it is so easy. Listening to music, not composing or performing it, but listening, unlike reading literature or even viewing visual art (which must at least be sought out to be seen), listening to music takes no skill or effort whatsoever. Music will come to you. This frightens some people.

3   What is frightening is never the art itself. It is important for this discussion that we agree on what art is. Put in the most simplistic terms possible, works of art are ideas made tangible. The only truly negative reaction to a work of art is total indifference. I say this because art's aim should be to inspire feeling. To have any opinion on the idea an artist puts forth validates the idea. To disagree, even strongly, with the artist's tangible idea (the art) means that the artist has provoked a feeling, which should be the goal. The stronger one argues against a work, the more validity one lends to it. Indifference to nonsense masquerading as art is the best defense, and one that should come naturally. The problem is that everyone reacts differently. What is art to me may not be art to another.

4   A few years ago, while in an art gallery, I was able to see this first hand in the form of people's reactions to a painting which consisted of a single, large red spot in the center of a white rectangle. Some wondered if it was a comment on the isolation of the American Indian from the rest of society, while others felt the red symbolized blood befouling the pure white backdrop of virginity. (I didn't get that either.) To me, of course, it was just the flag of Japan.

5   So talent, or at least skill, is not the issue. Anyone could have rendered the red dot on the canvas with equal aplomb. What we're discussing are ideas and provocation. People left the gallery wanting better relations with American Indians, or with a new-found respect for menstruation. Someone even walked out with the work itself, paying more than 900 dollars. So, the artist's role can be that of provocateur.

6   Let us also agree art doesn't necessarily require any great skill, nor does art have to possess any great beauty. It only has to express an idea. Artists like the man that painted "Red Dot" know that ambiguity invites interpretation. If the artist sits back and keeps quiet while the world finds more and more levels to their work, before long someone will proclaim them an artistic genius. Think of Andy Warhol. Was it really so brilliant to recreate a can of Campbell's soup on canvas? In the music world, three "deep" songs come immediately to mind: "American Pie" by Don Mclean, "Whiter Shade of Pale" by Procol Harem, and "Purple Rain" by Prince. Every one of these songs is considered a modern classic, and every one of them, due to their extreme vagueness, has been dissected and discussed on many levels, and therefore elevated to works of genius. In an essay on a popular group, Henry Louis Gates, Jr. does just this, claiming that 2 Live Crew are in fact brilliant young men engaged in "heavy-handed parody."

7   2 Live Crew expresses ideas through words that some find obscene, so obscene that they want the group banned. Yet to ban 2 Live Crew for their ideas is to pay them a great compliment. It is, ironically, to accuse them of being visionaries, the first artists to put forth their particular ideas in music. What are these innovative new concepts in music? None other than sex, sexism and violence. Sex or violence in art, including music, is certainly nothing new. Sex has been so prevalent in lyrics for at least the last 50 or 60 years it is hard to choose the best examples. "Makin' Whoopee" (1956's Sinatra version) is a pretty obvious example of a sexual song, as is "Whole Lotta Shakin' Goin' On" (1957). Even "The Tender Trap" (1955) could be a thinly veiled allusion to female genitalia.

8   Violence is nothing new either. Witness "Mack the Knife" (the 1958 Bobby Darin version), a swinging ode to a murderer for hire and womanizer. The opening lines of 1944's "Strange Fruit" concern a lynching tree in the "gallant south" with "blood on the leaves,

blood on the roots." Even the well-respected Nat "King" Cole, in a duet with Dean Martin, sings of putting a woman in her place, showing them who is boss and slapping them ("Open Up The Doghouse" in 1954). Now that's sexism.

9   So 2 Live Crew have no new ideas. They do use different words to describe their old ideas though. Would it be any less offensive if they were making whoopee (Sinatra) instead of f***ing (2 Live Crew)? If the lady were a tramp (Sinatra) rather than a bitch (2 Live Crew), would that smooth things over? If both phrases describe the exact same idea, why then should one be more offensive than the other?

10   I don't for one second believe that 2 Live Crew is "engaged in heavy-handed parody," as Gates claims, nor do I feel that "their exuberant use of hyperbole undermines . . . a too literal-minded hearing of the lyrics." In fact I seriously doubt that any member of the group in question even knows what hyperbole is. But Gates knows, and applies it brilliantly. His argument works because all we have to believe is that his interpretation is a valid possibility. If he believes this, or if anyone believes this to be the case with 2 Live Crew, then how can we ban it?

11   I cannot emphasize enough the concept of art equaling thought and not action. And thought control is bad. I cannot defend anything 2 Live Crew has to say because I disagree with the attitudes they sing about. I can, however, defend art, and in order to call 2 Live Crew art I had to define it: thoughts or ideas made tangible. Most intelligent people would probably dismiss what they've done as an attempt to shock, and therefore sell, but as Gates' essay beautifully illustrates, it may be taken on different levels. Art should be above banning. If we outlaw 2 Live Crew, how long before we are burning books? How about monitoring brain waves to make sure no one is thinking offensively? Art is not action, it is thought, and how can thought be punishable? There would have been no Stravinsky, no Presley and no Sinatra had we attacked them, and won, as was done with 2 Live Crew.

- "If a man is considered guilty for what goes on in his mind, then give me the electric chair for all my future crimes!"—The Artist Formerly Known As Prince, "Electric Chair" 1989.
- "Your honor I do believe I'd be better off dead . . . if you can take a man's life for the thoughts in his head."—Bruce Springsteen, "Johnny 99" 1981.

WORKS CITED

Gates, Henry Louis Jr. "2 Live Crew Decoded." *The New York Times* 19 June 1990, late ed., 23A.

Page, Clarence. "2 Live Crew's Lyrics: Vile, Not Dangerous." *St. Louis Post-Dispatch* 18 June 1990, three star ed., 3B.

"The Anatomy of a Crusade." *Los Angeles Times* 18 June 1990, home ed., 4F.

THESIS AND ORGANIZATION

1. What is the relationship between the headnotes and paragraph 1? What point is Slate making?
2. Slate uses definition in paragraphs 2 and 3 and example in paragraphs 4–6. In what ways are the definitions and examples critical to his argument?
3. What paragraph or paragraphs bring in 2 Live Crew? Summarize what Slate says about the group.
4. What paragraph or paragraphs bring in the essay by Gates? What does Slate's use of the Gates essay contribute to the essay?
5. Slate's essay argues against censorship in art. Supply the reasons behind his stand, and state the thesis in your own words.

TECHNIQUE AND STYLE

1. Slate opens and closes his essay with bulleted statements. In what ways do they frame the essay? Explain whether you find them effective.
2. Reread the essay noting Slate's use of the pronouns *I*, *we*, and *you*. What reasons can you think of for his using the different pronouns?
3. Consult a handbook on the use of the rhetorical question. Where does Slate use this device? How effective do you find it?
4. Where in the essay does Slate appeal to reason? To emotion? To his credibility? Which appeal is the dominant one?
5. Evaluate the effectiveness of Slate's last paragraph. How does it reinforce the essay's argument? Its organization? Its use of argumentative appeals?

SUGGESTIONS FOR WRITING

Journal

1. More likely than not, you have heard lyrics or seen films or television shows that some people, perhaps many, would find offensive. Did you? Use your journal to explore why you did or did not take offense.
2. Slate defines art in his third paragraph. Reread that paragraph and consider to what extent, if any, you find his definition accurate.

Essay

While there is no question that both rating systems and censorship are topics about which many people have strong opinions, what those opinions are vary greatly. Think about your own experience with ratings and censorship to identify the impact they have had on you. Perhaps when you were in high school a particular book became controversial, or perhaps your local newspaper has been running editorials and letters to the editor about what is or is not morally offensive or the banning of a popular music group. If you would prefer to do research, you might look into museum exhibitions that have been controversial (such as the 1999 square off between New York's Mayor Guliani and the Brooklyn Museum of Art), or look into what has been written about rap lyrics. Like Slate, you will want to focus on one area, perhaps even on one example. Some fields to consider:

books
lyrics
the Internet
films
dance
art

America Needs Its Nerds and Responses

Leonid Fridman, David Lessing, David Herne, and Keith W. Frome

> *Leonid Fridman's opinion piece appeared in the* New York Times *on January 11, 1990, as part of a continuing series of essays called "Voices of the New Generation." Appropriately enough, Fridman is a founding member of the Society of Nerds and Geeks, an organization that began at Harvard University where, at the time the piece was written, Fridman was enrolled in the doctoral program in mathematics. The reaction was immediate. The very same day, Keith W. Frome, a member of Harvard's faculty, fired off a response, and one day later, two Harvard freshmen, David Lessing and David Herne, also rose to the battle. The essay and the two letters reacting to it are reprinted below. Fridman's essay was accompanied by the drawing that Frome describes and attacks.*

> ***WHAT TO LOOK FOR***   *Although Fridman announces his stance toward his subject in his first paragraph, you can make a good case that he reserves his thesis for his conclusion. As a result, the reasoning in the essay is more inductive than deductive. As you read it, keep track of the line of reasoning and see if you can recognize the logical fallacies the letters to the editor accuse him of. You'll be able to judge for yourself whether their charges are just.*

America Needs Its Nerds

Leonid Fridman

1   There is something very wrong with the system of values in a society that has only derogatory terms like nerd and geek for the intellectually curious and academically serious.

2   A geek, according to *Webster's New World Dictionary*, is a street performer who shocks the public by biting off heads of live chick-

ens. It is a telling fact about our language and our culture that someone dedicated to pursuit of knowledge is compared to a freak biting the head off a live chicken.

3   Even at a prestigious academic institution like Harvard, anti-intellectualism is rampant: Many students are ashamed to admit, even to their friends, how much they study. Although most students try to keep up their grades, there is a minority of undergraduates for whom pursuing knowledge is the top priority during their years at Harvard. Nerds are ostracized while athletes are idolized.

4   The same thing happens in U.S. elementary and high schools. Children who prefer to read books rather than play football, prefer to build model airplanes rather than get wasted at parties with their classmates, become social outcasts. Ostracized for their intelligence and refusal to conform to society's anti-intellectual values, many are deprived of a chance to learn adequate social skills and acquire good communication tools.

5   Enough is enough.

6   Nerds and geeks must stop being ashamed of who they are. It is high time to face the persecutors who haunt the bright kid with thick glasses from kindergarten to the grave. For America's sake, the anti-intellectual values that pervade our society must be fought.

7   There are very few countries in the world where anti-intellectualism runs as high in popular culture as it does in the U.S. In most industrialized nations, not least of all our economic rivals in East Asia, a kid who studies hard is lauded and held up as an example to other students.

8   In many parts of the world, university professorships are the most prestigious and materially rewarding positions. But not in America, where average professional ballplayers are much more respected and better paid than faculty members of the best universities.

9   How can a country where typical parents are ashamed of their daughter studying mathematics instead of going dancing, or of their son reading Weber while his friends play baseball, be expected to compete in the technology race with Japan or remain a leading political and cultural force in Europe? How long can America remain a world-class power if we constantly emphasize social skills and physical prowess over academic achievement and intellectual ability?

10   Do we really expect to stay afloat largely by importing our scientists and intellectuals from abroad, as we have done for a major portion of this century, without making an effort to also cultivate a pro-intellectual culture at home? Even if we have the political will to spend substantially more money on education than we do now, do we think we can improve our schools if we deride our studious pupils and debase their impoverished teachers?

11   Our fault lies not so much with our economy or with our politics as within ourselves, our values and our image of a good life. America's culture has not adapted to the demands of our times, to the economic realities that demand a highly educated workforce and innovative intelligent leadership.

12   If we are to succeed as a society in the 21st century, we had better shed our anti-intellectualism and imbue in our children the vision that a good life is impossible without stretching one's mind and pursuing knowledge to the full extent of one's abilities.

13   And until the words "nerd" and "geek" become terms of approbation and not derision, we do not stand a chance.

Responses

1   While "America Needs Its Nerds" (Op-Ed, Jan. 11) by Leonid Fridman, a Harvard student, may be correct in its message that Americans should treat intellectualism with greater respect, his identification of the "nerd" as guardian of this intellectual tradition is misguided.

2   Mr. Fridman maintains that anti-intellectualism runs rampant across this country, even at the "prestigious academic institution" he attends. However, he confuses a distaste for narrow-mindedness with anti-intellectualism. Just as Harvard, as a whole, reflects diversity in the racial, ethnic and religious backgrounds of its students, each student should reflect a diversity of interest as well.

3   A "nerd" or "geek" is distinguished by a lack of diverse interests, rather than by a presence of intellectualism. Thus, a nerd or geek is not, as Mr. Fridman states, a student "for whom pursuing knowledge is the top priority" but a student for whom pursuing knowledge is the sole objective. A nerd becomes socially maladjusted because he doesn't participate in social activities or even intellectual activities

involving other people. As a result, a nerd is less the intellectual champion of Mr. Fridman's descriptions than a person whose intelligence is not focused and enhanced by contact with fellow students. Constant study renders such social learning impossible.

4   For a large majority at Harvard, academic pursuit is the highest goal; a limited number, however, refuse to partake in activities other than study. Only these select few are the targets of the geek label. Continuous study, like any other obsession, is not a habit to be lauded. Every student, no matter how "intellectually curious," ought to take a little time to pursue social knowledge through activities other than study.

5   Mr. Fridman's analysis demonstrates further flaws in his reference to Japan. He comments that "in East Asia, a kid who studies hard is lauded and held up as an example to other students," while in the United States he or she is ostracized. This is an unfair comparison because Mr. Fridman's first reference is to how the East Asian child is viewed by teachers, while his second reference is to how the American child is viewed by fellow students. Mr. Fridman is equating two distinct perspectives on the student to substantiate a broad generalization on which he has no factual data.

6   Nerdism may also be criticized because it often leads to the pursuit of knowledge but not for its own sake, but for the sake of grades. Nerds are well versed in the type of intellectual trivia that may help in obtaining A's, but has little or no relevance to the real world. A true definition of intellectualism ought to include social knowledge.

7   While we in no way condone the terms "nerds" and "geeks" as insults, we also cannot condone the isolationist intellectualism Mr. Fridman advocates.

David Lessing, David Herne

1   I am disturbed by Leonid Fridman's article (Op-Ed, Jan. 11) and its accompanying collage. The collage displays a huge football player saying, "I read a book once." He is adored by a diminutive cheerleader, who sports a pennant that reads "Yea."

2   The picture is, of course, sexist and a silly and immature insult. Then, both the article and the picture commit the fallacy of bifurcation, otherwise known as the black-or-white fallacy. According to Mr. Fridman, one is either a jock, who neither reads nor writes and who spends time away from the field house punishing intellectuals,

or a nerd, who totally devotes his time to learning at the expense of
"social skills and physical prowess."

3   This is reductive. Mr. Fridman's analysis ignores the marvelous
and rich field of humanity that lies between these poles. Rarely, if
ever, is a student one way or another.

4   I am an adviser, teacher and administrator at Harvard (the only
school Mr. Fridman mentions). I also live with 22 freshmen. Many
of my students are dedicated athletes, but they are in no way jocks
in Mr. Fridman's bifurcated sense of the word. The athletes I advise
and teach are reflective, hard working, polite and, yes, intellectual.
They read and discuss books, and even ideas.

5   In my expository-writing class, a hockey player has just handed
in a rigorously constructed essay on law, ethics and religion. He is
one of the best writers in the class. Another student, who plays
football for Harvard, just spent an afternoon in my study discussing
the metaphysical poets.

6   I could tell many more anecdotes of student-scholars I have
taught and from whom I have learned. But the point is this: our
pedagogic goal ought not to be to produce nerds or jocks, but human beings who are thoughtful, healthy and socially adept.

Keith W. Frome

THESIS AND ORGANIZATION

1. What paragraph or paragraphs constitute Fridman's introduction? What
   reasons can you give for your opinion?
2. Trace Fridman's use of examples. Explain whether you find them valid.
3. Where in the essay does Fridman use comparison and contrast? In what
   way does it support his argument?
4. Fridman also uses comparison and contrast to further his argument.
   Explain whether you find his comparisons accurate.
5. Combine the ideas contained in the title, the first paragraph, and the last
   paragraph. In your own words and in one sentence, state Fridman's thesis.

TECHNIQUE AND STYLE

1. Fridman's essay obviously elicited strong reactions. Reasoning aside, why
   do you think the letter writers responded as they did?
2. Lessing and Herne fault Fridman's reasoning, accusing him of shifting definition, false analogy, and hasty generalization. Are their criticisms valid?

3. Frome accuses Fridman of either-or reasoning, calling it the "fallacy of bifurcation, otherwise known as the black-or-white fallacy." Explain whether the charge is accurate.

4. Explain the extent to which the letter writers agree with Fridman's view that "a good life is impossible without stretching one's mind and pursuing knowledge to the full extent of one's abilities."

5. To what extent do all three pieces use the ethical appeal? Which one uses it most effectively?

SUGGESTIONS FOR WRITING

Journal

1. Define and describe a nerd, and the extent to which the term is or is not derogatory.

2. Write a response to one of the three arguments.

Essay

Although the characteristic Fridman attacks is anti-intellectualism, and the examples he uses are the negative terms used for the "intellectually curious and academically serious," he is hardly alone in decrying our society's "system of values." Consider other subjects that our society appears to value or not value, and draft an argumentative essay stating your position. You may well find that it's easier to start with examples and follow them to their subjects. Suggestions:

single-family homes
fast food
gadgets
television commercials
pets

High School, an Institution Whose Time Has Passed

Leon Botstein

The topic of education comes naturally to Leon Botstein, for since 1975 he has been the president of Bard College, where he is also the Leon Levy Professor in the Arts and Humanities. His administrational and teaching duties, however, have not kept him from being an active scholar and musician. He not only has continued his research in the field of history, having earned his Ph.D. in European history at Harvard, he also holds positions as Music Director of the American Symphony Orchestra, Co-Artistic Director of the Bard Music Festival, and Artistic Director of the American Russian Youth Orchestra. As a musician, he is known for his support of contemporary composers, many of whose works he has conducted in Asia and Europe as well as in this country. His two major interests are reflected in his latest books: Jefferson's Children: Education and the Promise of American Culture *(1997) and* The Compleat Brahms: A guide to the Musical Works of Johannes Brahms *(1999). Botstein has contributed articles and reviews on history, education, music, and culture to various leading newspapers in the United States. "High School, an Institution Whose Time Has Passed" was first published in* The New York Times *and then reprinted in the* International Herald Tribune *on May 20, 1999.*

WHAT TO LOOK FOR   *It's a toss up to figure out which is the more difficult to write—introductions or conclusions. Sometimes, you may find that what you have as your conclusion in your draft may work as an effective introduction, but rarely is the reverse true, which is one reason concluding paragraphs present difficulties. Summaries are apt to be predictable and, therefore, dull, yet bringing in a new idea can blur your focus. One solution is to do what Botstein does: bring in an argument that can be used to counter your proposal, dismiss it, and then end by reinforcing your thesis with a call to action.*

1   The national outpouring after the Littleton shootings has forced us to confront something we have suspected for a long time: The American high school is obsolete and should be abolished.

2   In the last month, high school students present and past have
come forward with stories about cliques and the artificial intensity
of a world defined by insiders and outsiders, in which the insiders
hold sway because of superficial definitions of attractiveness, popularity and sports prowess.

3   Indeed, a community's loyalty to the high school system is often based on the extent to which varsity teams succeed. High
school administrators and faculty members are often former
coaches, and the coaches themselves are placed in a separate, un-
touchable category. The result is that the culture of the inside elite
is not contested by the adults in the school. Individuality and dissent are discouraged.

4   But the rules of high school turn out not to be the rules of life.
Often, the high school outsider becomes the more successful and
admired adult. The definitions of masculinity and femininity go
through sufficient transformation to make the game of popularity in
high school an embarrassment.

5   Given the poor quality of recruitment and training for high
school teachers, it is no wonder that the curriculum and the enterprise of learning hold so little sway over young people.

6   When puberty meets education and learning in the modern
United States, the victory of puberty masquerading as popular culture and the tyranny of peer groups based on ludicrous values meet
little resistance.

7   By the time those who graduate from high school go on to college and realize what really is at stake in becoming an adult, too
many opportunities have been lost and too much time has been
wasted. Most thoughtful young people suffer the high school environment in silence, and in their junior and senior years mark time
waiting for college to begin.

8   But the primary reason high school doesn't work anymore, if it
ever did, is that young people mature substantially earlier in the
late 20th century than they did when the high school was invented. For example, the age of first menstruation has dropped at
least two years since the beginning of this century and, not surprisingly, sexual activity has begun earlier in proportion. An institution intended for children in transition now holds back young
adults well beyond the developmental point for which high school
was originally designed.

9   Furthermore, whatever constraints on the presumption of adult-hood existed decades ago have fallen away. Information and im-ages, as well as the real and virtual freedom of movement we asso-ciate with adulthood, are now accessible to every 15-year-old and 16-year-old.

10   Secondary education must be rethought. Elementary school should begin at age 4 or 5 and end with the sixth grade. We Americans should entirely abandon the concept of the middle school and junior high school. Beginning with the seventh grade, there should be four years of secondary education that we may call high school. Young people should graduate at 16, not 18.

11   They could then enter the real world of work or national service in which they would take a place of responsibility alongside older adults. They could stay at home and attend junior college, or they could go away to college.

12   At 16, young Americans are prepared to be taken seriously and to develop the motivations and interests that will serve them well in adult life. They need to enter a world in which they are not in a lunchroom with only their peers estranged from other age groups and cut off from the game of life as it is really played.

13   There is nothing utopian about this idea—it is immensely practi-cal and efficient, and its implementation is long overdue. We need to face biological and cultural facts and not prolong the life of a flawed institution that is out of date.

THESIS AND ORGANIZATION

1. Botstein starts his essay with the example of the shootings at the high school in Littleton, Colorado, and then generalizes about what caused them, focusing on the notion of elitism. What is he claiming about elitism?

2. Paragraphs 5–7 explore additional reasons that high school is ineffectual and present Botstein's views on learning. Summarize his ideas.

3. Botstein sets out the heart of his argument in paragraphs 8 and 9. What reasons does he give for high school being obsolete?

4. What paragraph or paragraphs argue for Botstein's solution to the prob-lems high school presents? State his solutions in your own words.

5. Summarize as fully as you can just what Botstein perceives as the problems with high school, together with his solution and its potential effects. Boil down what you have to one sentence for a clear statement of the thesis.

TECHNIQUE AND STYLE

1. Botstein devotes far more space to the problem than to the solution. What reasons can you find for his decision?
2. Take another look at what Botstein identifies as the problems with high school. In what order does he present them? Why might he have opted for that sequence?
3. The essay brims with assertions. Select one (paragraphs 2, 3, 6, and 7 are good hunting spots), and examine the evidence Botstein uses as support. Explain whether you find it adequate or not.
4. How would you characterize Botstein's tone? Is he blunt, condescending, reasonable? What evidence can you find for your view?
5. Reread the essay from the perspective of a high school teacher or parent. Would you find the essay offensive? Extreme? Why or why not?

SUGGESTIONS FOR WRITING

Journal

1. Reread Botstein's solution (paragraph 10). Use your journal to record your reaction to it. Given your experience in high school and what you know about the educational system, would it work?
2. What group or groups were the "elite" at your high school? Describe them.

Essay

Whether you agree with Botstein or not, you probably found his essay provocative in that he makes a number of assertions about a subject you know about. Consider some of his claims:

1. " . . . insiders hold sway because of superficial definitions of attractiveness, popularity and sports prowess" (paragraph 2).
2. "Individuality and dissent are discouraged" (paragraph 3).
3. " . . . it's no wonder that the curriculum and the enterprise of learning hold so little sway over young people" (paragraph 5).
4. "Most thoughtful people suffer the high school environment in silence . . ." (paragraph 7).
5. "At 16, young Americans are prepared to be taken seriously and to develop the motivations and interests that will serve them well in adult life" (paragraph 12).
6. Use any one of these statements (or any other from the essay that you prefer) as a point to argue a "yes-but" position or to disagree with. Use the experience of others in addition to that of your own to support your argument.

One Internet, Two Nations

Henry Louis Gates, Jr.

Henry Louis Gates, Jr.'s academic credentials and awards read like a scholar's dream: he was educated at Yale University and Clare College of the University of Cambridge; he has been a Mellon Fellow at Cambridge and the National Humanities Center, as well as being named a Ford Foundation National Fellow and a MacArthur Prize Fellow; he has been honored with the Zora Neale Hurston Society Award for Cultural Scholarship, the Norman Rabb Award of the American Jewish Committee, the George Polk Award for Social Commentary, and the Tikkun National Ethics Award.

Gates chairs Afro-American Studies at Harvard University where he holds the position of W. E. B. Du Bois Professor of the Humanities and director of the W. E. B. Du Bois Institute for Afro-American Research. Gates has written a number of scholarly books, of which the best known is probably The Signifying Monkey *(1989). Recently, however, he has edited the* Norton Anthology of African American Literature *(1996). But Gates is also that rare scholar who has also written for a more general audience in books such as his* Loose Canons: Notes of the Culture Wars *(1992), his autobiography,* Colored People: A Memoir *(1993), and* Thirteen Ways of Looking at a Black Man *(1997), and in the PBS television series* Wonders of the African World *(1999). He is also a regular contributor to the* New Yorker *magazine and serves on the Pulitzer Prize Board.*

The essay that follows appeared in the New York Times *on October 31, 1999, and as its title suggests, Gates turns his attention to the electronic media and the Internet. It's an area with which he's familiar, having coedited Microsoft's* Encarta Africana.

WHAT TO LOOK FOR *One way to think your way into an argumentative essay is to consider the subject from the angle of problem and solution. You'll see that's what Gates does in his essay, using a historical perspective to back up just how important his point is. Like Gates, you'll probably find more than one reason for the problem and more than one solution.*

1   After the Stono Rebellion of 1739 in South Carolina—the largest uprising of slaves in the colonies before the American Revolution— legislators there responded by banishing two forms of communica-

tion among the slaves: the mastery of reading and writing, and the mastery of "talking drums," both of which had been crucial to the capacity to rebel.

2   For the next century and a half, access to literacy became for the slaves a hallmark of their humanity and an instrument of liberation, spiritual as well as physical. The relation between freedom and literacy became the compelling theme of the slave narratives, the great body of printed books that ex-slaves generated to assert their common humanity with white Americans and to indict the system that had oppressed them.

3   In the years since the abolition of slavery, the possession of literacy has been a cardinal value of the African-American tradition. It is no accident that the first great victory in the legal battle over segregation was fought on the grounds of education—of equal access to literacy.

4   Today, blacks are failing to gain access to the new tools of literacy: the digital "knowledge economy." And while the dilemma that our ancestors confronted was imposed by others, this cybersegregation is, to a large degree, self-imposed.

5   The Government's latest attempt to understand why low-income African-Americans and Hispanics are slower to embrace the Internet and the personal computer than whites—the Commerce Department study "Falling Through the Net"—suggests that income alone can't be blamed for the so-called digital divide. For example, among families earning $15,000 to $35,000 annually, more than 33 percent of whites own computers, compared with only 19 percent of African-Americans—a gap that has widened 64 percent over the past five years despite declining computer prices.

6   The implications go far beyond online trading and chat rooms. Net promoters are concerned that the digital divide threatens to become a 21st century poll tax that, in effect, disenfranchises a third of the nation. Our children, especially, need access not only to the vast resources that technology offers for education, but also to the rich cultural contexts that define their place in the world.

7   Today we stand at the brink of becoming two societies, one largely white and plugged in and the other black and unplugged.

8   One of the most tragic aspects of slavery was the way it destroyed social connections. In a process that the sociologist Orlando Patterson calls "social death," slavery sought to sever blacks from their history and culture, from family ties and a sense of commu-

nity. And, of course, de jure segregation after the Civil War was intended to disconnect blacks from equal economic opportunity, from the network of social contacts that enable upward mobility and, indeed, from the broader world of ideas.

9   Despite the dramatic growth of the black middle class since affirmative action programs were started in the late 60's, new forms of disconnectedness have afflicted black America. Middle-class professionals often feel socially and culturally isolated from their white peers at work and in the neighborhood and from their black peers left behind in the underclass. The children of the black underclass, in turn, often lack middle-class role models to help them connect to a history of achievement and develop their analytical skills.

10   It would be a sad irony if the most diverse and decentralized electronic medium yet invented should fail to achieve ethnic diversity among its users. And yet the Commerce Department study suggests that the solution will require more than cheap PC's. It will involve content.

11   Until recently, the African-American presence on the Internet was minimal, reflecting the chicken-and-egg nature of Internet economics. Few investors have been willing to finance sites appealing to a PC-scarce community. Few African-Americans have been compelled to sign on to a medium that offers little to interest them. And educators interested in diversity have repeatedly raised concerns about the lack of minority-oriented educational software.

12   Consider the birth of the recording industry in the 1920's. Blacks began to respond to this new medium only when mainstream companies like Columbia Records introduced so-called race records, blues and jazz discs aimed at a nascent African-American market. Blacks who would never have dreamed of spending hard-earned funds for a record by Rudy Vallee or Kate Smith would stand in lines several blocks long to purchase the new Bessie Smith or Duke Ellington hit.

13   New content made the new medium attractive. And the growth of Web sites dedicated to the interests and needs of black Americans can play the same role for the Internet that race records did for the music industry.

14   But even making sites that will appeal to a black audience can only go so far. The causes of poverty are both structural and behavioral. And it is the behavioral aspect of this cybersegregation that blacks themselves are best able to address. Drawing on corporate

and foundation support, we can transform the legion of churches, mosques and community centers in our inner cities into after-school centers that focus on redressing the digital divide and teaching black history. We can draw on the many examples of black achievement in structured classes to re-establish a sense of social connection.

15   The Internet is the 21st century's talking drum, the very kind of grass-roots communication tool that has been such a powerful source of education and culture for our people since slavery. But this talking drum we have not yet learned to play. Unless we master the new information technology to build and deepen the forms of social connection that a tragic history has eroded, African-Americans will face a form of cybersegregation in the next century as devastating to our aspirations as Jim Crow segregation was to those of our ancestors. But this time, the fault will be our own.

THESIS AND ORGANIZATION

1. Paragraphs 1–4 focus on the relationship between African-Americans and literacy. Summarize that relationship.
2. The first sentence of paragraph 4 makes a claim. In what ways do paragraphs 5–9 supply evidence for that claim?
3. While Gates presents reasons the "digital divide" exists, he is careful in paragraph 5 to discount an economic reason. Why is it important that he include it?
4. You can analyze the essay in terms of problems and solutions, the first part dealing with problems. What paragraph or paragraphs focus on solutions? What are they?
5. Consider Gates' subject, the problems he perceives and the solutions he proposes. In your own words and in one sentence, state the essay's thesis.

TECHNIQUE AND STYLE

1. Gates refers to historical events in paragraphs 1–3 and 8. What do they add to his argument? To his persona?
2. In what ways is Gates' essay directed to an African-American audience? A white audience? A mixed one?
3. Where in the essay do you find Gates using an appeal to reason? To emotion? To his persona? Which appeal dominates?
4. Consider the paragraphs that both precede and follow paragraph 7. What is the function of paragraph 7?

5. Gates' last paragraph begins with a metaphor. In what ways is it appropriate for the essay's unity? For its subject?

Suggestions for Writing

Journal

1. Take a few minutes to jot down the various ways you use the Internet. What categories can those uses be placed in? Given how you use it, what effect does it have on you? If you don't use the Internet at all, explain why.

2. To test out Gates' argument, spend a half hour or so exploring web sites that are aimed specifically at an African-American audience. Record the results in your journal, and you will have the working notes for an essay that refutes or supports his argument. If you support it, make sure your argument is a "yes-but" type so you have an assertion.

Essay

You can't pick up a newspaper or magazine these days without running into stories about the Internet, stories ranging from praise (useful web sites and the like) to condemnation (web addiction and so on) with everything in between. Think about how it has affected you and the world you live in. To get started, here are some statements to mull over, each of which can begin with "The Internet has/has not . . . "

increased the gap between the haves and the have-nots
contributed to ethnic diversity
become the latest way to waste time
spread pornography
changed shopping as we know it
changed education as we know it

Like Gates, don't hold back from predicting the future.

For Further Reading
Pro and Con

10

ON HOME SCHOOLING

The three pieces that follow were published in the Denver Post's *Sunday edition on August 29, 1999, in the editorial section appropriately called "Perspectives." The first essay, by Angelo Cortez, an editorial writer and member of the paper's editorial board, sets the immediate context for the two essays that follow it, thus serving more as an introduction than as an essay by itself. Evie Hudak, writing in support of the public schools, has been on the board of the Colorado PTA for a number of years, spending much of that time as its public policy director. Kevin Swanson, writing in favor of home schooling, is the Executive Director of Christian Home Educators of Colorado. The issue they address is receiving more and more attention nationwide.*

Many Exploring the Option
Angela Cortez

1   In the weeks following the Columbine High School shooting, in which 15 people died and dozens were injured, the Colorado Department of Education received a 59 percent increase in inquiries about home schooling.

2   But although the requests for information about home study more than doubled in the wake of the worst school shooting in U.S. history, Department of Education officials do not expect an exodus

from public schools. Still, the numbers of people home schooling their children increases each year in every state in the nation.

3   Home-based education has more than doubled in the last five years. In the 1990-91 school year an estimated 250,000 children were home schooled nationwide. By the 1995-96 school year, about 750,000 children were being home schooled, or 1 to 2 percent of the total school-age population.

4   In Colorado, just under 7,000 students were registered as being home schooled in the fall of 1994. In 1998, home schoolers had increased to nearly 9,000. Officials in Colorado expect this school year's increase to be slightly higher than normal.

5   Traditionally, home schooling has been a valid option for parents who want to control their children's education in a home setting.

6   Home schooling in Colorado is deregulated.

7   Students test every two years, and as long as test scores are above the 13 percentile of public school students, they may continue with home study.

8   Parents who home school their children often do so because they feel their children are not being challenged, the classrooms are too big, or the child has special needs.

9   In addition to the quality of education children receive and religious and moral beliefs, the reasons for choosing home schooling are expected to include safety in the near future.

10   But statistics show that children are safest in public schools. More children are killed in their homes or neighborhoods each year than in school.

11   Another important trend in home schooling is that it has gone "mainstream." It's no longer considered a link to religious zealots who home school to shield their children from the evils of the world.

12   Many home-schooled children also take some courses in public schools. Many school districts like Jefferson County and Aurora allow home schooled students to take part in sports activities, art and music, or any other subject they can't get at home.

13   So what's the answer when trying to figure out what's best for children? It really depends on the child, parents and individual situations.

14   But everyone should strive to strike a balance, a combination of learning in the home and a public school setting.

15   Home schooled children need to interact with others. Children in public schools also need to be taught at home. That is where the most important lessons should be learned.

Public Setting Still Best

Evie Hudak

1   Public schools are still the best place for children to get an education. They promote student achievement successfully because of the strong system of accountability behind them, which home schools do not have.

2   Furthermore, public schools offer many worthwhile experiences and opportunities not available through home schooling.

3   The most important reason public schools provide an excellent education is that teachers are required to be highly qualified. They must acquire and maintain a license to teach. In order to earn this teaching certification, they must demonstrate proficiency in all basic skills, study their subject area in depth, learn effective techniques of instructing all kinds of learners, and get on-the-job training under the guidance of an experienced teacher.

4   To maintain their license, they must continue their own education and training throughout their entire teaching career. Teachers are also held accountable by an ongoing process of evaluation. State laws that provide the requirements for teacher certification and evaluation are regularly reviewed and updated. On the other hand, there are no requirements that parents doing home schooling be trained, experienced, ceritified or evaluated—or have any particular qualifications.

5   The accountability in public education is also extensive in the area of academic standards. Public-school students must demonstrate adequate academic achievement.

6   Colorado public schools have rigorous content standards required for all academic areas, and schools' success in upholding the standards is evaluated by regular statewide and district testing. This process has been strengthened by recent law directing the state to base its accreditation of school districts primarily on their performance in the assessment program.

7   On the other hand, home-schooled students are not required to demonstrate academic achievement on the state assessments, and their curriculum is not compelled to include any standards.

8   Public education in Colorado is enhanced by another kind of accountability as well, one that calls for involvement of parents and community members in school improvement planning. All schools and school districts in the state are required by law to have a committee of parents, teachers, administrators and community members. These "accountability committees" must evaluate the success of the school or district in providing for student achievement and a safe learning environment, and they advise on strategies for improvement. They are also charged with consulting on the use of taxpayers' money in the budget.

9   The input from the diversity of people making up these committees provides public schools with a kind of broad oversight and opportunity for new ideas not available to home schools.

10   Besides the kinds of accountability already mentioned, public schools also provide a commitment to building and maintaining the basic values of our society and our democratic system of government. The Colorado Constitution provides for a "thorough and uniform system of free public schools."

11   The people who govern public schools are elected by the public and expected to uphold the shared values of the community. School board members receive frequent and regular feedback from the public about their management of the district.

12   Also, principals, teachers and other school staff receive feedback from parents, parent groups and accountability committees. The public ensures that there is ideological control over public schools.

13   In home schools, there is no assurance that values such as citizenship and acceptance of diversity will be encouraged. The importance of these values to our nation's survival prompted our founding fathers to support the right to a free education.

14   In addition to instilling values related to citizenship and acceptance of others, public schools boost children's development of social skills and employability skills that are critical to their becoming successful adults.

15   Because the classes in public schools are large, students are not "spoonfed." They are forced to take more responsibility for their learning; this helps them gain more independence and initiative, which makes them better employees.

16   Children in public schools have to deal with many different personalities and temperaments, helping them acquire the skills to interact with the diversity of people in the world at large. They also

learn to adapt to the varied leadership styles of teachers. Home-schooled children experience a homogenous group of people, sometimes only their parents.

17   Public schools help children become more cultured, discriminating and enlightened because they have a wide variety of resources and activities. Schools have music, sports, clubs and other student groups that give children an opportunity to learn more than pure academics and have many kinds of experiences.

18   Despite the few recent incidents of violence, public schools do provide children with a safe environment in which to learn. In fact, many more incidents of children's gun deaths occur in homes.

19   Gully Stanford, member of the Colorado Board of Education, explains best why public education surpasses home schooling. "In an increasingly diverse and technological society, the paramount need is to prepare our youth for productive citizenship: No home, no matter how well equipped, can duplicate the nurturing and coping experience of a public school education," he said.

One-on-One Environment Is Beneficial

Kevin Swanson

1   While the cost of education in the United States has increased and academic performance has fallen, a bright star shines over America's academic landscape: home education.

2   While government schools spend an average of $5,325 per student per year to attain a 50th percentile performance ranking among the states, 1.5 million home-schooled children cost U.S. families only about $400 per student annually, to achieve test scores averaging 25 percent higher at the 75th percentile.

3   In the largest research study to date, completed this year by Dr. Lawrence Rudner of the ERIC Clearinghouse on Assessment and Evaluation, the average eight-grade home-schooled student performs four grade levels above the national average. This outstanding

academic performance by home-educated students makes home-schooling an attractive alternative to the traditional classroom.

4 A major factor in this achievement is intense parental involvement—a known key to exceptional academic performance. As a former teacher, I can attest that it is very difficult to achieve success in education without cooperation, reinforcement and abiding interest from the parents.

5 Home-schooling involves one-on-one instruction—known to be an ideal format in which to learn. With the efficiency of individual instruction, and without the distractions of a crowded classroom, parents often find their children accomplish more academic work in less time.

6 Cutting-edge technologies like CD-ROM, interactive video, satellite feeds, and on-line tutoring are bringing the best teaching tools and methods right into the home, increasing parental options exponentially. Home education may be a tried and true historical method of teaching, but it is now the wave of the future. Our top universities are actively recruiting home-educated students because of their love of learning and mature study habits.

7 A third advantage to home education is the opportunity to maximize the individuality of each child. As government education becomes increasingly centralized and bureaucratized, the inevitable result becomes a one-size-fits-all curriculum and classroom structure. Conversely, just as the small business can be more responsive to consumer needs, the home school can be incredibly flexible and adaptable to meet the needs of each child. Every individual child has his or her learning styles, interests and abilities. With the individual attention provided by a home education, each student's curriculum can be tailored to help him reach his fullest potential. There need not be any common denominator to which all students are reduced.

8 Not only does home schooling provide an excellent, individualized education, it also allows parents to determine the values on which their children's learning is based. All education is based on basic presuppositions, such as the origin of man and his nature, the purpose of life, and what constitutes proper human behavior. The predominant view of modern education places man as supreme over his own destiny, with a relative and changing set of ethics. For many families this undermines a strong faith in God. For them, home education provides the opportunity to pass on their family's faith and values to the next generation.

9   An issue closely related to family values is the socialization of the children. This question of "socialization" is the most frequently leveled criticism of those not familiar with home education. Ironically, the negative aspects of socialization, such as behavioral problems and unsavory peer groups, are driving increasing numbers of families toward home education. When you understand what it truly means to be socialized, this question readily answers itself. It has less to do with surviving in a room full of first graders, and more to do with honesty, respect, and the maturity to relate people of all ages and backgrounds.

10   Home-schooled children often have regular interaction with adults and siblings of various ages. Dr. Larry Shyers, in a 1992 study, found that the child's social development depends more on adult contact and less on contact with other children.

11   Not surprisingly, a nationwide study by Dr. John Wesley Taylor (Doctoral dissertation, Andrews University) revealed that, according to the Piers-Harris Children's Self-Concept Scale, the self-concept of home school students was significantly higher than that of public school students.

12   Proper social skills, making one fit for living in civil society, are not learned in large age-segregated classrooms, or in random contact with other people. They are the result of proper training, in which the parents play a crucial role. In fact, family socialization can be more effective in the long run than institutionalized socialization. Opportunity for teaching social skills can come through family interactions, community service, and extra curricular activities. A recent study showed that 98 percent of home educated children are involved in two or more social/community activities outside of the home each week.

13   Not only is home schooling reinventing education, it is reinventing families. Families have become so fragmented in our modern society, it is unusual for them to even eat dinner together! Home schooling reverses this trend and brings families back together. One mother told me, "Since we've been home schooling, I can actually talk to my teenage daughters." Since families are the foundation on which our society rests, they are well worth strengthening! There are numerous support systems for parents interested in home schooling.

14   Here in Colorado there are state conventions, workshops, news magazines, local support groups, graduation ceremonies, curriculum fairs, video and reading materials, and much more. Many of these resources can be accessed through the web site www.chec.org.

15   Home education is setting the new standards for academic achievement, character development, social skills, creativity, family, and responsible citizenship. The true impact of home education on our country's social, business, and political institutions will only be felt 20 years from now. Home education is definitely a bright star in America's future!

ON LEGALIZED GAMBLING

Both of the articles on legalized gambling were published in the Sunday edition of the Rocky Mountain News, *in its "Commentary" section, on December 10, 1995. At that time, Frank R. Wolf was serving in Congress as a representative (Republican) from Virginia, and Frank Fahrenkopf was president of the American Gaming Association. As you will see, the essays argue over whether a federal commission should investigate gambling and then focus on casinos in particular. Underlying the argument is a larger issue: Does gambling have a positive or negative effect? As you read the essays, keep in mind that legalized gambling covers a variety of forms, from lotteries run by the states to casinos Las Vegas style, with everything you can think of in between.*

Let's See Where Gambling Is Going

Rep. Frank R. Wolf

1   Twenty years ago, just two states had some form of legal gambling. Today, only two states don't.

2   Because of the rapid proliferation of gambling, I, along with 122 members of the House of Representatives, have introduced legislation to establish the National Gambling Impact and Policy Commission. Sens. Paul Simon and Richard Lugar have introduced similar legislation in the Senate.

3   The task of the commission is simple: to study the effects of one of America's fastest-growing industries and report its findings to the nation.

4   This legislation does not regulate or tax gambling and it imposes no new mandates on gambling. The sole purpose of the bill is to provide objective, credible and factual information so that elected officials and citizens alike can make their own informed decisions about bringing gambling into their communities.

5   Communities should know that business loss, corruption, crime and family breakdown often accompany legalized gambling. Without a doubt, different communities will encounter different results, but there are lessons that can be learned from others' experiences—and information that can be gleaned.

6   True, casinos pay taxes on their revenues. But a casino's gain is another business' loss. Consider that within a year of Atlantic City's casinos offering free food to patrons, more than a third of Atlantic City's restaurants went out of business.

7   Mississippi legalized casinos in 1992, yet last year more than $29 billion was wagered on gambling in Mississippi while taxable retail sales in the state totaled $27 billion.

8   And recent gambling establishments in Iowa partially accounted for the drop in attendance at the state fair.

9   Each person has only so many dollars to spend and money wagered in a casino is not cash available to spend in hardware stores, at the movies, in supermarkets, or elsewhere.

10   Gambling can impact our elected officials, too. Recently, the Federal Bureau of Investigation began an inquiry into the legislative influence wielded by the gambling industry in Louisiana. In August 1991, 17 South Carolina legislators, lobbyists and other officials were convicted of accepting bribes.

11   In 1990, six Arizona legislators pleaded guilty to accepting bribes in exchange for key votes on gambling. In Kentucky, seven legislators, including the speaker of the House of Representatives, were found guilty of accepting bribes, extortion, racketeering and making false statements. And in West Virginia, a former state lottery director was recently convicted of perjury, wire fraud, and mail fraud in the rigging of a state contract for video lotteries.

12   The Florida Department of Law Enforcement opposed casino gambling in the state because "casinos will result in more Floridians and visitors being robbed, raped, assaulted and otherwise injured."

13   Gambling is beginning to take a toll on our youth as well. In 1993, more people made trips to casinos than to Major League Baseball parks, replacing America's pastime with gambling. And that doesn't even count the more than 200,000 minors ejected from

casinos. *The Washington Post, USA Today, Sports Illustrated* and other publications have highlighted gambling's penetration into our colleges, high schools and junior high.

14   But communities often must make their decisions without information because there are precious few places that have collected it. The National Gambling Impact Commission will do that, and share its findings—good and bad—with the nation.

15   Opponents of this legislation claim that it is federal intrusion into a local dimension and driven by moral convictions. The claim is false. The commission's task is to study the issue and provide state and local governments with objective information.

16   America deserves the right to know the facts about gambling. It's time for Congress to create the National Gambling Impact and Policy Commission to find them.

Washington Insiders Are at It Again

Frank Fahrenkopf

1   "We're from Washington and we're here to help." How many times have people outside the Washington Beltway erupted in either riotous laughter or a quick rush for the doors when they've heard this comment? Well, the Washington insiders are at it again.

2   This time under the guise of a study, anti-gaming forces are seeking to bring Washington "help" to the states that might consider legalizing gaming entertainment.

3   Proponents of this study sell it as "only a study to help the states." As we in the industry are always asked, "If the industry has nothing to hide, why oppose the study?" Well, the industry wouldn't oppose a fair, balanced study. We have a great story to tell.

4   The problem is that the study being proposed would be neither fair or balanced. The outcome is predetermined.

5   If the rhetoric of the primary sponsors of the commission, which vilify gaming, isn't enough to convince you there is a predetermined outcome, then look at the language of the legislation.

6   Bills in both the House and Senate charge the commission to make "recommendations for such legislation and administrative actions as it

considers appropriate." In other words, federal legislation and regulation. The bill doesn't even suggest that the states are to benefit from this study. And interestingly, there is no long line of governors and state legislators begging for help from the federal government.

7   To support the "need" for a commission, gaming opponents have revived old stereotypes of the industry, conjured up statistics that seem to support their bias and have even managed to explain away the value of the billions of dollars in tax revenues and the more than 1 million jobs the industry has created.

8   The issues are always the same:

- The economic benefits are false. Ask the people of Tunica, Miss., the Quad City area of Iowa, or Alton or Joliet, Ill., what they think of the economic benefits—they have thrived.
- Gaming increases crime. There is absolutely no evidence to show the legal introduction of legal gaming, because of the nature of the business, increases crime. The increase in numbers of visitors to any community will bring more crime regardless of the venue. For example, Orlando, Fla., has a higher crime rate than Las Vegas—surely Mickey and Minnie cannot be fairly charged with increasing crime.
- Gaming breeds corruption. Sadly where there is money there is a potential for corruption, but it is by no means confined to gaming interests. The point is, where there is corruption, it needs to be rooted out and the culprits prosecuted.
- Gaming creates problem gamblers. Prominent leaders in the field report that the vast majority of Americans are social gamblers who can participate in gaming activity without harmful effects. Some gamblers cannot, however, and the gaming-entertainment industry accepts its responsibility to help those who cannot. We are doing a great deal now and we will do more in the future.

9   The real kicker to this debate is that no study is needed. For the last decade, state after state has considered the evidence and weighed the pros and cons of gaming without help from the federal government. In the process, hundreds of studies have been completed on every aspect of the gaming industry—studies by state legislatures, state research organizations and respected, independent consulting firms.

10   Critics of the gaming industry ask us to discount this wealth of existing information, to set aside the billions of dollars and jobs the

gaming industry supports, and ignore the public's consistent affirmation of gaming.

11   Instead they want to waste millions of taxpayer dollars trying to reach a different conclusion about gaming based on their own moral views. Is this national study commission really here to help—or is it just another example of a few Washington interest groups and individuals trying to tell the rest of us what we can and cannot do?

ON HUNTING

The three essays that follow were published in Sierra, *the magazine of The Sierra Club, an organization that promotes the conservation of wildlife, flora and fauna, and their surrounding ecosystems. Together with another essay (on hunting as an ethnic rite), they appeared along with a longer, expository essay that presented the various issues and groups involved in hunting. These three essays, however, are clearly argumentative. Their authors' backgrounds are as different as their immediate environments and reveal their positions on the subject: Dan Sisson lives in Oregon where he writes a regular column for* Field *and* Stream; *Steve Ruggeri works for Friends of Animals, an organization based in Newport, Rhode Island, and directs the group's wildlife policy; Humberto Fontova lives in Louisiana, where he works as a freelance writer, publishing his articles in magazines focusing on the outdoors.*

Why I Hunt

Dan Sisson

1   Hunting implies a relationship between man and animal, and as in any relationship, the layers of meaning that make it unique cannot be reduced to a single proposition or a simple-minded set of clichés.

2   Yet that is what has happened in the United States, where the debate between hunters and anti-hunters has been reduced to one question: How can anyone justify killing any animal?

3   As a hunter, I have felt hostility from people I know and respect who are anti-hunters. I have been told that killing any animal, ex-

cept in self-defense, is immoral; and I have been characterized as a social leper who belongs to a more primitive age.

4   But this view of the hunter as an anachronism ignores the histories of science and of humankind. It conveniently blots out the fact that in nature every species, no matter how big or small, is either predator or prey, the hunter or the hunted. This—not the preservation of all life at any cost—is the dynamic of existence on our planet.

5   In all predator relationships there is an inequality between the hunter and the hunted. The belief that all creatures have an equal right to life, and that therefore all killing is immoral, is a fallacy without precedent in science or the natural world.

6   The conviction of the anti-hunter that killing any animal is wrong may be based on the misguided concept that equality between hunter and hunted is the corollary of equality before the law. The equality of men and their right to life are *artificial* constructs of constitutional government and hold true only in the most civilized nations.

7   For me the essence of hunting is not the indulgence of the instinct to kill, nor is it to be found in the instant one kills. In fact, killing is no more necessary to a successful hunt than catching a fish is to a good fishing trip. If every hunt ended in a successful kill, hunting would be both boring and banal.

8   The essence of hunting for me is to pursue the animal ethically and in a manner that makes the possibility of killing or capturing it a genuine challenge. There is no certainty of killing when I hunt. Indeed, the *uncertainty* is what makes the sport interesting.

9   I accept limits on my ability to kill. The hunting seasons are carefully constructed so as to make the wit of the hunter and the cunning of the animal more truly competitive.

10   That is why we limit seasons to several days or weeks a year, limit the use of baits to lure unwary animals and birds, and limit the number of animals we kill, their size and age and sex. We limit our behavior by law in order to pursue game ethically and to make the challenge even more difficult. These odds I take on happily, knowing the elk herds will continue to flourish. Those who refuse to accept the odds—the poachers—are not hunters, they are outlaws.

11   Hunting is a complex activity involving undercurrents that are rarely articulated, but that nevertheless form the basis for one's actions. One of these unstated values is the attempt to establish a strong ethical position in life. Few activities in this world test ethical standards as does hunting.

12   There are no witnesses in the wilderness. The hunter knows in his conscience whether he has compromised the sportsman's standards. For an ethical hunter, hypocrisy and hunting are incompatible.

13   I have asserted that hunting involves much more than the act of killing. I hunt to nourish my aesthetic appreciation of nature; being in the field six months a year allows me to experience, personally, the most beautiful parts of America.

14   I hunt for food, and I do not choose to delegate my right to obtain it to a slaughterhouse. My friends go to supermarkets and buy packaged beef and lamb. I go into the wilderness and kill elk, venison, and wildfowl. Is there a moral difference between a cow being killed for market and a deer for my freezer?

15   I hunt because it deepens my relationship with my son. We have literally spent years in duck blinds, on deer stands, and around campfires—talking. I would not trade those conversations for anything on Earth.

16   I hunt because I can contribute to conservation directly. Last year I raised 5,000 valley quail. I killed 49 of them. This reflects a traditional value of giving more to the land and the environment than you take from it. How many anti-hunters can make a similar claim?

17   I hunt to simplify my life, away from the noise and the pollution of urban environments. What better way to ponder John Muir's axiom that every star is connected to every other star in the universe than by starlight after a day in the wilderness?

18   All this is why I hunt.

Why I Don't Hunt

Steve Ruggeri

1   Why did I hunt? From the time I was 12 until shortly after my 18th birthday, I pumped lead at the furred and feathered from Maine to Pennsylvania. I was the youngest member of the Newport Rifle Club in Rhode Island, where I was trained and disciplined as a small-bore competitive shooter. I was tutored by masters of the art, and I was given numerous opportunities to engage in my sport.

2   Despite my enthusiasm, I sought diversion from the rigors of competitive shooting. Trap and skeet shooting introduced me to moving targets, but I was anxious to sight down a barrel at animate ones. I looked forward to the pleasure of seeing birds plummet earthward. I knew I would delight in the contortions of small game, the end-over-end tumbling after the rabbit felt the sting of my .22. And I was confident that I would shrug and say, "Better luck, next buck," should I miscalculate shot placement and merely blow the lower jaw completely off a deer.

3   I didn't disappoint myself. I reveled in killing, maiming, bloodletting, and gutting. Never did I have the slightest thought regarding carrying capacity, overbrowsing, population dynamics, or any other game-management concept. The arguments that hunters advanced in defense of their sport were alien to me. I hunted in order to kill; I did not kill in order to have "the hunting experience."

4   Why did I stop? Social expedience: My pastime was deemed unacceptable by a circle of high-school mates from whom I sought acceptance. Would I have ever experienced an after-kill crisis of conscience of such emotional magnitude that I would hurl my weapon into the nearest lake? No, I was incapable of the visceral compunction that has triggered the moral rebirth of many who formerly exploited animals.

5   A couple of years after my guns had been silenced by peer pressure, I was dining on a hamburger so rare that the blood still appeared to be coursing through the animal tissue. While hurrying to finish so as not to be late for my cat's appointment with the vet, I was seized by the realization of how utterly inconsistent it was for me to be so solicitous of a cat, yet have no regard for the cow I was devouring.

6   Pain is pain, I reasoned, whether felt by the family feline or by the unknown steer shackled and hoisted above the killing-room floor. It became morally imperative for me to end my complicity in the infliction of any gratuitous pain and suffering upon either wild or domesticated animals. This ethical awakening led to extensive research and reading that enlightened me further as to the magnitude of our exploitation of nonhuman animals, and reaffirmed my resolve to embrace an ethic of moral consideration for all animal species. I recognized that my decision to stop hunting years earlier had been correct, though made for the wrong reason.

7   Why don't I hunt? I could allude to the fruits of exhaustive research into the ecological and biological consequences of hunting, and to the collective insight of biologists, ecologists, and naturalists who challenge the prevailing wildlife-management dogma. Yet, fundamentally, the answer can be expressed in simple moral terms: Hunting is wrong, and should be acknowledged to be so not only by those who espouse the strict precepts of the animal-rights credo, but by those who hold a common sense of decency, respect, and justice. When we have exposed the specious reasoning of the hunters' apologists and stripped their sport of its counterfeit legitimacy, the naked brutality of hunting defines itself: killing for the fun of it.

8   Although my current occupation requires attention to a wide array of animal issues, the subject of hunting is the predominant focus of my work. If I find my energy or motivation waning during the course of a day's work, I merely conjure up the image of my former self as a slayer of wildlife. The memory of stalking targets on the hoof or wing infuses me with renewed vigor in my labor against blood sports.

9   But obviously, no amount of dedication or energy expanded will atone for the suffering and death I visited upon the scores of animals I wantonly killed.

Why We Hunt

Humberto Fontova

1   Just once. My God, just once, I'd like to see hunters face up to the primal instinct that motivates us. But no, all I hear is:

2   "We're the top conservationists in the country."

3   "We put our money where our mouths are."

4   "We're nature lovers."

5   Hell, we'll pat ourselves on the back all day.

6   Yes, hunters are actually all these things. But no one (from our ranks, anyway) seems to want to point out that essentially we are killers of animals in the most direct way, and that what distinguishes us from everyone else who indirectly causes animals to die is that we take delight in it.

7   "Don't you eat meat?"

8   "How much did you contribute to conservation this year, Mr. Birdwatcher?"

9   Oh, how we love to retort to the anti-hunters. But they do have a point: If we're attracted by the beauty of nature, surely it's just as beautiful without a gun in hand. If the challenge is the key, why not sneak up on a bull elk and take a picture of it? If tradition and camaraderie are the inspiration, why pull the trigger?

10   And, of course, we all rush afield on opening day enraptured by the prospect of culling excess animals. The sleeplessness of the night before and the hollow stomach that morning are obviously caused by this opportunity to do our part for sound game-management.

11   I've never bought the classic hunting argument about the insignificant part that actual killing plays in the sport. If this were true, there would be no reason for the vitriol we hurl at the anti-hunters. These mushheads aren't out to stop us from walking in the woods and embracing nature. They're not out to deny us the challenge of stalking an animal. They're not out to prevent the friendship and the card games at the cabin. They're out to stop one thing: the killing. If it's such a tiny part of the total hunting picture, why are we in such a lather about the anti-hunters?

12   Let's face it: After we cut through all the embellishments, the one thing that distinguishes a canoeing trip or a nature walk from the hunt is the prospect of killing.

13   We *like* to kill animals. I can no more explain this predatory instinct to the satisfaction of Friends of Animals than anyone else can. But I won't throw up a smokescreen of rationalizations when confronted with this unnerving but unavoidable fact.

14   For a hunter to admit that there's something enjoyable about killing an animal is considered fantastic. The outdoor magazines are a perfect example: Their editorials constantly harp on sportsmanship, challenge, conservation ethics, nature worship, tradition, and camaraderie. These are showcased as the most genuine rationales for our sport; the killing is merely incidental—the "We kill in order to have hunted" syndrome. According to these editorials, it's the grueling hours of scouting, stalking, and honing our woodsmanship that count. We're led to believe that only a small minority of slob hunters forsake these principles.

15   Then the rest of the magazine's pages are filled with stories of guided hunts where, almost literally, all the hunter does is pull the trigger.

16   After a night of good-timing, the biggest challenge for the Texas deer "hunter" is to huff and puff his way to the top of a deer tower and keep his balance on the revolving seat. The "hunting" is a matter of gazing out over the corn-baited landscape and picking out which deer he wants.

17   The tycoon who roams over the African bush in a Land Rover, gets out, walks 500 yards, and kills a 60-year-old animal pointed out by a professional guide is not out to stock his freezer or display his woodsmanship. I know that this gentleman, with what he paid for licenses and trophy fees, probably contributed more toward the conservation of elephants than any of the do-good organizations, but still, he killed the elephant. And he enjoyed it.

18   I see absolutely nothing wrong with any of these scenarios, but let's recognize them for what they aren't and for what they are. They do not show the behavior of the conservationist, adventurer, master woodsman, naturalist, or philosopher of hunting-magazine mythology. Hunters are simply guys who get a thrill out of killing animals.

19   Yes, the love of the outdoors contributes to my urge to hunt. The challenge is definitely part of it. Studying the nature of the terrain and my quarry's habits, and then ambushing him fair and square, makes the kill more rewarding. Sometimes the fellowship is nice, although I usually hunt alone. Feeding my family year-round on what I kill gives a certain bounce to the step. But mostly, I recognize the urge as a predatory instinct to kill. Man is a predator—has been for tens of thousands of years. It's going to take a while to breed that out of us, and thank God I won't be around by then.

ON FILM

The Blair Witch Project *probably needs no introduction, for it was one of the leading money-earners of 1999, and if you calculated what the film earned compared to what it cost to make, it is probably the leading money-maker of all time. Money aside, the film also opened the door for other independent film-makers and helped create a market for low-budget productions. While the public loved it, or at least paid to see it, not all reviewers agreed on the worth of the movie. Kevin Thomas, who liked it, is a staff writer and movie reviewer for the* Los Angeles Times, *where his review was published on July 16, 1999. John Simon, who hated it, is known for acid reviews and regularly critiques films for the* National Review, *where his piece appeared on September 13, 1999.*

"Witch Project" a Mock Doc That Really Can Shock

Kevin Thomas

1   "The Blair Witch Project" has received so much advance press that you probably already know that it is a "mockumentary" that's received rave reviews on the festival circuit. And that's too bad since all that attention ultimately does a disservice to the audience. Those who go into the film cold are of course more likely to experience thrills and chills than those who know what they're getting into—the second group, however, can expect an unsettling experience, capped by a couple of jolts at the finish, as the film's twists and turns are impossible to predict and do generate low-key suspense. Some rave quotes suggest that you're in for a scare of "Exorcist" proportions, whereas "Blair Witch" is essentially an exceedingly ingenious diversion.

2   In short, the film is a clever, entertaining stunt, no more, no less, and a terrific calling card for its fledgling filmmakers, Daniel Myrick and Eduardo Sanchez.

3   An opening statement tells us that on Oct. 21, 1994, Heather Donahue, Joshua Leonard and Michael Williams hiked into Maryland's Black Hills Forest to shoot a documentary on a local legend of the so-called Blair Witch, a woman named Elly Kedward who was supposed to have caused half the youngsters of Blair village to vanish more than 200 years ago. In 1824, the town of Burkittsville was founded on the site of Blair; between November 1940 and May 1941, the town was rocked by the ritualistic slayings of seven children by a local hermit named Rustin Parr, who, after giving himself up, tells authorities that he did it for "an old woman ghost."

4   Once we're informed that the student filmmakers disappeared without a trace but that we will be looking at the footage they shot—found a year later—we are abruptly thrust into the quickly menacing world of that footage. The filmmakers have taken tremendous pains to bring to it enough coherence so that we can be involved in the students' plight as it unfolds yet maintain enough jaggedness so that "Blair Project's" fakery is utterly convincing.

5   Williams is the project's sound man. In the meantime Heather records the group's growing rifts on High–8 video and her comments on those rifts; this is an unobtrusive and persuasive

device that provides a crucial narrative flow in a completely natural way.

6   Heather, whose project it is, comes off as headstrong and determined to maintain control of her shoot at all costs. She's strong on using all the correct terms for the shoot-from-the-hip kind of documentary she's trying to make. There's something highhanded, a little condescending and insensitive about Heather as she goes about interviewing locals before she and her crew enter the forest, where they quickly get lost and soon become subjected to a series of mysterious and malevolent incidents.

7   The men become outraged at Heather for the predicament she got them into, but all three young people are smart enough to know that if they are to have a hope of making it out of the forest they've got to pull together.

8   All three are playing roles, although they use their actual names, and the way in which Myrick and Sanchez make improvisation work within their outline, keeping their cast in the dark and off balance as much as possible, is nothing less than amazing. You can, if you want, buy into the possibility of supernatural forces acting as the prime mover or believe the trio has fallen victim to some unseen person or people who simply are in the grip of madness. Donahue, Leonard and Williams are as absolutely believable as everything else about the film.

9   If you're willing to look beyond the fright tactics in "Blair Witch," you can enjoy it as a kind of mordant commentary on the presumptuousness of brash and inexperienced documentary filmmakers who, in this extreme instance, plunge into a forest wilderness with woefully inadequate preparation and who actually think they will somehow be able to record supernatural manifestations on film. In the final analysis, "Blair Witch" is perhaps more amusing and satisfying as a cautionary tale deflating a certain kind of filmmaking arrogance than it is as an offbeat horror show.

Of Witches and Muses

John Simon

1   Why are people so benighted as to think *The Blair Witch Project* a terrific movie? Is it because it was made by five young kids?

Because it cost only $35,000? Because it was a hit at the Sundance Festival (the worst possible reason)? Because they find it truly scary? For that, it would have to be, on some level, plausible; have characters that are, in some way, appealing. I find neither to be the case. Or because it is being sold with a monstrously effective hype? Now that is scary.

2   An opening title card announces that three young filmmakers vanished into a Maryland forest, where they had gone in search of a reputed witch. A year later, this film shot by them was found, and tells their story. The very first absurdity is that, as the two young men and one young woman each had a video camera, the film would really have to be three films. Edited into one, it predicates the work of editors, undercutting its documentary authenticity.

3   Next, these Maryland woods seem neither thick nor extensive enough to warrant such a disappearance. The young people, moreover, have only one map, which they read with difficulty, and which one of them, for no good reason, throws away. They also have only one compass, which they don't resort to till late in the game. When they come across a stream, they do not have brains enough to follow it; it would surely lead them to human habitations. Further, they keep fighting among themselves, which, under the circumstances, is imbecile. And finally, they keep shooting their film with their cumbersome equipment instead of jettisoning it and facilitating their escape.

4   The strength of the film supposedly resides in the invisibility of the enemy; the witch, or just some locals having fun with the trio. Only disturbing nocturnal sounds are heard, and disquieting manikins made of twigs hang in the trees near the campsites in the morning. That may, perhaps, be scarier than actual sightings, but when certain key things are shot so we can't quite make them out even up close, that is cheating.

5   What is imposing is the extensive and manifold hype the movie is getting. The press, TV, the Internet are full of it. I just read in the *New York Times* that "the voodoo doll-like stick figures . . . were based on an ancient runic figure called the Burning Man [plagiarized from a 1973 film, *The Wicker Man*] . . . [and] are drawing as much as $300 on the Internet" That is a bit steep; but if someone could inform me where I could get them for, say, $250, I would gladly order a dozen.

Additional Writing Prompts

What follows is a list of possible topics that you can use or that may suggest ideas of your own. The aim of the essay, its thesis, and its audience is up to you, but keep in mind that these modes are means to an end—your major assertion—not an end in themselves.

1. Describing and Narrating

Describe a person so that you convey the person's character: friend, family member, student, teacher, coworker.

Describe a place so that you create a specific point about it: neighborhood, workplace, classroom, where you live, restaurant.

Write a narrative about an event that had an emotional impact: embarrassment, joy, remorse, grief, anxiety.

Write a narrative about an event that changed your opinion: product, music group, television show, person, place, political candidate.

Write a narrative that explains a conflict: parent vs. child, brother vs. sister, boss vs. worker, human vs. animal, human vs. nature.

2. Defining and Using Examples

Define an abstract term: morality, honor, pride, humility, friendship.

Define your taste in: music, art, film, books, television, friends, pets.

Define the qualities you most admire in a person: parent, teacher, religious leader, sibling, political figure.

What does it mean to be a "good" employee, student, parent, friend, citizen, co-worker, leader?

What is your idea of a "perfect" day, class, celebration, vacation, meal, date, pet?

3. Dividing, Classifying, Comparing, Contrasting

Consider the types of locomotion associated with sports: skateboard, Roller Blades, surf board, skis, snow shoes.

Consider what ads tell us about products and ourselves: cars, lingerie, liquor, beer, men's cologne, men's underwear.

What is the ideal house pet? Dog, cat, gerbil, snake, exotic animal, guinea pig?

Explain a subject by drawing an analogy: work, politics, football, boredom, homework, friendship.

Compare two dissimilar subjects to make a satiric point about one of them: going to a party vs. studying, raising a garden vs. children, playing poker vs. football, owning a bicycle vs. a car, eating junk food vs. cooking.

Compare two ways to accomplish the same goal: studying day-by-day or cramming, winning an argument by logic or emotion, agonizing over a decision or making a snap call, reacting immediately to a situation or mulling it over, planning some fun or opting for the spontaneous.

4. Analyzing How and Why

Explain a familiar chore in such a way that you make it less boring: washing the car, mowing the lawn, painting a room, cleaning out the bathroom closet, preparing for an exam, vacuuming.

Explain a positive approach to an usually negative action, such as how to procrastinate, tell a white lie, stay awake in class, hide dislike, keep from screaming.

Explain how to survive a difficult or unpleasant job: weeding a garden, learning a computer program, filing, reviving a computer crash, recycling, changing diapers.

Consider a problem that can arise in a setting you are familiar with and its solution, a problem that might occur at work, school, home, a sports event, between friends, within a marriage.

Analyze why you like what you like, your taste in music, sports you play, sports you watch on television, friends, food, films.

Writing Prompts by Theme

1. Scenes and Places

Personal Essay The concept of *setting* includes not only what a place looks like but also everything associated with it: the times, artifacts, and atmosphere. Mario Suarez's "El Hoyo" (30), for example is set in the late 1940s, and Ellery Akers "Left Sink" (38) takes place in October during a drought. The idea of *artifacts* is a broad one that encompasses both Jason Holland's quite real bridge (26) and Mary Ruefle's quite hypothetical bench (167). *Atmosphere* is equally elastic, for it is the emotional tone arising from the setting, the sense of loneliness and strangeness, for instance, that Barry Lopez creates in "The Raven." Think of an atmosphere you want to create and write an essay that conveys it to the reader. You can use time and various artifacts to help build that atmosphere. One place to start is with a specific emotion. What scares you? What do you find exciting? Depressing? Stressful? What do you look forward to? What do you dread? Once you've chosen the emotion about which you want to write, you've probably thought through many details about the setting—what it looks like, the time of day or year, specific events, or people. Those are details you can use in your essay.

Response to Essays Would you like to join the group on the bridge (26) or live in El Hoyo (30)? Write a response to one of the essays, using details from the piece to support your opinion. If you prefer, reread "Left Sink" (38) and "The Raven" (195) so that you can analyze whether you would want to visit either place. Again, use the details from the essay to explain your position. If you enjoyed "The Bench" (167), however, write an analysis of the essay. Here are some questions to consider: Is the essay a satire on arguments? On marriage? Is it a comment on the imagination, and, if so, what is it saying about it?

Research It seems that you can't read a newspaper without running into a story about an environmental issue that raises questions about the places in which we live. To turn some of those questions into possible topics for research, consult the index of your local or state newspaper, looking for what is listed under key words such as *acid rain, air pollution, chemical spill, phosphate runoff, water pollution,* and the like.

Once you find a news story that interests you, you'll be in a position to do further research as you'll know what to look for—news stories usually provide sources. In addition to the newspaper, you can consult popular journals (*Time* and the like) and academic publications in the field. The Internet is also an excellent source.

2. Gender

Personal Essay If you were to reread the four essays that deal with gender, you would find they share a common thread: survival as a woman. Maya Angelou spells out what women should be, "tough, tender, laugh as much as possible, live long lives" (82); Gloria Naylor argues that the idea of the African-American matriarch is a harmful myth (94); Caryn James discusses how women are treated as sex objects (155); and Naomi Wolf advises women on how to fight against powerlessness (216). Consider putting together your own survival kit, as woman or as man. More likely than not, you have had to deal with issues of gender, so think about where those issues arose. Perhaps the notion of gender came out in a classroom or a workplace. Perhaps it affected how your parents treated you. Perhaps it dictates your interests or choice of career. How has the idea of gender affected you in those situations? Choose one of them to explore in an essay—your survival kit.

Response to Essays Choose one of the statements below and write an essay that agrees or disagrees with it, citing evidence from the essay and from your experience to support your points. If you agree with the statement, qualify your agreement so that you are not simply repeating the information in the essay. The easiest way to do that is to think in terms of "Yes, but . . . ." What you supply after the *but* is the heart of your thesis.

It is imperative that a woman keep her sense of humor intact and at the ready (Angelou, 82).

What's more, 30 years of raised feminist consciousness has taught us all that when men yell out to women on the street, whether to comment on a smile or issue a crude invitation, no compliment is involved (James, 156).

Never choose a profession for material reasons (Wolf, 216).

Research Gloria Naylor's essay (94) makes a number of assertions about slavery: that women who were slaves had contradictory roles

(95); that they worked "regardless of the advanced states of pregnancy" (95); that "The need to view slavery as benign accounted for the larger-than-life mammy of the plantation legends" (96). Use the resources of your library to examine the relative truth of one of these statements or of any other in the essay.

3. The Individual

Personal Essay "Who am I?" is an ancient yet topical question, one that is apt to have a number of answers depending upon the situation. Caroline Hwang (62) and Bharati Mukherjee (190) ask it in terms of culture: Korean or American? Asian or American? Scott Harpt (182) explores answers by comparing his life to that of a fictional character, and Gary Soto (67) relives his brush with "sin" to discover who he was as a child. To consider your own answer to the question, think about yourself in relation to your generation, your parents, your ethnic background, your childhood, your "ideal." Perhaps you would prefer to think about who you were or who you want to be. Once you have a general topic, the essays noted above will be helpful. Maybe a particular event raised the question for you, as it did for Caroline Hwang and Gary Soto, or perhaps, like Scott Harpt and Bharati Mukherjee, you were struck by similarities and differences.

Response to Essays All of the essays in this section (xv) depict individuals caught in some kind of conflict, both internal—the person in conflict with himself or herself—and external, in conflict with culture, religion, or ethics. Choose one of the essays and respond to it, explaining why you would or would not like to be that person. Summarize and quote from the essay to support your point.

Research Except for Native Americans, the United States is a nation of relatively recent and very recent immigrants. Choose one ethnic group and research its traditions, listing them. Then take one of those traditions and write an essay explaining its history and practice. If you choose an ethnic group you are close to, you can augment your research by interviewing friends and relatives. If you prefer, write an essay explaining the history and practice of a local tradition, one that has developed in or been adapted to this country.

4. Relationships

Personal Essay "Where do I fit in?"—the idea of belonging or not belonging underlies many of the essays listed under "Relationships" (xv).

What is it like to watch one's mother grow old, asks J. Merrill-Foster (34). What does it mean to be part of a "crew," like Henry Han Xi Lau, (85) or, like Brent Staples, perceived as a threat (252). Thomas B. Stoddard (279) and Suzan Shown Harjo (274) explore what it means to be outside of the mainstream culture, while Flavius Stan (58) examines family relationships. Think about the various ways you do or do not belong to a group. You might want to mull over how you fit into family relationships or groups at school or work. Are you on the outside looking in or vice versa? How do you define your role in the group? Your relationship to it? Like Bjorn Skogquist (241), you may want to write about a time from your past or perhaps you want to explore present relationships, such as those at work or in school.

Response to Essays Switch roles with one of the persons in one of the essays in this section (xv). How might J. Merrill-Foster's mother feel about her daughter? Flavius Stan's brother feel about him? A noncrew member feel about Henry Han Xi Lau? A customer about Stacey Wilkins? Tiffany Stephenson (now) about Bjorn Skogquist? Choose one of the essays, and write a response to it from the perspective of the other person.

Research While marriage between two people of the same sex is both controversial and topical, restoring the relics of Native Americans to their tribes rarely makes the headlines, yet both subjects lend themselves well to research. Choose one to explore. Your thesis will grow out of what you find: What problems do you discover? What solutions have been proposed? What are the major arguments for and against various positions? What legal and ethical questions are tied to the issue?

5. Society

Personal Essay The essays in this section (xvi) can be grouped together by the common theme of action versus inaction. Tania Nyman (71) takes action when she buys a gun, while Dan Sisson (315) and Humberto Fontova (319) take action in the form of hunting; Robert C. Maynard (186) and Frank Wolf (311) propose actions to solve problems; Frank Fahrenkopf (313) and Steve Ruggeri (317) are against action; and Edna O'Brien (100) analyzes waiting, the ultimate form of inaction. Think about what affects you and consider what action, if any, would be an appropriate response. You might start with rules and regulations: Are the requirements for your major too difficult? Too easy? How about the general degree requirements? Or consider your day-to-day life: If you live in a dorm, what would you like to see changed? How about the campus book store? The cafeteria? The campus newspaper?

Response to Essays Select one of the essays and analyze it, quoting from the essay to back up your points. Is the problem the essay addresses a real problem or concern? If a solution is proposed, how realistic is it? Are the definitions used in the essay adequate? Are there points or objections the author ignores or glosses over? Are the examples used appropriately? Is there adequate evidence to support the author's view?

Research Gambling, gun control, hunting, poverty—all are subjects that bristle with opinions. Choose among them and use research to explore one of the topics. For legalized gambling, for instance, you might inquire first about the status of legalized gambling in your state? How is it defined? What effect has it had? Where does the revenue go? Does it do more harm than good? Is there such a thing as an "ideal" blueprint for legal gaming? If gambling is not legal, should it be?

6. Science and Technology

Personal Essay You can look at the essays in this section (xvi) as being about how things do or do not work. The things in question range from the nose (Ackerman, 22) to the fly swatter (Cuppy, 210) to the right kind of pasta (Hazan, 179), all of which work. Russell Baker, however, writes about inanimate objects in general, which don't work, while the more serious essays address the strange components of lipstick (Gandhi, 221) and who is left out of the Internet (Gates, 299). If you want to take the humorous route, you can model your essay after Cuppy or Baker, writing a psuedo-scientific piece about your battle with a pest or machine. Mosquitos, no-see-ums, the dreaded cockroach, all are common insects with which we do battle using various weapons. And surely you have been frustrated by the candy or soft drink machine or pay telephone that refuses to work, though it works well enough to take your money. Then there's the computer, which knows infinite ways to frustrate. If you prefer to take a serious approach, then you might take up the Internet. Should products carry sales tax? Should certain sites be subject to censorship? Should college students be required to have computers? Should term paper sites be regulated? The questions go on and on.

Response to Essays Choose one of the statements below and write an essay that agrees or disagrees with it, citing evidence from the essay and from your experience to support your points. If you agree with the statement, qualify your agreement so that you are not simply repeating the information in the essay. The easiest way to do that is to think in terms of "Yes, but . . . ." What you supply after the *but* is the heart of your thesis.

Nothing is more memorable than a smell (Ackerman, 22).

The goal of all inanimate objects is to resist man and ultimately to defeat him . . . (Baker, 163).

Unless we master the new information technology to build and deepen the forms of social connections that a tragic history has eroded, African-Americans will face a form of cybersegregation in the [21st] century as devastating to our aspirations as Jim Crow segregation was to those of our ancestors (Gates, 302).

Research If you are interested in food or agriculture, you might consider researching what we eat and how safe it is. Various pesticides, for example, are outlawed in the United States but used in other countries, countries that export produce that is sold in our markets. Hormones, however, are legal here and used to fatten cattle but are outlawed in Europe's Common Market. Is the food we eat really safe? What is meant by "organic" products? Are "organic" products regulated? What steps can we take to make sure fruit and vegetables are safe? Or perhaps your interests run to the technological, in which case the computer is the ideal subject. Are we really in a new Gutenberg age? Is there such a thing as Internet addiction? How safe is it to send credit card numbers over the Net? Who has access to the information we send and receive? How real is the "Digital Divide"?

7. Language and Education

Personal Essay Your personal resources on this topic are vast, for you have at least 12 years of experience with formal education and you have been learning language all of your life. How would you evaluate your education? Were you adequately prepared for college? What strengths and weaknesses do you note? Are there subjects that are not taught in high school that should be? What arguments can be made for single-sex schools or colleges? For religious teaching in the schools? The danger in writing on this topic is that you may take on too much, so if you are choosing to write in response to one of these questions, make sure you narrow your topic to a manageable size. You might note, for instance, a number of weaknesses in your high school education, but then analyze one in detail.

Response to Essays Almost all of the essays in this section (xvi) are full of assertions that can be tested against your own experience. Select one of the statements below or any other assertion from one of the essays, and analyze it in terms of your own experience and the evidence from the essay:

> [O]ne of the heaviest burdens black Americans—and black children in particular—have to bear is the handicap of definition: the questions of what it means to be black (Raspberry, 90).

> There is something very wrong with the system of values in a society that has only derogatory terms like nerd and geek for the intellectually curious and academically serious (Fridman, 289).

> The American high school, is obsolete and should be abolished (Botstein, 295).

Research If you are interested in how children learn, you might want to research the current debate about the first three years of a child's life. Some experts maintain that those years are the critical ones for learning, while others find that children continue to learn at a rapid rate well beyond that time. There's little argument, however, about childhood being the ideal time to learn a foreign language, so perhaps that topic appeals to you. If you're interested in education at a later time, you might want to research some of the issues currently receiving much attention: prayer in the schools, the "zero tolerance" policy, public funds for private education, the voucher system, the teacher certification process, and the like.

8. Popular Culture and the Media

Personal Essay As several of the essays in this section show, popular culture has its drawbacks: Steve Martin points out that CD packaging and its ilk (54)—"improvements"—can make a situation worse; Barbara Ehrenreich finds that slasher films and the like suggest we hate our bodies (257); Peter Steinhart says that the animal shows we see on television have misinformed us about our relation with nature (135); and Daniel Slate examines the controversy caused by a popular musical group (283). You can use any of these essays to analyze the effect an example of popular culture has on you. Perhaps you also find an "improvement" that isn't, or that a particular film, television or radio show, musical group, or advertisement affects you strongly.

Response to Essays Choose one of the essays in this section that interests you and analyze it. You may find you disagree with the thesis or that some of the assertions are not adequately supported. If you agree with most of the points the author makes, again try the "yes-but" response so that you don't repeat what has already been said. If you prefer, analyze one of the statements below, testing it against your own experience and the support provided for it in the essay:

> George Felton's explanation of why he loves pro wrestling (247) fits other "bizarre" forms of entertainment, such as Jerry Springer, Howard Stern, Marilyn Manson, slasher films, Thomas Harris's Hannibal Lecter novels.

> Michiko Kakutani is right that advertising has saturated our lives, "blurring . . . the lines between art and commerce," making "us increasingly cynical about everything else" (132).

> What Edna Buchanan says about mysteries, that they are "an escape, a sanctuary, in an increasingly chaotic world overtaken by unresponsive government agencies, rush hour traffic, voice mail and other unspeakable torments" (238), is true of other forms of popular culture such as film, television, books, and music

Research Use research to explain the popularity of running, health clubs, or country music. For a different project, choose a popular film you liked that is also available on video and look up a number of reviews, checking newspapers, popular weeklies such as *Newsweek*, and magazines such as *The New Yorker*, *Atlantic*, and *Harper's*, along with a few film journals. Choose several reviews that strike you as unjust, and write a paper to show that they are wrong. Because the film is available on video, you can rerun it to check your points.

CREDITS

Page 22: "The Mute Sense" from *A Natural History of the Senses* by Diane Ackerman. Copyright © 1990 by Diane Ackerman. Reprinted by permission of Random House, Inc.

Page 26: "The Bridge" by Jason Holland. Reprinted by permission of the author.

Page 30: "El Hoyo" by Mario Suarez for *Arizona Quarterly*, Summer 1947, vol. III, no. 2. Copyright © by the Arizona Quarterly. Reprinted by permission.

Page 34: "At 85, Frightened by a Loss of Power" by J. Merrill-Foster from the *New York Times*, January 31, 1988. Copyright © 1988 by the New York Times Co. Reprinted by permission.

Page 38: "Left Sink" by Ellery Akers from *Sierra*, 1990. Reprinted by permission of the author.

Page 54: "Designer of Audio CD Packaging Enters Hell" by Steve Martin. Copyright © 1999 by Steve Martin. Reprinted by permission of International Creative Management, Inc. Originally published in *The New Yorker*.

Page 58: "The Night of Oranges" by Flavius Stan from the *New York Times*, December 24, 1995. Copyright © 1995 by the New York Times Co. Reprinted by permission.

Page 62: "The Good Daughter" by Caroline Hwang from *Newsweek*, September 21, 1998. All rights reserved. Reprinted by permission.

Page 67: "The Pie" from *A Summer Life* by Gary Soto. Copyright © 1990 by University Press of New England. Reprinted by permission of the University Press of New England.

Page 71: "I'm Frightened, Angry and Ashamed: I Have a Gun" by Tania Nyman from the *Times-Picayune*, April 21, 1990. Reprinted by permission of the Times Picayune Publishing Corporation.

Page 82: "In All Ways a Woman" from *Wouldn't Take Nothing for My Journey Now* by Maya Angelou. Copyright © 1993 by Maya Angelou. Reprinted by permission of Random House, Inc.

Page 85: "I Was a Member of the Kung Fu Crew" by Henry Han Xi Lau from the *New York Times Magazine*, October 19, 1997. Copyright © 1997 by the New York Times Co. Reprinted by permission.

Page 90: "The Handicap of Definition" from "Instilling Positive Images" by William Raspberry. Copyright © 1982 by the Washington Post Writers Group. Reprinted by permission.

Page 94: "The Myth of the Matriarch" by Gloria Naylor from *Life* magazine, Spring 1988. Copyright © 1988 by One-Way Productions, Inc. Reprinted by permission of Sterling Lord Literistic, Inc.

Page 100: "Waiting" by Edna O'Brien from the *Los Angeles Times Magazine*, 1994. Copyright © 1994 by Edna O'Brien. Reprinted by permission of David Godwin Associates.

Page 224: "Inspiration? Head Down the Back Road, and Stop for the Yard Sales" by Annie Proulx from the *New York Times,* May 10, 1999. Reprinted by permission of Darhansoff & Verrill.

Page 237: "Still a Mystery" by Edna Buchanan from the *New York Times Magazine.* Copyright © 1996 by Edna Buchanan. Reprinted by permission of Don Congdon Associates, Inc.

Page 241: "Tiffany Stephenson—An Apology" by Bjorn Skogquist. Reprinted by permission of the author.

Page 247: "Wrestling with Myself" by George Felton. Reprinted by permission of the author.

Page 252: "Black Men and Public Space" by Brent Staples. Reprinted by permission of the author.

Page 257: "Why Don't We Like the Human Body?" by Barbara Ehrenreich from *Time,* July 1, 1991. Copyright © 1991 by Time Inc. Reprinted by permission.

Page 274: "Last Rites for Indian Dead" by Suzan Shown Harjo, President, Morning Star Foundation, Washington, D.C. Appeared in the *Los Angeles Times,* September 16, 1989. Reprinted by permission of the author.

Page 279: "Gay Marriages: Make Them Legal" by Thomas B. Stoddard from the *New York Times,* March 14, 1989. Copyright © 1989 by the New York Times Co. Reprinted by permission.

Page 283: "But Is It Art?" by Daniel Slate. Reprinted by permission of the author.

Page 289: "America Needs Its Nerds" by Leonid Fridman from the *New York Times,* January 11, 1990. Copyright © 1990 by the New York Times Co. Reprinted by permission.

Page 291: "All Work and No Play Makes Jack a Nerd" by David Lessing and David Herne from the *New York Times,* January 1990. Reprinted by permission of the authors.

Page 292: "Multiple Choices" by Keith W. Frome from the *New York Times,* January 28, 1990. Reprinted by permission of the author.

Page 295: "High School, An Institution Whose Time Has Passed," originally published as "Let Teenagers Try Adulthood" by Leon Botstein, from the *New York Times,* May 17, 1999. Copyright © 1999 by the New York Times Co. Reprinted by permission.

Page 299: "One Internet, Two Nations" by Henry Louis Gates, Jr. from the *New York Times,* October 31, 1999. Copyright © 1999 by the New York Times Co. Reprinted by permission.

Page 304: "Many Exploring the Option" by Angela Cortez from *The Denver Post,* August 29, 1999. Reprinted by permission of The Denver Post.

Page 306: "Public Setting Still Best" by Evie Hudak from *The Denver Post,* August 29, 1999. Reprinted by permission of the author.

Page 308: "One-on-One Environment is Beneficial" by Kevin Swanson from *The Denver Post,* August 29, 1999. Reprinted by permission of the author.

Page 311: "Let's See Where Gambling is Going" by Frank R. Wolf from the *Rocky Mountain News,* December 10, 1995. Reprinted with permission of Denver Rocky Mountain News.

INDEX